Praise for *Uncon*

"Just when you thought the *lost thing the world needs is another* business management book, *Uncommon Sense Management* arrives like a breath of fresh spring air after a long winter. I have been a business executive for 25 years, so when I first sat down to read *Uncommon Sense Management*, I was a little skeptical. However, Dan has tapped into the wisdom of leading and inspiring people in the workplace with a very practical and easy to grasp approach that makes these pearls of wisdom easy to apply. Dan speaks to us as a peer who has been there and his passion to boil leadership training down to its essence is refreshing and inspiring. I expect *Uncommon Sense Management* will inspire my leadership team when I share it with them."
—Mark Kettering – President & CEO, Brightlight Consulting

"Dan Purkey's conversational style makes this an engaging read. Full of practical advice for young managers and important reminders for business veterans who may have lost their way."
—Robert Graham - retired Boeing executive

"Buy this book. What Dan has managed to do here is to develop, present, and fully explain a game plan of management and action that is nothing less than inspirational. This is a book to be absorbed and adopted. It is a book to form up around. Be it at the level of daily operations, symposia, charrette, or any other melee, these processes will bring about productive, cogent, and tangible results. The game of business is at its best when every player knows their role, goals, and responsibilities, AND how they impact the end game. Adopting Dan's book will build teams where every player knows how very critical they are to the outcome."
—Doug McElroy - Owner, Two Mac, Inc.

"Purkey presents many pertinent fundamental management principles in a fresh writing style that can be of benefit to new and experienced managers. A fun and entertaining read which I could not put down."
—Kevin Person - CEO, Wagstaff, Inc.

"After nearly 40 years in business I have found common sense to be anything but common. In *Uncommon Sense Management*, Dan Purkey outlines a strategy to achieve results through a system of simple steps that are critical to the success of any business. Mission Statements that are simple to internalize, Values that every team member can identify with, and simple, measurable goals are at the heart of Dan's plan for success. Working with Dan for nearly two years demonstrated to me that Dan believes deeply in this process and truly "Walks the Talk." I highly recommend that you read and share the principles in this book with your team and take Dan's advice to measure the results you experience as you execute your new-found plan for success."

—Bob Pentico - President, Protocol Communications

"Dan Purkey's *Uncommon Sense Management* is a great read for both new managers who will get good insight into what makes a good leader and seasoned management veterans who can be reminded of the simple fundamentals that are required to be successful in management. The straight-forward and story-telling style that Dan uses makes it an easy read. I recommend this book to anyone in a business environment."

—Rick Hess - President and CEO, Hittite Microwave

UNCOMMON SENSE MANAGEMENT

Move Yourself and Your Business from Chaos to Calm with Practical Techniques

Dan Purkey

NOTE TO READERS
People and companies portrayed in this book are, for the most part,
illustrative examples based on the author's experiences. They are not
intended to represent a particular person or organization.

The Open Door Group, LLC is a management consulting firm that
specializes in teaching organizations how to be more efficient,
effective, and profitable using the techniques portrayed in this book.
For more information on how The Open Door Group can help you
and your business, go to
www.TheOpenDoorGroup.com

ISBN-13:
978-1483967974

ISBN-10:
1483967972

*To my friends, family, and
fellow travelers in the world of business.
Sources of inspiration all.*

Dan Punkay

Table of Contents

INTRODUCTION

Here's the basic premise for this book: virtually all business ills can be traced back to ineffective communication of some type. If you can identify and fix the communication breakdowns, you can fix your business ills.

In a survey from June 2013, Gallup published a report that showed 70% of Americans hate their jobs or have "checked out," costing U.S. businesses as much as $550 billion per year. This book gives you the tools to solve that problem and gives you the tools to break away from the "too busy to do my job" syndrome.

Ineffective communication takes many, many different forms that can appear to the untrained eye as something other than a communication issue. The key to success is to have the realization that if you can't associate the root cause of a given problem with some type of communication, then you haven't dug deep enough.

In the movie *Fallen* with Denzel Washington, the demon Azazel can possess any person or animal merely by touching them. Throughout the movie, Azazel constantly transfers himself from person to person, shifting and manifesting himself in different forms as Detective John Hobbs chases and tries to kill him. Ineffective communication is like Azazel, constantly shifting and manifesting itself in different ways that wreak havoc on you and your business. The result is inefficiency, ineffectiveness, and low or negative profitability.

It's a case of true root cause analysis. Managers, as a general proposition—from entry level to CEOs—don't have either the training or the discipline to follow problems back to the ultimate root cause and then successfully address them. Consequently, there's a lot of dust created in an attempt to fix things (which, ironically, further contributes to the overall problem), but little actually gets solved. In this book, you'll get not only the necessary tools and insight to see the true root causes of problems, but methods to help with your discipline so that you can actually put the training to use instead of just talking about it. The result will be improved efficiency, effectiveness, and profits for the business and a calmer work life for you.

Identifying where the ineffective communication takes place is much like the Six Degrees of Separation game, which theorizes that any two people on earth are a maximum of six acquaintance links apart. You just need to find that path to connect them. For example, you can connect Kevin Bacon with Rudolf Valentino in this way: In 1922, Rudolph Valentino starred in the silent movie *Beyond the Rocks* with Gertrude Astor. Astor acted in *Daddy Long Legs* in 1955 alongside James Cromwell. Cromwell worked with Kevin Bacon in 2009 on *Beyond All Boundaries*. Valentino has three degrees of separation from Kevin Bacon.

In the same fashion, poor profits might be linked to dissatisfied customers, caused by technicians showing up late to do work, caused by order creators not providing/communicating correct customer order info to the techs.

Communication is the transfer of information from one entity to another. Any time you have a transfer point, you have a potential point of failure. The reality is that in everyday business life, there are millions of instances of those potential points of failure, like person-to-person, department-to-department, team-to-department, etc. The goal is to minimize the percentage of times that failure occurs in order to make your working life easier and your business better.

~~~~~~

The Universal Truths of Business Management
We hold these truths to be self-evident:

1. Communication is the source that enables a society to form and exist. Without interaction between two people, those two people wouldn't be able to inform and grow from each other. Society wouldn't be able to develop beyond one person. By definition, interaction requires communication, regardless of what form that takes. A business is a society.

2. Everyone Prioritizes; not everyone realizes they do.

Few understand the consequences of that lapse of realization.

3. As a general Principle, something simpler is easier to do than something more complex.
4. The more you and your organization can stay in alignment with your business Principles, the more your business will behave like your vision, whatever that might be.

If this is the first management book you've ever read, you've picked the right one. If you've read lots of management books, you'll find this one's different and will give you insights you may have never experienced.

Whether you're a C-level executive (CEO, COO, CFO, etc.), a frontline employee, or any management in between, you'll find a use for the practical actions and perspectives in here that'll open your eyes to a better way to work and manage. You'll find that you can gain more control over your work life.

The root cause of virtually all business problems comes down to a failure to execute on one of the four universal truths shown above. What are some common symptoms seen when one of these universal truths is in play? Among others, see if these sound familiar:

1. Daily fire drills
2. Frequently changing policy, structure, or process/procedure direction
3. Too busy to do your job
4. Overabundance of priorities
5. Low profitability
6. Inefficient operations
7. Ineffective operations

We'll explore the causes that are the real drivers—the root causes—of why people are too busy to do their jobs and why businesses as a whole have such a frantic, frenetic pace, jumping from one fire drill to another. This all drags down efficiency, effectiveness, and profits.

At the center of those root causes is management. More specifically, poor management. Fix management and you fix everything because a company's culture reflects leadership style and decisions from the top down.

Do you find yourself jaded by most management books? Are they not really digestible? Do they give you lots of information, but little that you can put to use in real life? Seen enough four-box models and giant, graphic, curved arrows that connect pithy word bites in a circle to last you a lifetime?

This book is presented from the perspective of a teacher with the intent to have the student truly understand, the flair of a novelist with the intent to entertain, and a businessperson with the intent to increase efficiency, effectiveness, and profits. While this approach is somewhat unique in the field, make no mistake that this is a practical, put-it-to-use-now book. It uses a casual coaching conversation as the format versus a formal, textbook approach. It appeals to the everyman in most of us.

We won't complicate things as can happen with management models like Lean, Six Sigma, Total Quality Management, Just-in-Time, Quality Circles, or the Shingo Model for Operational Excellence, among others. We'll distill that information down to what you can actually use and easily implement to make a real impact. This is really a toolbox for everyone to use, filled with lots of tools as well as instructions on how to use them.

Even if you work in a Top Ten Best Places to Work (and congratulations if you do), *Uncommon Sense Management* will still give you more of what you need to continue on the path of continuous improvement.

Why the title *Uncommon Sense Management*? After thirty years of interaction with a variety of companies, I realized that common sense is not so common. (Well, I actually knew it before thirty years, I just hadn't written about it.) I heard many people question, at some point, why others couldn't just apply a little common sense to situations to make things easier. I began to wonder why it's called "common" at all, since it certainly doesn't seem prevalent.

I concluded that what we need more of is, apparently, uncommon sense. Few acknowledge or effectively incorporate the four universal truths to help them move from a chaotic to a calm environment. Those truths must be uncommon since few use them, although there's certainly nothing mystical or rare about them. It's as though people who live next to a lake die of thirst because they won't drink the water, as readily available as it is.

In their zeal to produce profits, management frequently focuses on the finance and neglects the people. What they're missing is that it's the people that ultimately feed the finances, whether the people are employees or customers. Consequently, when profit goals aren't met, management gets frustrated at their own inability to move the needle. A better plan is to find and fix the root causes of the things that feed (or don't feed) the profit.

By the time you reach the end of the book (or even at the end of various paragraphs), you'll feel empowered to take steps to improve your work situation. You'll have the confidence needed to take informed action, no longer daunted by the ostensibly impossible task of finding time to do your job.

"Some books are to be tasted, others to be swallowed, and some few to be chewed and digested." —Sir Francis Bacon

"This is a book to chew and digest." —Dan Purkey

"It's what you learn after you know it all that counts."
—John Wooden (college basketball coach)

CHAPTER 1—BASICS
How to Understand the Rest of the Book

Let's have a talk, you and I.
"I'm too busy to do my job." How many times a day have you heard that? How many times a day have you thought that to yourself? You just start on a task and the phone rings with some urgent matter dumped on you from a co-worker or a customer. Then a hot email comes in that needs immediate attention. Then your boss assigns you some chore that has to be done by tomorrow or the world as we know it will end. Then the phone rings again, followed by an instant message from a colleague wondering where you are for the meeting that started five minutes ago, just as one of your direct reports comes in yammering about the disagreement he just had with another department. Finally the end of the workday comes and you've accomplished—nothing. Or at least that's the way it feels.

If you're too busy to do your job, there's a good chance you've developed the habit to focus only on the immediate fire drill that's in front of your face right now. From an overall company health perspective, that's bad, as you forget to make the customer satisfied, forget to coach employees, forget about why the company hired you, and forget to improve your situation. You just want to get the current issue behind you so you can address the next issue in line. What a dreary existence.

If you and everyone you know are too busy to do your jobs, that must mean that no jobs get done, since everyone's otherwise busy. Which raises the question: How does American business ever survive? It's really pretty miraculous that businesses produce any goods or services at all that customers want to buy, since no one does their job. They're too busy! How does anything ever get finished? No results, no business. No business, no jobs. It seems an impossible equation, since companies' payrolls are proof that there are jobs in spite of no one producing results. The practical reality of how businesses operate just doesn't stand up to common sense.

> "You humans. Sometimes it's hard to imagine how
> you've made it this far."
> —Prot (Kevin Spacey), from the movie *K-PAX*

Yet somehow we claw ourselves along through our stressful daily grind, but feel like we take two steps back for every one step forward. Despite it all, eventually things do get done. It's incredible. Some tangible product at the end of the line actually does get produced, whether it's a car, a desk, or an idea for some new software, but no one, from their own individual perspective, knows how it happened. In the face of this, the business deems itself successful—since something got produced—regardless of *how* it got produced.

Left in the dust of this "successful" business are the stressed out and frustrated employees who created those results and who wonder what and how they actually contributed to that success. Maybe better stated is that the workers themselves are the dust—the end product of being ground down every day by relentless pressures they feel powerless to control.

Or maybe you don't even worry about how you contribute to the business results. You're too busy. You just show up for work every day, ready to endure the same routine all over again, jumping from crisis to crisis as you drown in your sea of frustration. Work could be so, so much better.

Does this chaotic situation sound familiar? Would you like a different house, a different reality? Let's make it better. If a job change doesn't appeal to you, then let's start a remodel of the house you work in. Let's fix both you individually and the entire organization by identifying some guiding Principles and then acting in alignment with them.

~~~~~

Root Cause of the Mess (a.k.a. Blame)

Let's begin with the understanding that you being too busy to do your job is only a symptom of the root cause. We need to figure out why you're so busy and attack the problem at its source. You also need to understand that there's no single silver bullet that'll fix everything.

So why do you feel like Sisyphus pushing the boulder up the hill for all eternity when you're at work? Well, it starts with management. Let's not pull any punches. Let's place the blame squarely where it belongs: management. We'll talk about root causes in more detail later in the book, but poor management is the root cause reason you, as an employee and/or a manager, are too busy to do your job. We'll talk about the poor management actions that lead to your situation and how you can reverse them.

I need to throw in a little clarification, since you, the reader, are most likely a manager of some type. You might think, "Hey, wait a minute. I'm a product of the situation, not the cause." Managers are employees, too, in kind of a dual role. Let's assume that you're someone who wants to help fix the mess. So, by "management," I mean anyone who's at levels equal to or above you on the organization chart. Now, if you're the CEO, sorry, but you're it. Accept it and read on if you'd like to make your business run better, because more than anyone, you have the power to change things.

Management creates the structure in which employees operate. Management, either overtly or, more likely, unwittingly created the framework in which you operate. They set up the departmental structure. They set up the reporting structure. If you're too busy to do your job, it's most likely that management has set up the system that doesn't allow you to shine. Management set up the processes and systems that either 1) constrain you from being your best, or 2) support you to help you be your best. They built the house that you work in. They installed the faulty roof that leaks. They designed the bathroom to be an outside pit toilet instead of an inside flush toilet. The good news is that the house can be remodeled. From your perspective as an employee, the selfish result from fixing management is that you'll have time to do your job and do it well.

A facetious one-liner that's sometimes heard when something goes wrong and it has to be escalated to the next level of management is "Well, if things worked right on their own, we wouldn't need management." Witty, but let's take a more serious look at the logic of the statement. The fact is that every organization has management and it's integral to the operations of a business. Therefore, things can't just work on their own because management exists and meddles in everything. So, the conclusion must be that things go wrong because of management, not that management is the savior. The more things work badly, the more management is needed and the more management gets involved, the more things work badly. Sounds like an infinite loop that produces gainful employment for management to me, even though problems persist.

Doesn't it feel great to have someone to blame?

~~~~~~

I feel your pain, but I've also fixed that pain for others, so let's get started on the fix-it path. We quickly have to get off the finger-pointing, blame-placing path and move to some actions that'll repair the mess, otherwise it'll just continue. The actions I propose are specific, concrete steps to take to put an end to the otherwise endless cycle of "too busy to do my job." To do that, we need to work on two primary entities—all employees (to include all levels of anyone in the company) and, separately, managers (to include anyone who has direct reports). It's possible to work them in parallel and fix both at the same time.

There's a lot of foundational work that needs to be presented in order to facilitate a true understanding of the Principles presented, but I can hear you: "I'm too busy for that right now. I haven't got time to spend on some theoretical, textbook information. Give me something practical that I can do right now, or I'll set this book aside because my phone's ringing."

Fine. We'll feed the "right now" beast in the very next chapter to give you a taste of how to fix your dilemma. Some practical knowledge that you can put to instantaneous use should de-stress you at least enough so that you can better absorb the rest of the book. However, know that in order to implement the practical fully, it's important to understand the theoretical—the why. If you don't, the practical will eventually fail because no one understands the foundation, making it easier to get knocked off the true path to efficiency, effectiveness, and profitability. Kind of like your current situation and we can see how well that works. If you understand both the practical and the theoretical, you can be *sustainably* successful in your endeavors.

~~~~~~

STOP RIGHT THERE. I gotta know right now. Before we go any further . . . (with a nod to Meatloaf).

I understand you're probably in a hurry to get some practical advice. It's likely why you bought the book. If you're in that much of a hurry, skip the rest of this chapter for now and proceed directly to Chapter 2. It has some Practical Actions shown in **bold** that you're looking for. The goal is to get out of the survivor mode (too busy to do your job) you're in and move towards productivity (the ability to produce something), followed by the next level of efficiency (the ability to produce something with a minimum of effort), and finally the proficiency level (the ability to produce something well and easily). Go there, learn, and then come back to this spot. Go ahead; it's okay. Really.

(Musical interlude.)

~~~~~~

For those of you just returning to this spot from Chapter 2, welcome back. For those who stuck with me in a linear fashion, I admire your discipline. There are some foundational, background items that relate to the stuff in the rest of the book that you should be aware of before you delve too deeply into the material. The rest of this chapter will give you the basis to make more sense out of what we'll talk about later. While the topics may seem somewhat disconnected, remember that their purpose is background for the rest of the book. Chapter 1 is really kind of like a basic training course, if you've been in the military, or spring training, if you follow baseball. (Feel free to fill in your own analogy for whatever activity interests you.) It's stuff you learn now, but won't actually use until later. So, here's the rest of Chapter 1.

~~~~~~

My Intent

Okay, I know the road to hell is paved with good intentions. Nonetheless, if I communicate (in alignment with the Principle of Effective Communication) the intent of what I'm trying to accomplish, maybe you'll have a better grasp of the points made because you'll be less likely to form unfounded assumptions. Much of that intent was seen in the Introduction, but here are a few additional perspectives.

You've probably already noticed that the tone of this book is a bit different from what you usually see in other management books. That's by design. I believe (based on experience and education) comprehension is enhanced when the reader's engaged in what they read. I've minimized dry tables and charts and replaced them with, among other things, Dilbert cartoons, eye-catching slides, and thoughtful quotes from the likes of Homer (not Simpson, although I'm sure there's wisdom to be found there) to Babe Ruth to Steve Jobs to reinforce important points.

It uses a more casual, approachable, familiar style of a friend-to-friend conversation versus a formal, textbook approach. You'll find some tongue-in-cheek remarks thrown in for effect and maybe just my own amusement, because that's what I do when I talk to people. While I'm not sure "entertaining" is the right word for any management book, I've tried to err on that side of the equation to hopefully keep you interested and want to know what comes next. I hope you learn and enjoy it.

So, let's have a conversation, as much as an author and a reader can have at any rate. If you can incorporate even half of this stuff into your personal and work lives, your life and company will run more smoothly and efficiently than you ever dreamed possible.

~~~~~~

What This Book Fixes

We'll examine the components that should be Prioritized to the best benefit of your business so that not only is profit maximized, but the people that produce that profit are happy to do so instead of resentful that they have to show up to work. By the end of the book, you'll have discovered:

- How to get control of your work life and reduce both personal and work stress
- How to increase efficiencies
- How to increase effectiveness
- How to be a better leader

- How to make the organization better
- How to institute a culture of Effective Communication
- How to institute a culture of continuous improvement
- How to improve profitability
- How to move your business from chaos to calm
- Practical steps to change your reality

To be fair and set expectations up front (one of the topics we'll discuss later that helps break the cycle of "too busy to do your job"), we won't stop all of the fire drills that occur daily. Life happens. Real emergencies do occur and must be dealt with. But there are ways to reduce the number of false emergencies and take control of your work life. You can sure put a big dent in the number of fire drills so that those that still do make it to you will be worthy of your attention. Then, you'll actually have time to address them calmly. By the time you turn the last page, you'll understand the way it could be and, more importantly, how to get there. With this knowledge in hand, you'll find you can actually fix abysmal customer satisfaction, leave your work day with a sense of accomplishment, and have a stronger, healthier business to boot.

~~~~~

Lean Management Demystified

Lean Management is all the rage in the business world as I write this. It's based on the much-ballyhooed (with good reason) management techniques developed by W. Edwards Deming, popularized and put into practice by Toyota.

Initial Lean efforts focused on waste elimination to produce just-in-time products most effectively in a manufacturing environment. Waste is defined as any activity that doesn't produce customer value (i.e., something a customer will buy) or contribute to critical internal business information. There's a lot involved to reach this state of affairs and the "how" of it is important, but it's not my intent to make this into a Lean Management seminar. However, a short review of the basics is in order.

Lean, because of the name itself, implies to the uninitiated that it's just some spin to put on staff reductions. When many people hear "Lean," they think slash and burn cost cuts and they put up defenses immediately in fear for their jobs. Relax. When properly implemented, the result of Lean techniques is a workplace that people want to come to and stay and where efficiency, effectiveness, teamwork, logic, learning, and profitability all thrive. In fact, studies have shown that employment increases in companies that utilize Lean more than at companies that don't. The reason is that Lean makes a business grow more than normal, which means more employees are needed.

Lean is an attitude, an approach, a way of thinking, something that's in the forefront of all employees' minds in whatever task they undertake. It focuses on the important, not the urgent, even while the urgent is acted upon. It's about sustainable, behavioral change. It's a culture where it's safe to question conventional wisdom with inquiries like "How do you know that?" and where the person questioned doesn't worry about the ulterior motives of the questioner, other than the motive to make things work better.

Lean takes norms, standards, values, Principles, and strategies and moves them from theoretical constructs gathering dust on a shelf to vital, practical actions within the work force. It requires accountability at all levels of the company to keep everyone in alignment with the stated norms, standards, values, Principles, and strategies based on actions, not words. Although the origins of Lean (and maybe more correctly, Six Sigma) come from manufacturing, the Lean philosophy broadly applies to most other types of non-manufacturing businesses as well.

Lean focuses on waste elimination—just those things that are non-value added costs. After all, it's tough to argue for a particular process to stay in place when the process doesn't significantly contribute to make something a customer will buy. It's smarter to redirect those resources into processes that produce customer value so that customers will buy more of your product or service.

While I'll make some direct references to Lean here and there, this book really is a new way to present the theory of Lean in practical terms. I won't spend time to give you a specific Lean Principle and then tell you how that applies when it comes to, say, Prioritization. Just know that True Prioritization and the other Principles presented are in alignment with traditional Lean.

~~~~~~

The ABC Company Versus the XYZ Company

I'll refer to the ABC Company and the XYZ Company frequently in this book. While they're fictional company names, they really are a conglomeration of all the real world events of the companies I've worked for or consulted with, as well as real world events that took place in companies I've heard or read about. The situations aren't fictional and the management lessons to be derived from those situations also aren't fictional. The stories are presented in an effort to allow you to avoid or apply similar circumstances as you travel through your career. The ABC Company is generally the "good" company, the one you should emulate. The XYZ Company is generally the "bad" company, the one you can learn lessons from on what to avoid.

~~~~~~

The Big Four Principles

There are some key concepts that run throughout this book, primary among them are what we'll call The Big Four Principles. They show up in instance after instance on how to either avoid something bad or embrace something good. They're so important that I'll draw your attention to their applicability over and over, since they play such a large role to make a business run more smoothly, efficiently, effectively, and profitably—if understood and adhered to. They're Principles that, when you can relate them to your immediate work, will provide clarity and direction to whatever endeavor you engage in. They'll help you get your "busyness" under control.

Principles are the mom and dad of business. In the classic case of siblings in an argument with one another, one of them eventually says, "Oh, yeah? Well, I'm telling Mom." Mom would usually settle it, though sometimes not in an expected way. When you get into a conflict or disagreement with a peer or anyone in the company, the first place you need to go to for advice is the Principles. You need only ask each other if whatever action under discussion is in Alignment with Principles. If it is, then proceed. If it isn't, then do something different that *is* in alignment. If you can train your team, your peers, and your superiors (level-wise, not necessarily talent-wise) to rely on the Principles first of their own volition, you'll have fewer people knocking on your door who need your input.

Learning takes repetition and practice. As I present information in alignment with that truth, you may feel hammered over the head with the Big Four Principles, but it's only because so many different situations arise with spectacular regularity that involve them. If something's wrong, look to a misalignment with one or more of these four Principles as the cause. If you want to take the next step and *fix* something, look to employ one or more of these Principles. Then all will be right with the world. Well, maybe it's a bit more complicated than that, but hopefully you get my point. If you get nothing else out of this book, understand and internalize these four Principles to build your work around. They'll last you a lifetime. Here they are:

- True Prioritization (detailed discussion in Chapter 2)
- Alignment with Principles (detailed discussion in Chapter 4)
- Effective Communication (detailed discussion in Chapter 5)
- Simplification (detailed discussion in Chapter 7)

In order to help your mind remember and grasp the importance of these Principles, you'll find these terms are capitalized throughout the book whenever they're used.

~~~~~

Practical Action #1
Resolve to turn words into actions.

If you jumped ahead to Chapter 2 at the decision point earlier, your stress might be slightly reduced at this point, since you've now got some concrete steps to take around Prioritization. The most important thing you can do now is move from simply understanding something to a state of action. It's become cliché to say to "walk the talk," but get past the cliché to the real lesson. Great to understand the concept of Prioritization, but if you don't do anything with it in an actionable form, then what good is it? Nike had it right—Just Do It.

"A little less conversation; a little more action."
—Elvis Presley (rock 'n roll performer and philosopher)

How many meetings have you sat through or training sessions attended in which the audience sits passively and nods their heads in agreement with whatever really good point the speaker made? Can I get a hallelujah? While head nods are a start, it's all so much hot air, time that you'll never get back, unless you turn it into action, whatever "it" is.

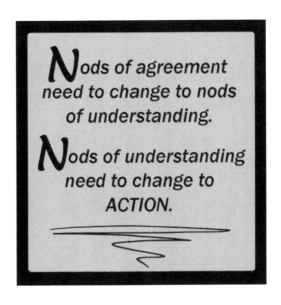

Nods of agreement need to change to nods of understanding.

Nods of understanding need to change to ACTION.

Priorities are nothing without action. Plans are nothing without action. Business and personnel evaluations are based primarily on the actions that are taken and the results of those actions (at least the good ones are). In the real world, no one's evaluated on how good a game they can talk, except maybe political pundits. The results are what matter and there can't be results without actions. This practical action to put words into action is totally up to you. It simply isn't good enough to talk endlessly about how things could be better. You and your business deserve more.

Practical Action #1 is the one that has the most room for a lamentably ironic outcome. Resolving to do something and actually doing it are two different things. The resolution is nothing but words, as powerful as the typical New Year's resolutions. So, yes, you need to resolve first, but then you actually have to do it or it's all for naught.

~~~~~

The Role of Profit

How healthy your business is depends on many components—notably profit, management, employees, and customers. While your success is driven in large part by employee and customer satisfaction, the real measure of business health is profit. Make no mistake about that. As crass as it sounds, profit rules. Logically, it can't be any other way. No profit, no business; no business, no employees. So, get past the idea that profit is bad.

"You only do that to make a buck" is a common accusation spit towards management. My somewhat sarcastic answer usually is, "Well, yes. What's your point?" Profit gets its bad reputation in some circles because the stereotype of management is profit at all costs, in disregard for human well-being. Unfortunately, most stereotypes have some basis in reality.

Never lose sight of the fact that this whole endeavor you're engaged in for forty or more hours a week is all in the interests of making money. While the operations hierarchy in Chapter 8 has at its foundation Effective Communication, note that the item at the top of that hierarchy is profit.

The great things you'll learn in this book to make you and your business better are all well and good, but without profit, they'll ultimately prove pointless if the business fails. The good news is that all of the great things you'll learn in this book about management and employee techniques for success will directly improve your profitability—a true win-win situation.

~~~~~~

Introspection, Logic, and Reality

Let's see if I can overwhelm you with logic. Because once you say, "Well, that makes sense," you'll be committed to a different, better way of working—a way that'll lead to fewer headaches, greater profits, and both job and customer satisfaction. There'll be no going back to the old ways because the logic's irrefutable. So follow along with me as we explore . . .

Understand that this book isn't some Kumbaya book whose goal is to make everyone happy and create world peace through some esoteric psycho-babble. That said, let's look at a series of questions that, subject to your perspective, may appear to fall into the Kumbaya category. Keep in mind that to find the root causes of problems, you need to examine the visible parts of the tree first. If the leaves are green and healthy, the roots are probably (maybe) fine. But if you see some brown spots on those leaves, or some wilting, you might want to take a deeper look for a solution other than just to keep your attention on the leaves. It's all interconnected.

Are you happy at work? Are your co-workers happy at work? Are your employees happy at work?

Are you as productive at work as you can be? Are your co-workers as productive at work as they can be? Are your employees as productive as they can be?

The answers to these questions are quite likely all the same—no—otherwise you probably wouldn't have bought the book. While there are more studies than necessary that show more job satisfaction leads to more job productivity, it really only takes common sense to understand the direct correlation. Two conditions exist that relate to that concept: 1) Good businesses strive to increase productivity and efficiency in order to produce ever greater profit; and 2) Good employees want to be satisfied at their jobs. Really, who wants to come to work if you're miserable all day? Who can do their best work when you feel like the wretched refuse?

Logic dictates that management should want both productivity and employee job satisfaction in order to maximize the chances for profit. That's clear enough, but that's also where the train often falls off the rails. Managers know what they want, they just don't know how to get it. They go about it like a teenage boy fumbling with his girlfriend's bra for the first time—eager, but no skill. In the rush to get profits, management rushes to get productivity. In that rush, they illogically ignore the fundamentals that get that desired productivity. The adage "The beatings will continue until morale improves" has its origin in the reality of thousands of real-life, real-time businesses. There is a better way.

Think about your business for a minute. Whether you're an owner or employee—think about it. If you were in charge, think about what you would do with the business. If you already are in charge, think about what you *could* do with it. There must be countless things that could be improved, both big and small. Pick one—one that really bugs you, big or small. Then, consider what would or could you do to change it? What if there were no boundaries on your ability to change it? What would you do?

You're the one reading this book. So, when I'm speaking (writing), I'm talking just to you, because this is a very personal endeavor, calling for a personal commitment. It's been said that ***personal change precedes organizational change***.

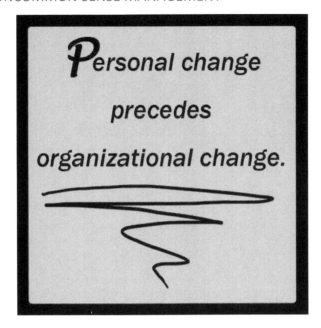

Pause a second for a point of reflection and really take in the significance and logic of that concept. It plays a central role in much of what we'll talk about in this book. Together, you and I will work to make this happen. It won't happen all at once, so set your expectations accordingly. But as we walk hand-in-hand through this book, you and I will form a bond of determination, backed by irrefutable logic, that'll bring about fundamental changes in the way business conducts business. We'll apply a certain *uncommon* sense to the process, since common sense apparently lacks in some or even most businesses.

Don't think for a minute that you and I are the only ones involved—it just starts with us. Along the way, we'll need to enlist or convert more like-minded business people. Once we achieve a critical mass, business as a whole will become a point of pride instead of a target of derision.

Think "derision" is too strong? Pick up the business section of any newspaper on any given day. Inevitably you'll find articles on fraud, mismanagement, failing businesses, inefficiency, personnel lawsuits, and a hundred other things that make you wonder how American business survives at all. Scott Adams, the creator of Dilbert (see notably *The Dilbert Principle*, his version of a management book) became a millionaire because of the pervasive ineptitude of business.

Beyond the "get what's mine at the expense of others" mentality that stereotypically permeates the business culture, there's enough out and out plain bad management to fill every office on Wall Street. (Some might cynically suggest those Wall Street offices are already full of bad management and we should look for office space somewhere else, but I digress.) Unclear direction. Backstabbing. Hypocrisy. Inefficiency. Finger-pointing. Unrealistic expectations. Lack of support. Lack of respect. Incompatible goals. Inconsistency. Subjectivity over objectivity. Style over substance. Why can't managers see these and hundreds of other practices that drag their businesses towards doom? At the risk of a bit of self-aggrandizement, maybe no one's shown them until now, so now the time has come.

Television shows, movies, magazines, blogs, and books all are replete with examples of how not to run a business. Yet it persists. Read the comic pages in the newspaper. If not for the more than adequate supply of bad management practices, many of these comics wouldn't even exist. I already mentioned Scott Adams, but *Blondie*, *Doonesbury*, and *Sally Forth* are just a few others that spring to mind. While they make you laugh at the obvious foibles of inept managers, somehow the obvious isn't so obvious when it comes to real world management. There are none so blind as those who will not see.

While some rebel against the use of sports analogies, I'm not one of them. They provide some of the best examples of which organizational characteristics lead to success and which lead to mediocrity or even failure.

Take the Dallas Cowboys in the 2008 season . . . please. They were a team (or perhaps more correctly characterized as a collection of individuals instead of a team) that purportedly thrived on chaos. Players calling each other out. Players saying if only they would get the ball more than the other guys, then they'd win. Players with off-field problems that bled over into the locker room. Coaches not in control. Constant turmoil. Ownership deliberately injecting potential problems in order to "stir things up." Or, as my old commercial fishing skipper once told me, "A certain amount of pollution is good for the environment." Hmmm . . . (editorially speaking). The Cowboys, despite massive amounts of individual talent and a huge payroll, failed to make the playoffs, in large part because they had too much "pollution."

Now look at virtually any championship team. Words that come from those locker rooms are words like Unity, Focus, Unselfishness, Commitment, Vision, Buy-in, Chemistry, Love, Teamwork, Execution, Character, Harmony, Consistency, Effective Communication, and Accountability. These aren't concepts unique to sports champions. They're directly applicable to profitable business teams. Yet so much of business refuses to embrace these winning concepts. They either ignore them or they mouth the words, but fail to truly incorporate them. Remember Practical Action #1.

These championship ideas aren't rocket surgery [Note: That's sort of a joke, not a typo.]; they're just uncommon sense. Simple in theory, yet apparently too complex to implement for many businesses. If you don't believe these championship attributes are important components in the overall success of a business, then please work really hard to keep an open mind about the rest of this book, because if you read to the end, you'll have a changed and better perspective on business and, perhaps, life. Focus on the logic of what's presented and examine your preconceived notions in the light of new information.

A note about logic. It's not all it's cracked up to be. While a primarily logic-driven business would no doubt exceed all financial and personnel objectives, Vulcans, those fictional paragons of logic from *Star Trek*, don't run businesses—humans do. In David Rosenfelt's novel *Play Dead*, his main character says, "I like dogs considerably more than I like humans. That doesn't make me antihuman; there are plenty of humans I'm very fond of. But generally speaking, if I simultaneously meet a new human and a new dog, I'm going to like the dog more. I'm certainly going to trust the dog more. They're going to tell me what they think, straight out, and I'm not going to have to read anything into it. They are what they are, while *very often humans are what they aren't*." (Emphasis added.) Dogs are straightforward; humans are full of emotional contradictions and not always susceptible to logic.

So as you proceed down the merry path to set your work life and business right, remember nothing happens unless you have buy-in from the people that make up the business. It'll take ten pieces of logic to overcome one piece of emotional resistance, and even that may not be enough. Logically, then, a business leader must incorporate the human, emotional factors into whatever direction the leader leads.

~~~~~~

Personal Life Impacts

Along the way to controlling your work life via this book, you'll find that a bonus is in the application of these Principles to your personal life. They'll provide a smooth path to better relationships and whatever activities you do outside of work. Some of the most gratifying experiences I've had as a leader are when someone comes to me and says "You know, I used one of your management ideas with my spouse the other night and it actually prevented an argument that we would have had otherwise." That's powerful stuff.

~~~~~~

Okay, *now* let's get to work.

CHAPTER 2—PRIORITIES
How to Truly, Effectively Prioritize

Practical Action #2
Resolve to Prioritize your work and then act in accordance with your stated Priorities.

Discount what follows at your own peril, regardless of whether you've heard it before. There are thousands of management books out there that say the same thing. Listen to them and to me. We're right. But what I'm about to give you is a different way for you to make practical sense out of it, a way to actually implement it and change your work life.

People tend to throw around the word "Priority" without any conscious thought to what it really means. Its common and loose usage diminishes its importance.

Using the term "Priority" lightly is analogous to people giving 110%, or if they're better than that 150%, or if they're really, really good 200%. C'mon. It's simply not mathematically possible to give more than 100% of what you've got. The challenge is to get up to the 100% level. But in an effort to puff out their chests, people get carried away in nonsensical statements in an assumed battle of one-upmanship. "Oh, you only gave 100%? Well, I gave 150%. You suck."

The same type of misuse happens with "Priority." Ever hear people say, "Oh, that's a Priority for me" and "Oh, this is a Priority, too" and "Oh, look at that Priority over there." If someone says they've got Priorities, why that must make them an important person; they've got their act together because they have Priorities. And the more Priorities they have, the more important they must be. Pretty soon they've got about a hundred Priorities, but nothing ever happens on any of them. They're basically full of hot air, but don't bother them; they're too busy with their Priorities and inflating giant hot air balloons.

Most people don't even hear the word when it's used anymore because it's thrown out all the time with even the most insignificant of projects. People generally don't follow through to ensure the completion of a given "Priority." Therefore, why should anyone drop whatever they're otherwise doing to focus on this issue—particularly true if there aren't consequences of not acting on the Priority?

Language is important and the words chosen to communicate need to be selected with care. Limit how often the term "Priority" is used. Reserve it for things that fall into the category of single-minded focus until completion—to use an extreme example of the concept. Replace the word "Priorities" with "tasks," unless you actually talk about True Priorities. You'll help create a culture at work that has people jump with purpose when the word is used, that attaches genuine significance to the term.

Here's a dictionary definition of PRIORITY:

1. The right to precede others in order, rank, privilege, etc.
2. The right to take precedence in obtaining certain supplies, services, facilities, etc., especially during a shortage.
3. Something given special attention.
4. Highest or higher in importance, rank, privilege, etc.: *a priority task.*

Notice the first two definitions say that a priority has *a right* to take precedence, not that it *does* take precedence. It's up to you to make it actually have precedence in an actionable fashion.

The third and fourth definitions are more how Priorities should be treated, seen with the phrases "special attention" and "of the highest importance." These imply a bit more action. Priorities without corresponding action are simply ineffectual words.

Here's my more practical definition: *A True Priority is whatever you're doing at this exact moment.* At this very point in real time as you now read this book, you've chosen, for whatever reasons, to set aside all other potential activities in favor of doing what you're doing right now. Your current and immediate Priority right now is reading this book. You've chosen to forego all other activities—phone calls, emails, TV, golf, exercise, meetings—to spend your valuable and limited time focused on improving your lot in life by reading this book. That's a True Priority.

True Priorities are defined by actions, not words.

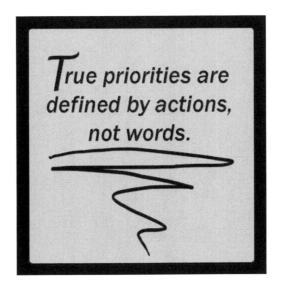

The question then becomes whether this action you're now involved in really is the Priority you should work on. A fair inquiry of an employee (and yourself) is "Why do you spend your time on A when B is the Priority?" This question can, and should, be applied to any activity before you undertake it.

Now, there can be valid reasons for such an allocation of time, but the question forces the employee to make conscious choices about how their time's spent instead of just working on things as they come along. A leader engages their employees in their work and deadlines help maintain that engagement.

What if you forsook all other actions (for now, at least) to perform in sickness and in health, for richer or poorer, the task you're about to undertake? That deliberately sounds like marriage vows because when you take on a task/Priority, you need to be committed to it and work it until death do you part. Don't freak out. In this case, "death" simply means completion of the Priority. Once you complete it, it's over and done with and you can move on to the next Priority.

The problem is that people generally don't keep their Priorities clearly in mind. They let the daily workaday world take command and obscure the real Priorities. It's not a conscious thing, it just happens.

In the song *Virtual Insanity*, Jamiroquai sings:
"It's a wonder man can eat at all
When things are big that should be small."

True Priorities need to be so ingrained into your consciousness that every time you do anything else, you'll stop and question why you're spending time on a task that's not a Priority. It's a case of you managing the job or the job managing you. Sometimes it's just easier to tidy up a stack of papers or sharpen your pencils than attack the hard things that are the real Priorities, but those avoidance tasks are actions that should be avoided like the plague. Spend your time on the real stuff.

If it's a True Priority, treat it as such. The first time you deviate from that Prioritized task, you've just moved that item from a Priority to a non-priority. Is that really what you meant to do? Did you really mean to devalue a True Priority? Do you understand that you set the example for others (and yourself) when you don't act in congruence with your talk? Do you understand that your credibility and integrity are now at issue?

Don't move True Priorities around on a whim. Make a commitment to your Priority and keep that commitment. Treat Priorities as Priorities. Handle with care, not indifference. However, the practical reality is that life will intrude at some point. A rigid adherence to your Priority to read this book while the water in the bathtub overflows might not be in your best interests. Priorities need to be flexible, based on changing or reevaluated conditions. What if you generally resisted any rearrangement of Priorities? You could still assess the new information that comes in, but only clear and conclusive evidence would knock you off the path you initially set.

This all presupposes that you actually know what your Priorities are. Now that we know to treat Priorities as True Priorities, let's figure out how to determine what those Priorities are.

~~~~~

Three Flavors of Priorities

Priorities come in three different flavors: Strategic, Tactical, and Task.

A Strategic Priority is a bigger picture view of what you'd like to accomplish and is supported by Tactical Priorities, which in turn are supported by Task Priorities. Strategic Priorities are strategic only relative to the work you do or what you want to accomplish, but the thing here is to think big. Big might be getting your installers to their jobs on time or it might be solving world peace. A Strategic Priority will likely have multiple, supportive Tactical Priorities. Each Tactical Priority will likely have multiple, supportive Tasks.

One way to think of Task Priorities is that they're the things that aren't dependent on anything other than you to take a specific action. For example, if you want to take the family to the movie as your Strategic goal, that depends on you eating dinner on time (Tactical), which depends on you picking up the kids from school on time and finishing cooking dinner on time (Task). Only after your Task Priorities are resolved can you move up a level to the Tactical. In theory, after all of your Tactical Priorities are achieved, the Strategic Priority will be accomplished without any more effort.

Assume our goal/Strategic Priority is to solve world peace. A Tactical Priority that supports it might be to establish a place where people from around the globe can come together and communicate. Hey, let's build a United Nations. Then one of your Task Priorities might be to meet with the ambassador from China on Thursday. Of course, you could get even more detailed and have some key points planned ahead (Priorities) that you want to discuss with the ambassador. These Tactical and Task Priorities are all in alignment with the master, big picture Strategic Priority of world peace and so work together to achieve your goal. Work on an appropriate Task Priority and you effectively work on all three levels of Priorities. Your overall plan is simply composed of various Priorities at various levels.

It really doesn't matter that you categorize your Priorities as Strategic, Tactical, or Task. That's maybe too textbook and, after all, who has the time to categorize? It's not a Priority. Don't get too hung up on the labels. That'll sort itself out as you dig into the process. It's the order and dependencies of your Priorities that are the important things.

Practical Action #3
List your potential Priorities.

For now just list potential Priorities. Take a piece of paper (or a computer, if you've moved into the twenty-first century) and just write down the things you'd like to make happen. Everything. Think of it as a release of sorts. Take all the troubles that you'd like to solve and write them down without a thought to how important they are, just that they're things you want to fix at some point. It can even include the things that you do that constitute the daily grind of what makes you frustrated because you're too busy to do your job, like answer emails. Everything. Go ahead. It may take some time (maybe days) if you really think it through, but I'll wait . . . .

Finished? Great.

Practical Action #4
Prioritize your potential Priorities.

If you used a computer to compose your list, this next action will be easy. Let's say for discussion's sake that you've listed five potential True Priorities—A, B, C, D, and E. You'll have many more in your real world list, but I just want to simply for the example. Compare two of the potential True Priorities. Any two, let's just say A and B. Which of those two is the more important in your mind? No ties. Pick a winner and a loser. Be decisive and ruthless. Can't decide? C'mon. You're a manager. Step up and make a decision. If they really are equal in your mind, then flip a coin. The important thing to remember is that you simply don't have time enough in the day to do everything (or anything, if you're the cynical type), so if you can only do one, just one, which do you need to solve the most?

Say you've decided B is more important than A. Now rearrange your list of potential Priorities so that now it shows B, A, C, D, E. (If you're old school, then maybe you use your pencil (or, if you're fancy, a pen) and write a 1 next to B and a 2 next to A.) Take the next potential Priority, C, and compare it to each of the Priorities you've rearranged thus far, starting with the one you've currently got in the number one slot. Is C more important than B? No? Then drop down to the number two slot and compare whether C is more important than A. No? Now C becomes Priority number 3. Your list is now in this order: B, A, C, D, E.

More as an FYI than anything, this process is called a Bubble Sort because, in the process, the truly important items bubble to the top. It's widely used, particularly among computer programmers, who, according to a knowledgeable friend of mine, believe they rule the world. Hey, if it's good enough for world rulers, it's got to be good for the rest of us.

The process should be clear now, so just continue it. Take D and compare it to B. More important? Yes, so now your list looks like D, B, A, C, E. Then take E, start at the top, work down, and compare it to the others. If you come to the comparison decision that E's more important than A, now your final list looks like D, B, E, A,

C. You're done. Take a break, because if you did this right, with a lot of thought, it probably took a while.

Just a word of caution in regard to your newfound ability to Prioritize. There's the issue of good judgment in Prioritizing. Just because you've determined your Priorities, that doesn't mean you're done. You also need to validate (over time) that the items are in the right order. A rigid adherence to the original list in the face of new, important information could result in disaster. You need to have flexibility with your Priorities in order to modify them if you don't achieve the results you want or if you determine after further review that a shakeup's in order.

For example, I once saw a title of a seminar session at an IT conference that was "Why Leaders Place IT Strategy before Business Strategy." I'm sure the speaker wanted to create a bold, marketing, grabber headline to draw in session participants and, on the surface, it sounds great. On closer examination, though, the Priorities are backwards. He confused the strategic and the tactical Priorities.

Let's think about it. Suppose you want to start a business. You don't know what kind of business, but you think to yourself, "Well, I don't know exactly what I want to do, but I'd better go out and get myself a really cool Information Technology system." Really? How can you know what IT system you need if you don't know what functions it needs to serve? If there's no business strategy in place, you won't know what functions are needed. Clearly, IT supports the business; it doesn't drive the business, unless you want to drive your business into the ground.

This type of thoughtless approach to Prioritization goes on daily. And this speaker taught this approach to an audience of hundreds. If you wonder what's wrong with American business, there's a clue.

~~~~~~

Follow Up and Follow Through

Priorities are nothing without follow up and follow through.

Dilbert By Scott Adams

Funny, huh? Far-fetched? Not so much. Scott Adams gets many of his ideas from people in the real business world. He may exaggerate them for comic effect, but the sad fact of the matter is that the same type of thing as depicted above happens in the real world on a daily basis.

LACK OF FOLLOW THROUGH EXAMPLE: The XYZ Company finally, after neglect of many years, conducted an employee satisfaction survey to see how things stood with the worker bees. Interestingly (and glaringly, in hindsight), management never released the results. Management failed to follow through on its own initiative. Maybe it was simply a case where the CEO really didn't care, like the CEO in the Dilbert cartoon above, and did the survey only because it was expected of him. The common, water-cooler theory was the results came out so negatively that top-level management rebelled at making them public, so they didn't. "Sweep it under the rug and it'll go away, I'm sure," we could almost hear them say.

Of course, we didn't really need a survey. We could see the dissatisfaction daily as people slogged their way through their pathetic work lives, too busy to do their jobs. What a golden opportunity for management to step up with some open and honest communication about the state of affairs and Prioritize some actions to fix the problems. Instead, they chose to climb back into the proverbial ivory tower and, in the immortal words of (allegedly) Marie Antoinette, "Let them eat cake." Employees felt betrayed, used, and disrespected.

ANOTHER LACK OF FOLLOW THROUGH EXAMPLE: According to the Army Corps of Engineers, an earthen dam had the possibility of collapse. If it gave way, the area below the dam would flood. The Corps, the county, and the insurance companies encouraged businesses in the potential flood zone to take precautions during dam repairs. The Vice President of the XYZ Company made it a Priority to get some flood protection for a critical office. Seems a reasonable action on the surface. Who wants their critical facilities flooded? So, the VP spent thousands of dollars to buy a compact barrier that could be unfolded and deployed around the entire building to stave off the floodwaters. Problem solved. Well, sort of. Some questions remained that weren't addressed in midst of the self-congratulations done to celebrate the great management decision to put flood protection in place. For example:

- Exactly how would the barrier be deployed? [No one was trained to do it.]
- How long would it take to deploy the barrier, assuming someone was trained, versus how much notice would there be before the collapse? [The county could only give a four-hour notice of an imminent flood and, even under ideal conditions, the barrier would take longer than that to deploy.]
- What additional equipment was needed to deploy the barrier? [Water pumps, high capacity hoses, and forklifts were required, none of which the business owned or bought.]

While some apparently felt comforted that they had flood protection after the purchase, it wasn't really any protection at all. The VP had Prioritized the big picture, but failed to Prioritize the necessary follow through tactics. Ironically, management later found that the area in question had never flooded in recorded history.

QUASI-REAL WORLD EXAMPLE: I can't vouch for the veracity of this example, but local Seattle lore has it that prior to the Great Seattle Fire of 1889, which essentially wiped out downtown Seattle, city leaders saw the potential danger posed by a lack of fire protection. Now, fire hydrants were a relatively new invention back then, but those leaders quickly saw the value of the concept. City officials announced the Prioritization of a portion of city funds to ensure that protection. They further Prioritized funding the installation of fire hydrants throughout downtown, which were duly installed. However, the leaders didn't follow through on actually funding the *connection* of those shiny, new fire hydrants to the water lines. Because of the lack of follow through on their stated Priority, the city burned.

LESSON: As a manager, if you say you'll Prioritize something, have the perseverance to follow it through to completion. Know or research ahead of time if you and the organization will have the mental and time bandwidth to bring the Priority home. If you're not prepared to address all aspects of making a Priority a reality, don't announce the action as a Priority in the first place. Instead, spend your limited energies on something that deserves True Priority status. How many figurative fire hydrants do you have in your business that have never been hooked up to the water lines?

Practical Action #5
Resolve to be okay with things falling off your plate.

At this point, you're closer to gaining control of your life than 95% of the population. Congratulations. But don't get weak now, because the next step will put you to the test. Remember that you can't do everything, regardless of how much you try. Internalize and live this notion. Believe it in your heart of hearts. Logically you know it's true, yet somehow most of us feel like Superman and act as if we can do it all. I need to pound on this point because many of you might just skip right over this concept, thinking it doesn't apply to you. Believe me, it does.

YOU CAN'T DO IT ALL, SO DON'T. Be ready to say "No." With a nod to Bill Murray's character Phil in the movie *Groundhog Day*, ask yourself if you're a god—not *the* God—a god. If your answer is "No," then what if you considered not trying to be a god and doing it all?

You've got to be okay with this concept or you'll go crazy and continue to be forever frustrated. Everyone has their figurative plates piled high with stuff and every day it seems more stuff is piled on higher and deeper. A plate is only so big. Eventually something will fall off, even if you can balance with the best of the Cirque du Soleil. You want to be able to control what falls off and what stays on.

As Clint Eastwood famously said in his role as Dirty Harry, "A man's got to know his limitations." To know your limitations requires a bit of self-evaluation for you to get a realistic assessment of your capabilities—a completely separate topic, but relevant nonetheless. You need to know how much you can genuinely take on at one time and still produce meaningful results for all the tasks you've chosen.

The key here is to recognize what's falling off your plate and where it fits on your newly constructed list of Priorities. When one more piece of stuff attempts to weasel its way onto the pile, take the weasel by the scruff of the neck, hold it out away from you, and examine it closely. Then go back to your sparkly, new list and do the same comparison process you did for Practical Action #4 and see where its importance really lies.

See already how you've begun to take control? You're the one to make the decisions on what you'll take on and what you'll let slide. Don't let the rush of power get to you. As the Romans said, at least according to the movie *Patton*, "All glory is fleeting."

After a critical evaluation, suppose your weasel (let's call it potential Priority W) actually turns out to be more important than Priority C. Now your Priority list will look like D, B, E, A, W, C. For all intents and purposes, C has now fallen off the plate, if you've self-assessed that you only have the bandwidth for five items.

A quick word about changing Priorities and flexibility.

Dilbert By Scott Adams

Dilbert demonstrates one of the typical great faults of management: a lack of will or skill to make Priorities sustainable, particularly in the face of some new, perceived, hair-on-fire crisis that becomes the hot new Priority. It's as if management has attention deficit disorder, much like the boss in the Dilbert comic above. It's fine to start something, but don't start the something if you won't follow it through to its completion. Flexibility's good and necessary, but changing Priorities on a willy-nilly basis only leads to a confused, cynical workforce and a lack of confidence in leadership. If you say it, then do it.

Practical Action #6
Communicate early with the people to whom you committed a result if the Priorities change and you can't meet the commitment.

One of the main reasons why you're too busy to do your job is that people either have to check in with you to get a project status or you've missed a deadline and now the people interested in that project are incensed and need escalated action. Or, maybe you're the person escalations come to and the project now has a higher sense of urgency because someone else missed a deadline and you're the one that has to figure out what to do.

Practical Action #6 is designed to take a step towards decreasing panic-mode, hair-on-fire escalations/expedites across the company, but it starts with you. Control what you can control.

While the owner of Project C may be dismayed to get bumped down the Priority ladder, it's really a matter of respect to let that person know your decision and the reality of the situation. That person will at least appreciate knowing where Project C now stands and from there you can negotiate a new due date. This is addressed in more detail later, but for this Prioritization chapter, understand that it's important to Prioritize communication with your co-workers as one of those strategic Priorities.

As Stephen Covey teaches, we oftentimes lose sight of what's important and unfortunately Prioritize what's urgent. "The key is not to prioritize what's on your schedule, but to schedule your priorities."

~~~~~~~

ROOT CAUSE ANALYSIS

Dilbert By Scott Adams

How do you know that what you've Prioritized is the right thing to concentrate on? The initial out-of-the-box list of potential Priorities is definitely where to begin, but once you start actually Prioritizing the Priorities, you'll likely need to do some further investigation to make sure you've got the right problem in mind—that is, the most important problem to solve. Issues seldom have just a single cause that can be easily identified and attacked.

Many managers would like to think that issues are standalone. ("Gee, if we could just fix this one thing, everything else would work correctly.") Those managers are delusional. They typically look just at the surface symptom in order to find an easy answer. Then they can cross off an item from the list, move on to the next topic, and more quickly congratulate themselves for being good managers. They may not consciously have this thought process, but their behavior would certainly reinforce that view. It's like they say, "I'm too busy to spend any quality time on this issue, so we'd better find a solution—any solution—fast so that I can get to the hundred other Priorities that need to be addressed." Just check the box and move on to the next item. A problem transferred is a problem solved. Break this pattern. You need to be better than that.

Particularly with existing processes that you've Prioritized for improvement versus new ones you'd like to develop, you need to dig down into the depths of the process to find all the interconnections and see the real situation. Only after this due diligence is complete should you set up the final order of your issues as D, B, E, A, W, C. Without a closer look, you may not realize that D (the nominal number one Priority) actually depends on A. If you don't fix A, D can never be fixed. Therefore, corrective actions need to be put against A first and not D directly.

At XYZ Company, most blamed the frontline installation technicians for virtually all the ills that could beset an installation. After all, when customers called in with complaints that usually started with "When the tech came out here . . . ," who else could be to blame? The easy target became the Installation department. In internal departmental meetings to discuss customer complaints, all departments started with the standard, politically correct, self-deprecating line of "Well, we've certainly got some issues in our department . . ." since they didn't want to appear holier-than-thou. But, they immediately followed with ". . . but those installation folks are out of control."

The finger squarely pointed at the technicians and everyone knew it. The techs chafed under this burden for years and futilely pointed out that most of the problems they encountered weren't in their control. The management team didn't want to hear it—particularly those managers of other departments who were too busy dealing with their own more immediate (from their perspective), internal departmental issues. They didn't have time to worry about the Installation department's woes.

With a new approach, however, the finger began to waiver and turn a bit. The techs identified their number one problem as frequently inaccurate orders with issues such as types of services to be installed, the customer's address, contact information, equipment needed, appointment time, etc. Customers saw unprofessional installations, if the installations got completed at all. Techs, the face of XYZ Company to the customer, bore the brunt of the dissatisfaction, since they were the ones eye-to-eye with the customers.

The first step of the turnaround came when an Installation manager finally not only listened to the techs, but also took some actual action. What a novel concept. The Installation manager Truly Prioritized this issue. He tracked the percentage of orders that reached the field that contained inaccuracies and found over half didn't have the right information. Armed with data, he then went to the Order department's management to find out what could change to get accurate orders. They bristled at the audacity of the Installation department daring to insert itself into their Order department's processes. In short, turf war issues made the Order department unresponsive. (We'll address turf in Chapter 8.)

With perseverance and some additional support from the Installation department's upper management, interdepartmental meetings started to take place about the issue. Remarkable what a little Effective Communication can accomplish. In the same way that the Installation department believed most issues were out of their control, the Order department ironically believed the same thing about input coming to them from their upstream department partners.

This confluence of issues prompted a review of all departments' roles in getting an accurate order to an installation tech. The concept for the analysis was simple: start at the point when the order comes in the door from sales and follow it through the system. See which departments touch the order along the way and how they touch it; look at the time each department takes to move it along to the next department and why. The root causes relatively quickly became apparent. Interestingly, after this analysis began, they found that the starting point—when the order came in the door, which seemed logical at the time—wasn't the right place. The right place appeared even earlier in the process—when the salesperson walked through the customer's door and made promises (set expectations), which often were out of alignment with what the company could actually produce.

This "follow the bouncing ball" process uncovered many more Priorities to add to the list. It moved the initial number one Priority to fix the installation techs to the back of the line, as various departments finally awoke to the havoc they caused through their own problematic processes. It also reprioritized Priorities within those various departments as they began to understand the impacts from their efforts (or lack thereof) on customer satisfaction.

While this real world experience wasn't all quite as neat and tidy as portrayed here, that's the essence of it. The lesson learned, that can be applied in most all industries, is that if you start at the real beginning and follow an order through in detail to the end (however you define an "order" for your business), you'll gain both a better awareness of your business and what to Prioritize.

~~~~~~

A Surface Symptom Example

Let's take another example at the XYZ Company in which management couldn't (or at least didn't) take the time to figure out the real problem and took the "easy" way out. They just looked at the surface symptom and jumped to a conclusion.

There are essentially two ways fix a business problem: 1) attack the problem directly (e.g., low sales means to spend more money on marketing or hire more sales people to generate more customer purchases) or 2) attack the root causes (e.g., low sales could mean poor service reputation, installation problems, can't fulfill promised orders, sales people are poorly trained, you have a bad product, etc.). Essentially, you can cut off the visible part of the weed or you can destroy the roots. Most everyone knows that the weed will regrow if only the part above ground is removed. When the weed regrows, you have to spend additional time to cut the weed again, and again. The weed really never goes away and now you've spent considerable time and attention on that weed. That's inefficiency in all of its glory. The same concept is true for business issues. Inefficiencies are created when the wrong problem is attacked or the right problem is attacked in the wrong way.

At the XYZ Company, sales slumped. Sales management, inside their walled-in silo and not needing anyone else's help in their view, decided to sell their way out of the problem of slow sales. Put more feet on the street and pound the pavement; inundate customers with a true sales force ("force" meaning both power and a group). So, they hired like crazy, doubled the number of salespeople, and threw them out there with the directive of "Just go sell."

They failed to consider that the number of potential customers remained the same. Now with twice the number of salespeople and no controls over who had responsibility for which territories or customers, it became a wild frenzy of sales activity.

The backlash soon began. Potential and current customers began to complain about multiple sales calls from different salespeople within just a few days. Salespeople complained that they spent their time with customers who'd just been talked to a couple of days ago. Total sales actually started to decrease. Sales per salesperson took a dramatic fall, given that they now had twice the salespeople but the same number of potential customers. Turnover among the sales force increased dramatically, since they couldn't sell enough to make quota (so they were fired) or make a livelihood (so they quit). Stress exuded from every corner of the sales department. Company costs increased as training staff had to be beefed up to train all of the new hires coming in to replace those who left.

XYZ didn't lack salespeople. The deeper, root cause problems like poor service reputation, installation problems, inability to fulfill promised orders, and poorly trained salespeople (this latter root cause being magnified by the revolving door of new salespeople) all contributed to fewer dollars coming in the door.

Find the true root cause.

~~~~~~

Characteristics of a True Priority

So how do you recognize a True Priority when you see it? If people constantly spout off about the various Priorities they have and the term's frequently used without any real thought, how do you separate the wheat from the chaff?

A True Priority must have action attached to it, essentially:

- WHO (the accountable person)
- will do WHAT
- by WHEN?

The "what" is really the statement of the Priority itself in clear and succinct language. If a stranger comes up to you on the street and asks you about your number one Priority, what if you were able immediately to recite it in clear terms that anyone could understand? That would indicate the Priority is firmly lodged in your brain. The more you can state your Priority with numbers attached, the better off you are, since numbers provide clarity. If you talk about a strategic Priority, it may be harder to attach a number to it, but the more you work with tactical and task Priorities, numbers become critical to provide a connotation to what you want to do. Let's see how a good Priority statement can be built with these components.

First, state the Priority in the format of "We will move from X to Y." This is a simple, clear way to communicate. In this format, X is the current state of affairs—where you are with your current metric. (If you don't have a metric (i.e., a number), we'll get to that later in the book.) Y is the future state of affairs that you want to achieve (i.e., your goal), again in terms of a number.

For example, a good starting-point Priority statement could be "We want to move our current on-time installation performance from 70% to 95%." Now you've got something tangible you can grab ahold of and do something with. As you continue to measure, chart/track, and focus on changing the start number to the end number, you'll graphically see your progress. If you publish that tracking chart for all to see, you'll have a powerful motivator to improve.

Second, inextricably linked to the Priority statement must be who's accountable for the completion and success of the Priority. The "who" can't be a department or organization, since that dilutes and deflects true accountability. The more nameless "who" is, the more people can hide behind a screen of anonymity and not do what they've been charged to do. They can always blame it on someone else because they personally haven't been identified as part of the effort. Use names. If you don't know who's driving the boat, you can't effectively point out when you see the boat veering off course in order to do something about it. Let's say Jane Smith's the lead for the team to accomplish this Priority. The preliminary Priority statement could be "Jane Smith will lead the effort to move our current on-time performance from 70% to 95%."

Third, a goal is worthless unless it's Prioritized with an associated deadline. Deadlines really are the essence of Priorities. They force you to take action and plan because time's a finite quantity. Actions take time. Seems obvious, but if you don't really understand and incorporate that concept into your plans to accomplish the goal, you'll never get there. Your "Priority" will be relegated to a lower level in the practical world. A deadline makes it a real, tangible entity with meaning. A deadline moves the task from the theoretical, pie-in-the-sky realm to the practical, real world. Add this component and you have a complete Priority statement.

"Jane Smith will lead the effort to move our current on-time performance from 70% to 95% by June 30, 2013."

Clear, succinct, accountable, and actionable.

An interesting exercise for you would be to ask some key questions of people when they throw out statements like "I'm too busy to work on that because I've got other Priorities." "Oh, really?" you might say. "What's your number one Priority? Who's the lead for that effort? What metrics do you want to change? When do you plan to get that finished?" Now, you'll probably want to avoid the impression of a police interrogation, but if you ask those types of questions in a culture that truly understands Priorities and embraces open and honest communication, it'll help keep people focused on the tasks/Priorities that they've agreed to focus on.

~~~~~~

Inefficiencies

When the Priorities are wrong, you work on the wrong problems, and so inefficiencies are created. It's simply wasted effort and time that you could put to better use to create customer value. You might say, "Inefficiencies? Inefficiency really is only wasted time, not real money. So what?" Well, the "so what" is that inefficiencies do equal lost money. Money thrown down a rat hole by paying for and using up precious, limited personnel resources on tasks that don't result in customer value means that profits are lower than they otherwise would be. Period.

Too often management misunderstands the connection between inefficiencies and real, bottom-line costs. They view inefficiencies dismissively as opportunity cost and misunderstand what opportunity cost is. They take the stance that it's just a theoretical construct that doesn't affect profit, created only to provide gainful employment to economists and not worthy of real use. From Wikipedia, "opportunity cost is the cost of any activity measured in terms of the value of the next best alternative forgone (that is not chosen). . . . Opportunity cost is a key concept in economics . . . and plays a crucial part in ensuring that scarce resources are used efficiently. Opportunity costs aren't restricted to monetary or financial costs." From this definition, you can see that opportunity costs are real monetary costs. What if they were treated as such and used as justification to eliminate inefficiencies?

Here's an equation for your edification: Inefficiency = extra work = too busy to do your job = less profit.

For example, suppose a change in process is proposed that would save a given department 100 hours a week. The ABC Company manager, steeped in Lean philosophy, would jump on it and look for ways to put that freed up 100 hours to use to create more customer value. The XYZ Company manager would say one of two things: 1) I'll still pay those people to come to work, so I haven't really saved anything. Why should I implement the proposal? 2) Great! Let's implement the process and fire three people to reduce staff cost.

Because management ultimately is graded on profit, many managers jump right to the Profit and Loss (P&L) statement to justify their decisions. They ignore the fact that they've been hired not as accountants, but as thinking beings who can see and consider all aspects of a situation, who can look ahead and consider consequences of actions. Decisions based solely on a short term, immediate financial impact are usually misguided. For example, if you reduced inventory, you'd save money directly by not spending so much on product. That's a direct, hard cost savings, but many managers stop there and pat themselves on the back for a job well done.

In an effort to reduce inventory costs at the XYZ Company, management decided to reduce the amount of parts that techs carried on their trucks. Sure, they thought about the inefficiencies they introduced by requiring more trips to the warehouse to restock parts, but they stopped there. "Inefficiency" floated in the ether as a vague concept to them, not a real cost. After all, what's a little inefficiency put into the system when we can reduce inventory costs?

They failed to consider the opportunity cost of increased drive time due to the more frequent trips to the warehouse to pick up parts that they formerly carried on their trucks. They failed to consider the customer impacts of missed appointments because techs drove to the warehouse first instead of to customers to get their work done. Time and customer impacts could have been quantified, but even if they had been, they would have been dismissed as "just" opportunity costs.

Inefficiencies, labeled as opportunity costs (and thinking they don't really count), became just another buzzword at XYZ. They labeled these costs as opportunity costs versus recognizing them as real costs—really only a poor rationale not to take any action that would otherwise create customer value. "Yeah, yeah. You want to eliminate inefficiencies. Show me the direct cost savings, not some theoretical paper savings." Use of that type of rationale about opportunity costs is the first step of a company towards a slow death spiral.

~~~~~~

Just a quick reminder to those of you who skipped ahead to Chapter 2 from the middle of Chapter 1. Now's the time to go back to Chapter 1 and read the rest of it from where you left off. That'll give you the context and insight to help you better understand the rest of the book.

CHAPTER 3—LETTING GO

How to Decide What Can Fall Off Your Plate

L et's take a minute and talk about Practical Action #5 in Chapter 2 because to many this premise will seem sacrilegious. The idea of purposefully allowing tasks to be incomplete is a totally contrarian philosophy, akin to the rule to not mash down on the brakes to stop when you drive on a snowy road. People, maybe even you, will be worried about things falling off their overfull plates. The problem's that employees in every industry are expected not to let anything drop off their plates—ever. They're subtly (or sometimes overtly) trained that if something drops off, then by definition they're not doing a good job. They may be worried about what their boss or co-workers will think that could lead to them being fired. It's ingrained in our work culture. Consequently, in situations where there actually *is* too much on their plate, they can only fail as they try to juggle everything.

Well, if you're likely to fail anyway, why not fail on your terms instead of someone else's? However, if you use the contrarian philosophy, you'll be more likely to succeed. Stuff falling off your plate's okay, as long as the stuff is non-prioritized items and your plate's otherwise filled with True Priorities.

Management needs to set this expectation clearly and create the culture in which everyone's playing by this new set of rules. As a manager, you need to keep track of what and how much falls off people's plates because you need to beware of the use of "falling off the plate" as a crutch or excuse to disguise the fact that they simply are just poor performers.

It's a truism that few pay attention to, but *if everything is a Priority, then nothing is a Priority*. In a Truly Prioritized environment, people stay focused on those True Priorities and don't worry about those lesser "Priorities" that fall on the floor. Fix first things first, then move on to the next tier of items. In an environment of stress, overworked frontline employees, and overworked managers, Prioritization becomes the critical factor to get out of that environment. Everything may *feel* like a Priority at any given time, but a successful manager will realize that's not true and modify expectations accordingly.

Choosing One Over Another

In successful companies, there are a number of basic metrics that drive the desired behavior of frontline employees, like on-time performance, percentage of customer complaints, sales quota, etc. However, sometimes these metrics vie for position on the Priority list. In companies with installation technicians or manufacturing companies that build anything from a watch to an airplane, quality control (QC) inspections are done after the work has been completed in order to ensure customers get good, quality service/products. Let's look at an example of competing Priorities.

While the pass or success rate varies widely by industry or task, let's look at an example that has a 95% QC pass rate as the goal. One metric that may conflict with the QC inspection pass rate is the completion percentage—of the jobs assigned for the day, the percentage that is actually completed. Say 95% is the goal for this metric, too. However, the faster a tech goes, generally the lower the quality of the job.

Are they both important? Sure. But you, as the Prioritization-aware manager that you are, have determined that QC pass rate's more important than completion percentage. The practical implication of this is that you'd rather have the jobs that do get done get done well versus making sure all scheduled customers are attended to, even if not in a quality fashion. Your obligation as a manager is to make sure that your Prioritization order is crystal clear to the techs and staff. Now, when Tom the tech has a 95% QC pass rate, but only a 75% completion percentage, you've implicitly agreed basically to be okay with that.

I say "basically" because not showing up to one out of four appointments really shouldn't be acceptable, particularly if the goal for that second metric is also 95%. Customers certainly won't like it if they're the one of four. A solution is to have a coaching discussion with Tom along these lines: "Tom, you do a great job with your QC pass rates. Thanks for Prioritizing that. It looks like you're consistently able to meet the goal of 95%. Now I need you to take it to another level. Your completion percentage is only 75% versus the goal of 95%. I know one of the reasons you run out of time at the end of the day and miss those later appointments is due to the fact that you make sure the work you do is high quality and that takes extra time. But we get too many customer complaints about us promising to be there and then us not showing up. That particular metric seems to have fallen off your plate. So let's talk about ways that you might be able to keep up the quality and still get through your route more quickly."

It's not enough to Prioritize and fix a problem, then move on to the next Prioritized item, but lose sight of the original Priority. Inherent in the concept of letting stuff fall off your plate is to also keep stuff on your plate—the True Priorities. A problem isn't fixed unless the fix lasts over time. The theory's that once you've incorporated the number one Priority fix into a business-as-usual environment, then you won't need to spend as much time on it. With the new free time, you should be able to add a new Priority to your plate and work on it without any loss of fidelity on the number one Priority (which is still the number one Priority, even after you fix it).

Letting stuff fall off your plate really isn't that hard, even for the super-conscientious. Everyone does it all the time in their everyday life, but most don't even notice it. Think about all of the sensory input your brain receives every second of every day. Your brain has a natural "significance filter" that's in the on position all the time. Not everything in life is significant; in fact, most things aren't. An unchecked assault on the brain by all five senses on every little thing that crosses your path during the day would make a person insane. So, the brain sorts out what is and isn't important and processes only the significant (at least according to the brain). That gives people the ability to enjoy the many colors of a rainbow without having to place consequence on each and every subtle shade.

Your brain's an automatic Prioritizer. You just need to tap into that inner, natural tendency to Prioritize and apply it to your work life.

> "The main thing is to keep the main thing the main thing."
> —Steven R. Covey

CHAPTER 4—PRINCIPLES
How to Build the Launch Pad to Effectively Manage

Time for true confessions. I misled you a bit by beginning the book with how to Truly Prioritize. However, you were in such an all-fired hurry to get something you could sink your teeth into and actually use to relieve your current situation of being too busy to do your job, that I felt it best to feed your need. It's all about customer satisfaction and hopefully you, being the customer in this case, are at least somewhat satisfied now. If you've calmed down a little, hopefully been able to implement some of what you've learned in the first three chapters, and gotten into somewhat of a groove in reading this book, let's take a different look at what Prioritization encompasses. Let's start back at the start.

How do you know what to Prioritize? There have to be reasons for the goals you set and the actions you take, but where do they come from and what are they? Logically, something had to come before Prioritization in order to have something to relate your Priorities to. For example, you might Prioritize customer satisfaction, but why? If you have the value of profitability, timing-wise that really came before customer satisfaction. It's kind of a "Which came first, the chicken or the egg?" issue. (By the way, the answer is the egg.) You can't have just random, disconnected Priorities. It's inefficient, for one. There needs to be a context—a glue—that holds them together and gives them meaning.

That glue is Values and Principles.

Back in Chapter 2, we talked about the three flavors of Priorities—Strategic, Tactical, and Task. Now we need to factor in Values and Principles to get a complete picture of how everything interacts. It starts with Values.

- Principles are built based on Values.
- Strategies are built based on Principles.
- Tactics are built based on Strategies.
- Tasks are built based on Tactics.

If you like diagrams, here's a simple one for visual effect.

Fig. 4-1

Even though Values are at the start of this dependency chain, the reason this chapter's titled "Principles" and not "Values" is that you need a bias for action in this world. See Practical Action #1 in Chapter 1. Principles are states of action while Values are states of being. Therefore, the chapter title's in alignment with the Principle of a bias for action.

Values are more character attributes, like honesty, respect, integrity, accountability, and profitability.

Principles describe big picture actions that'll be taken, like Communicating Effectively, Truly Prioritizing, Simplifying, and Aligning actions with Principles.

Let's talk about Values first.

Values, from BusinessDictionary.com, "are important and lasting beliefs or ideals shared by the members of a culture about what is good or bad and desirable or undesirable. Values have major influence on a person's behavior and attitude and serve as broad guidelines in all situations." Values are a bit more esoteric and Principles are a bit more practical.

Although many companies don't have a defined set of Values, the trend is for more and more companies to embrace the benefits of them in order to drive their vision of a defined culture at work. A Values statement creates expectations for everyone. Like Principles, they need to be incorporated into the language of daily work and reiterated in as many forums as possible. Not that the Values need to be recited like the Pledge of Allegiance before or after every meeting, but what if they became a natural part of discussions when ideas are thrown around? "Hey, Jean, your idea to involve the sales department on our team was right in alignment with our value of respect. Thanks."

There are tons of potential Values you could have for your company, but here again, in alignment with the Principle of Simplification, don't go crazy and have a list of fifteen. Five isn't a magic number by any means, but people need to be able to know and recite what the company's values are. You don't want it to become a contest to see who can memorize the most Values. Prioritize your laundry list of potential Values, then Simplify.

At the XYZ Company, they started out on the right path. They created a nice, short list of six Values and put them on a piece of paper people could keep at their desks. They even created some posters that showed the six Values and hung them visibly around the office so everyone could keep them in mind.

Over time, however, management didn't reinforce them. The Values never became incorporated into daily conversation. As happens in many companies, the posters became background wallpaper and most people ignored them. Management didn't acknowledge or consistently work one of the Values in particular—integrity. Ironically, they didn't have the integrity to do what they said they would do—namely make the Values a part of the culture. They turned their backs on Values and left the company adrift.

A Principle, per the Encarta World English Dictionary (1999), is

1. an important underlying law or assumption required in a system of thought, or
2. a standard of moral or ethical decision making, or
3. the primary source of something.

Principles are the foundation for virtually any action you take in your business. Once Principles for a business are defined, then the management challenge is to keep everyone's actions and Priorities in alignment with the Principles.

Steven Covey gave a very cogent description of what Principles are in his book *Principle-Centered Leadership.* He wrote,

"Correct principles are like compasses: they are always pointing the way. And if we know how to read them, we won't get lost, confused, or fooled by conflicting voices and values. Principles are self-evident, self-validating natural laws. [Purkey's note: Often principles are not so self-evident.] They don't change or shift. They provide 'true north' direction to our lives when navigating the 'streams' of our environments. Principles apply at all time in all places. They surface in the form of values, ideas, norms, and teachings that uplift, ennoble, fulfill, empower, and inspire people. The lesson of history is that to the degree people and civilizations have operated in harmony with correct principles, they have prospered. At the root of societal declines are foolish practices that represent violations of correct principles. . . . Centering on principles provides sufficient security to not be threatened by change, comparisons, or criticisms; guidance to discover our mission, define our roles, and write our scripts and goals; wisdom to learn from our mistakes and seek continuous improvement; and power to communicate and cooperate, even under conditions of stress and fatigue."

When you create a business or want to change an existing one, here are some basic steps to work.

- The first order of business should be to come up with a list of Values. Write down lots—everything that comes to mind. Then Prioritize and Simplify those Values down to just the strongest few.
- The second order of business should be to come up with a list of Principles. Write down lots—everything that comes to mind. Then Prioritize and Simplify those Principles down to just a few.
- Once that's in place, then you can Strategize and set goals—high level, mid-level, and low level—and the associated Prioritization exercise that comes with that development.
- Then you move to Tactics—the processes that make the goals achievable. These are daily activities and metrics to track to keep your Priorities on the rails. All of this must be in alignment with your original, high level Principles.
- Finally, you can start to produce something that customers want to buy with Tasks.

It's all a natural, logical flow if kept in order, but without the initial, guiding Principles, it turns into a chaotic mess.

What's the first Principle? Where does it all begin? Easy. It starts with why the business formed in the first place. Henry Ford wanted to build and sell cars. The entire Ford empire exists today because of that one driving Principle (see definition number 3 above)—we build and sell cars. (Some might say this is more of a mission statement, but mission and vision statements fall under the broad category of Principles. Don't get hung up on splitting hairs here. We're talking about the background to practical actions in this chapter for the most part, so knowing the technical differences between vision, mission, values, and Principles isn't critical. Just understand the big picture concept.)

Once you set that first Principle, then it becomes a little more complicated. The brain almost automatically kicks into overdrive and spits out ideas in any creative process, so don't be surprised that when you think of creating Principles, a bunch of them will pour out of your head. The ability to harness those ideas into a somewhat coherent plan is what separates a successful company from a failed company. That's where Prioritization comes into play. What if once you see you have multiples of anything to analyze, Prioritization always popped into your head as the best tool to use? Principles, Simplified in quantity by using Prioritization, provide that solid framework from which everything else flows.

So, back to true confessions, Prioritization is *almost* the first thing to do when you want to get a business to run efficiently, but not quite. I didn't steer you too off course because if you don't have the Principle or concept of True Prioritization in mind first, then you'd just be left with a bunch of random, useless Principles that you created but that didn't form a cohesive story, didn't provide that "true north" compass that Covey wrote about.

Principles give you the ability to answer the question "Why am I doing this task?" This leads to efficiency and productivity, as you discover whether you're in alignment with the stated standards. If you can't relate your actions back to a given set of Principles, then you just randomly go through work and life without meaning. The Ten Commandments is one of the more widely known set of Principles. The United States Constitution's another, for the most part. These documented Principles have demonstrated their importance over time to provide order and structure for the groups that profess to act in the fashion described by the Principles.

Take training, for example. You're not just training staff for training's sake. You're training with a specific organizational goal in mind to improve some defined something. *Every individual action/task is taken because it will directly impact the strategic or tactical objectives established from the Principles.*

What if every individual action had a defined, specific purpose behind it described by a Principle? For a simplistic example, you don't just answer the phone; you answer the phone because you're in alignment with customer satisfaction. Principles and Strategies would become the drivers, not things that gather dust on a shelf. If you can't make that connection between the individual action and the strategy served, then you shouldn't waste time on the individual action.

Principles can be vague and ambiguous at times if not well conceived or constructed, but your job's to make them clear by not only acting in alignment with them, but overtly commenting on how others' actions are or aren't in alignment. Management is continuous coaching, or at least good management is. It gets back to one of the Big Four Principles of Effective Communication (discussed in greater depth in Chapter 5).

Another way to clarify Principles is to provide a definition of what you mean by the Principle. For example, on any documents that proclaim your company's Principles, you could have something like this:

ABC Company's Guiding Principles

- **Effective Communication**

  Employees take extra care to ensure that all parties have the same understanding of whatever issues are discussed. They particularly use paraphrasing and identify potential assumptions.

- **True Prioritization**

  Employees effectively identify the truly important issues that deliver high customer value and focus primarily on those for resolution before they address issues of lower importance.

- **Simplification**

  Employees focus on just a limited number of items at a time that'll have the most impact on providing customer value. Employees minimize process steps. Employees communicate plainly.

- **Accountability**

  Employees do what they say they'll do.

- **Alignment with Principles**

  On a daily basis, Employees' actions are congruent with stated company Principles.

Where's the real benefit from a practical standpoint to clearly state Principles and Values? It allows management to coach desired behavior more effectively. Just the very existence of Principles and Values, combined with Effective Communication, tells everyone that "We've got standards around here and everyone's expected to live up to them in their daily actions." As a manager who coaches your staff, now you've got something to explain the "why" of your employee's performance, either good or bad. Principles take away some of the subjectivity associated with evaluations and provide something concrete and actionable that you can refer back to.

With a Principle of "We build and sell cars," when a department starts to investigate selling goldfish, you can ask how selling goldfish relates to building cars and put everyone back on track. Rigid adherence to any given Principle, however, may not be in the company's best interest. It may be that selling goldfish could be a new profit center for the company in addition to building and selling cars. After an appropriate business case is constructed and examined, what if the company revised its main Principle to keep current with new conditions? What the Principle does is give you a starting point against which to have an intelligent discussion to evaluate each new proposal.

Converting plain, old management into Principle-based Management gets everyone to row in the same direction, with the same set of guiding beacons shining on a parade in which everyone marches to the same drummer—to mix some metaphors. Principle-based Management puts the organization into alignment so that it can operate in a true team environment.

~~~~~~

More Big Picture Concepts

Let's pause for a minute and talk about the concept of the big picture and its role in business. Principles certainly fall into that big picture category because they're applicable to a wide variety of specific situations. They're relatively broad and somewhat undefined and squishy, at least compared to the day-to-day tyranny of urgent problems.

Some things in business really don't need to be urgent. Really. If you can start with a calm, planned, considered base and then move into action from there, you'll be well ahead of the game. That's the big picture. You want employees who see the big (or at least bigger) picture versus having their nose so close to the grindstone that that's all they can see. Those employees won't be able to help the company improve processes because they can't see where they fit in the grander scheme. Just because your title is assembler doesn't mean that you shouldn't be able to also see the finished product, know how you contributed, and come up with ideas on how to improve the process to get to the finished product.

So let's talk about some of those things in business that take longer to happen, but that can't be overlooked in your drive to get less busy.

~~~~~~

Vision and Mission Statements

You've got to start somewhere and starting at the beginning

is best. That beginning is a single, guiding light that shows the way to what you envision—a vision statement, as it were. Everything in the company is in the service of achieving the vision. Everything. The mission of management, regardless of the company, is to keep everyone in the company in alignment with the vision.

Vision and mission statements often sound pretentious, to my ear anyway. They're often grandiose statements about achieving something akin to world peace, without practical import or application to the employee body as a whole. I'm not saying not to have them, but if you have them, make them practical and then use them consistently with all levels of employees and customers. They are Principles after all, so treat them the same. If you won't exercise them, then it's really a waste of time to develop them. Many companies don't even have vision statements or, if they do have them, don't actually tie their activities to them. Most gather dust in some public relations or marketing office.

Do you really need them? Well, in short, yes. If you don't know where you're headed, you'll never get there. Define the big picture, even if only in general terms. That gives relevance to daily activities. When employees know the vision and mission statements and focus their work efforts to be in alignment with them, employees will be more engaged and customer satisfaction will follow. What if an employee could say, "I know that what I'm doing right now contributes to accomplishing the vision or mission because . . .?"

Vision statements are grand and global and represent the ideal state of affairs. Relative to each other, the vision is the strategy while the mission is the tactic. The key is to balance the verbiage of the statement between the grand and global versus the practical and relevant.

Example Vision Statement: ABC Company will be the nation's premier broadband installation services company that is sought out by broadband cable systems for their contract installation needs.

Mission statements are purposeful and state how the vision will be accomplished, although still grand and global.

Example Mission Statement: ABC Company will help

broadband cable systems achieve their corporate goals by providing responsive, competitively priced, high quality, customer-focused broadband installation services.

Looking at the mission statement example above, an employee can easily ask "Do I help provide quality service? Do I help keep costs down so we can be competitively priced? Am I responsive to requests?" If the answers are all "no," then you've got to wonder why that employee position even exists. This example mission statement also has the concept of customer satisfaction clearly in play, since ABC Company will help its customers achieve those customers' goals. Here, an employee can ask "Do I help my customer get better?"

~~~~~~

Strategizing

A strategy's a plan of action or a policy designed to achieve a major or overall goal in alignment with established Principles. It's big picture by definition. Development of strategies isn't limited to just executive management. Middle and upper management also need their fingers in the pie of strategy development. Not only will more synergy be added to the process with more people involved, but those levels will also be more engaged and invested to see that the strategies are executed properly versus sitting on a shelf.

Just as with Prioritization, Principles, and Values, one of our Big Four Principles comes into play with strategies: Simplification. Yes, there should be fewer of them rather than more of them, but also don't "complexify" the ones you do choose to have. Keep them simple and understandable. As one of my Montana friends says, bring the food down to where the dogs can eat it. Make the strategies relevant. If they can't be directly related to front line work, then they won't be of much value. Strategies should help the front line keep their eye on the ball, not be reserved for boardroom discussions. What if employees lived and breathed the strategies?

At the XYZ Company, typical departments had 15-20 strategies. That's too many for people to grasp and implement effectively.

~~~~~~

Culture

Culture is the behaviors and beliefs characteristic of a particular social, ethnic, or age group. Culture forms over time and often without conscious thought, which is part of the problem in business. There's often no deliberate effort by upper management to construct a pre-defined culture or even modify a current one to conform to an ideal. Management can't simply decree a culture or flip a switch and expect different behaviors. Culture change takes time, generally with years of consistent focus by management to make it happen. Years. You might make a dent in a culture in six months with the right people in the right positions, but you shouldn't really expect a true, sustainable change in that short time. However, you have to start somewhere and there's no time like the present.

In fact, culture change usually happens so slowly that you might not even notice it until it's already happened, unless you're the driver of it or specifically look for it.

Culture change is difficult at best for a variety of reasons, among them:

- A natural human resistance to change
- It's time consuming and many so-called leaders aren't prepared for the long haul to see it through. ("So-called" because if a "leader" is ineffective, then they aren't much of a leader.)
- It requires dedication and patience, which many so-called leaders lack.
- Change is measured in terms of generations for societies. The time advantage for businesses versus societies is that a generation in business is only as long as it takes to turnover personnel. While not ideal, major changes at the top of the management hierarchy can jump-start the process for culture change.

These characteristics of company culture mean that, as attributed to Peter Drucker, whom *BusinessWeek* called "the man who invented management," culture eats strategy for breakfast. Culture is to strategy as a glacier is to a boulder.

Yet management, as a stereotype, spends little time to make the culture receptive to whatever strategies they design. They just force the strategies down the employees' throats and then typically don't provide the necessary follow up and support. Consequently, while administrations come and go with different approaches, often a business in need of change simply can't because culture isn't considered in the equation.

True change happens when people internalize the positive culture changes and truly believe in them. In this environment, you'll hear different phrases (like "under promise and over deliver," "accountability," and "How do you know that?") in common usage that didn't used to be spoken. Overt behaviors can change more quickly than a true internalization, but if no one believes, follows through, and works to maintain the new, desired culture, then the behaviors will soon revert. You can teach a dog to shake hands, but there's no belief in its intrinsic value to the dog. If you're not there to reinforce the behavior, the behavior disappears over time.

The inherent, natural resistance to change is also a challenge to overcome. Western-style toilets have been around since the late 1800s and are pretty much ubiquitous in Western countries. They were introduced in China decades ago. Yet despite the apparent advantages of the Western-style (granted, my personal bias), squat toilets are still the main waste disposal system in China. How do you change a culture of 1.3 billion people accustomed to squat toilets for over 5000 years? If you wanted to change how Chinese eat, how do you change 5000 years of chopsticks to forks or, from the opposite perspective, how do you change 2000 years of forks to chopsticks? The answer is time and continual focus on the issue.

I think it's a fair statement that, as a societal whole, racism in America has declined over time. But the end of slavery over a century and a half ago didn't end racism. Gradually, slowly, more and more people have come around to the true equality proposition and its inherent fairness. However, not everyone did (or has done) so at once. We're now seven generations removed from the end of slavery, but racism isn't yet gone, only diminished. Time.

The point is you can't just declare that you have a Customer Satisfaction Culture. You must put events into place that'll cause that to happen. You must be proactive, you must be vigilant, and you must be patient. Keep in mind the glacier analogy from earlier and and the acronym CURP—Constant, Unrelenting, Ruthless Pressure (discussed in more detail in Chapter 8).

CHAPTER 5—COMMUNICATION
How to Communicate Effectively

"For a communications company, we sure don't communicate very well."
>—Cliché comment from employees of virtually all telecom companies

Effective Communication is the foundation for every function associated with business or even life as a whole. Lack of communication can be a disaster and bad communication may be even worse. In this chapter, we'll dig deeper into how to make communication effective—some of the nuts and bolts that help us find that common ground.

~~~~~

What Is Effective Communication?

Research has shown that most of us spend 70%-80% of the time we're awake in some form of communication activity. You'd think with all that practice, we'd all be good at it. The reality is that very few of us are. Why is Effective Communication so hard? As a friend told me, "I've been talking since about a year after I came out of the womb and usually get my point across, I think. I got fed. I tell people what I want done and if they don't get it, they're probably stupid, belligerent, or just don't listen. Sounds like their problem to me."

And therein lies the problem. It's never "my" fault; it's always the other person's fault when communication fails. Changing that outlook to take more responsibility for your own part in the play is a major component to make communication effective. We'll talk about that concept in more detail in a bit.

Another problem with achieving a real mutual understanding is that communication's so ingrained in life that most just take it for granted. "Communication" is one of those idle, throwaway words that everyone uses, but no one really works to make happen, kind of like "Priority." Everyone assumes it'll just occur; that it's like breathing—it just happens. Well, I'm here to tell you that it doesn't "just happen." Or it doesn't "just happen" effectively at any rate. Underestimate the impact of communication in your life and treat it cavalierly and you'll find your life much more complicated (i.e., busy) than it might otherwise be.

The dictionary definitions of the word "communication" generally only talk about "imparting," "transmitting," "disclosing," or "exchanging" information. This is only half of the equation. Imparting information inherently means that there's a sender who's imparting, but who's receiving? I can impart information to a tree, but that doesn't mean the tree's able to do anything with the info.

~~~~~

The real world definition of Effective Communication is the achievement of mutual understanding among participants.

~~~~~

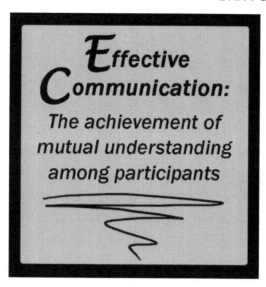

Effective Communication: The achievement of mutual understanding among participants

To differentiate the communication of imparting from the communication of mutual understanding and to provide a significant reminder of what we really want to accomplish, I add the word "effective" when I mean that a mutual understanding, a meeting of the minds, has taken place. The goal—the Principle—is *Effective* Communication, not just communication.

What does Effective Communication look and feel like? We, as managers, try to build effective teams. People need to understand their roles. Teamwork's impossible without Effective Communication. In teams that Effectively Communicate, you'll see attention paid to the speaker with good eye contact. Heads will nod and thoughtful expressions will appear. You'll hear phrases like "Let me see if I've got this right . . ." and "Is what you really meant . . ." and "Let me summarize what I heard . . ." Questions will fly and no one will take offense at them.

The key word here is "effective." It's easy to talk about teams and teamwork, but few put the energy into what it really takes to make effective teams. I'm sorry to use a football analogy for you non-football fans, but too bad. The 1976 Tampa Bay Buccaneers claimed to be a football team. The media guide said so. Since they ended the season with zero wins, they could hardly be called an effective football team. No wins, fourteen losses.

So, when you talk about teamwork at your company, what if you were more specific about what you really want, which is *effective* teamwork? Words are powerful things. Insert the word "effective" in front of "team" or "teamwork" every time you say it. It takes away the idleness of the word, the throwaway phraseology, and gives it some meaning, some focus. It says what you really mean. Say what you mean and mean what you say. That's Effective Communication.

≈≈≈≈≈

Filters and Experience

We talked briefly in Chapter 3 that the brain has natural filters that ignore stimuli that have little impact on you. The reason's obvious – if everything you saw, heard, tasted, smelled, and felt took on the importance of, say, having your hair on fire, then you couldn't function. You simply couldn't cope with all of the sensory input if everything was a number one Priority and you had to react to every little thing. "The solution to world peace is . . . oooh, look at the puppy!"

It's an understanding and awareness that this phenomenon exists that's the important thing. Filters are insidious, though. It's usually easier to see when filters are in operation in others than it is to know that they're at play inside your own head. That's because it's easier to be an observer than a participant. It's why there are so many more pundits and commentators than actual world-class athletes or politicians.

Your ability to be introspective, look objectively at your inner workings, and then modify your behavior to get more in alignment with the Principle of Effective Communication is the difference between an excellent manager and an also-ran.

Let's take a look at a real example of how filters impact decisions.

So there I was, riding along on my bicycle on the ten-foot wide bike path when I approached two people who walked in the same direction as I biked. Per the customary rule, they had placed themselves on the (my) right side of the path. A few meters farther ahead, two more people also travelled in my same direction, but on the left side of the path. In order to pass the first couple, I had to move to the left lane—the normal lane of travel for passing—but there, just ahead, the second couple walked out of position and sort of in my way. Irritated, I thought (other than "Be careful"), "These irresponsible people are on the wrong side of the path."

In the space of about five seconds, the filters in my brain categorized this situation for me (or it—"it" being my brain). Without any conscious thought and in the blink of an eye, I developed some judgments about these people that I'd never seen before in my life. Primarily, I had the emotional reaction of irritation towards these numbskulls. First of all, they broke the rules. Now despite the fact that I've been known to break a rule or two, I generally respect the rules. I'm a well-ordered, logical kind of guy. Who were these people to put themselves above the rules that everyone should follow? Why I oughta . . .

Don't worry. No one crashed. No animals were harmed in the making of this scene. In an exhibition of my bike handling skills, I safely negotiated my way around both couples. But let's put ourselves in the left-side couple's place. If the people had a legitimate reason to walk on the left side, who am I to get irritated? Thinking more openly, maybe these people came from a country where the custom is to drive/walk/bike on the left side of the road/path. Had I known that, instead of being irritated, I might have been more inclined to help them out and educate them on the custom in the United States. Maybe they were searching for a lost item. Had I known that, instead of being irritated, I might have helped them look. Maybe they saw some unusual animal and wanted a closer look. Had I know that, instead of being irritated, I might have gone to look with them.

Now let's throw in some more considerations. Does it make any difference to the story that I'm a male? What filters come into play now? How does the situation change with that piece of information? Or does it? How about if I add that the "irresponsible" people appeared (to me) Asian? How about if you know that I'm of something less than 100% European descent? If the "irresponsible" people were both females? If the "responsible" couple was a man and a woman? If the "responsible" couple was of senior age? If the term "couple" doesn't necessarily mean two people in a relationship?

All of this and more went into the reaction I had and all in the blink of an eye. It's a wonder that humans are ever able to Communicate Effectively.

Consider this (revising Aldous Huxley, intellectual and author of *Brave New World*): Experience is not what happens to you. Experience is how you interpret what happens to you.

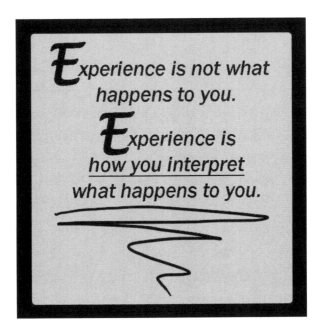

Simple recognition of this fact can lead to true understanding. The question is do you believe what you see or do you see what you believe.

Attorneys will tell you that there's nothing as unreliable as an eyewitness. The classic case is the car accident at an intersection. There's only one event, the accident, but there are many interpretations of the event. Sure, everyone saw it happen at the same time, but the accounts of the event all differ. Those pesky filters come into play and suddenly, twelve observers saw twelve different accidents. It's twelve different individual interpretations of events based on each individual's own set of beliefs, history, preconceived notions, etc. The event goes through many filters that you've unconsciously (or consciously) set up before the event even happened.

Donna Bridge, a postdoctoral fellow at Northwestern University's Feinberg School of Medicine, scientifically documented *that the brain does two things with memories: it alters them, and it believes it hasn't.*

No one has "knowledge" of anything. You only have knowledge of things based on what your brain has filtered and allowed through. Factor this into any attempt you make at Effectively Communicating.

I once led a group of about twenty technicians who notoriously jumped to conclusions and talked past one another. Group meetings were often unproductive as everyone saw their own point, but couldn't seem to see anyone else's points. We'd talked about how experience is how you interpret what happens to you in order for them to take into account the other person's perspective in discussions, but the group as a whole didn't get it. I needed to do something dramatic to help them see what they did to themselves. Now, a two-by-four upside the head would have been frowned upon by Human Resources, so I opted for something completely different.

I drew on a psychology experiment I'd learned from an earlier time and asked Kim, one of the techs, to help me out with a little role-play. We set it up beforehand that he would come into our regular staff meeting a few minutes late, I'd berate him for always being late, he'd respond in kind, we'd argue back and forth a short while, and he'd finally storm out of the room in a huff. We agreed on two rules of engagement—no physical contact and no profanity. Our total interaction lasted probably two minutes. Silence enveloped the room after he left, looks of astonishment everywhere.

"Composing" myself, I turned to the group and said, "I'm sorry you had to witness that. I think this could easily turn into an

HR complaint. I'll need documentation. Would everyone take out a piece of paper and write down what just happened here? I'll need eyewitness accounts of what happened. I don't need anything elaborate, just jot down the events as you saw them."

After receiving all the written, eyewitness statements, I retrieved Kim and we revealed the hoax. Then we began a discussion of filters and experience and Effective Communication. I read the statements to the group without the authors' names to protect the innocent. One event, nineteen eyewitnesses, and nineteen different accounts of the event. Some said I swore at Kim. Some said we swore at each other. A couple of techs said shoves took place.

Depending on the tenor and resiliency of the group you manage, I'm not sure I'd recommend this particular method of education, but it was certainly interesting and impactful. One tech in particular may still hold a grudge about the charade, but then, that would be how he interpreted that particular event and turned it into his experience.

You, personally, have to know without a doubt that your thoughts are clouded by filters and you, personally, need to account for that in any communication if you want to have any hope to be understood for exactly what you mean to say. Accept the reality that you might be wrong and your filters might have deceived you.

If you'd like more evidence of this phenomenon, check out the three part National Geographic TV series called *Test Your Brain*. You may be surprised to learn how fallible your brain is. But it's not enough just to understand that point. You have to take the next step and incorporate that reality into your actions around Effective Communication.

~~~~~~

Effective Communication Is 50% Sender and 50% Receiver

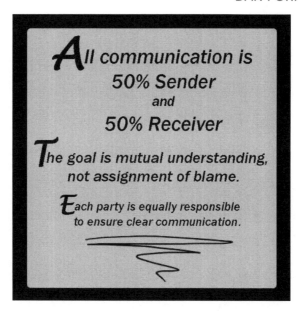

All communication is 50% Sender and 50% Receiver. The goal is mutual understanding, not assignment of blame. Each party is equally responsible to ensure clear communication.

"What we have here is failure to communicate."
—The Captain (Strother Martin) in *Cool Hand Luke*

That failure the Captain lamented is usually due to the fact that either or both of the parties in a given conversation don't understand that they share an equal responsibility to achieve the goal of mutual understanding. All communication is 50% sender and 50% receiver. Think about it. If the sender of information asks the receiver to do A, they finish the conversation and walk away, and the receiver ends up doing B, who's at fault? Certainly the sender likely thinks the receiver screwed up. The receiver correspondingly will respond with ". . . but you told me to do B." The work that the receiver did now needs to be redone to get the desired outcome. No wonder you're too busy to do your job, since you constantly have to redo your job.

These types of inefficiencies that are the result of poor communication permeate American business. They drag down productivity and negatively affect the bottom line of profit, yet few companies really make an effort to get Effective Communication ingrained in the culture. They don't provide their employees the tools necessary to succeed, but you're in luck. This chapter is filled with key tools that'll help you in your quest to become not so frantically busy.

The first key tool is the knowledge and understanding that all communication is 50% sender and 50% receiver.

I once had an HR manager tell me that statement's wrong. He said both parties need to put in 100% in order to have Effective Communication. From my perspective, his analysis looked at the individual components (sender and receiver) as totally separate entities. His interpretation of my 50/50 analogy was that neither party individually did their best (i.e., 100%) to contribute to the success of the engagement. If each party only puts out 50% effort, no wonder the communication wouldn't work.

I actually meant that if we want to be 100% successful at Effective Communication, then the responsibility for that result is *equally* shared between the parties. Certainly each party needs to give 100% from their individual perspective, but their full effort is each only half of the bigger picture—to have a mutual understanding. Ironically, this matter of perspective led to a disagreement between us, even though we both meant the same thing.

The use of some paraphrasing (parroting back in your own words what you just heard) by either of us might have corrected the problem, but at that point I disengaged. I deemed it not worth the effort. I'm not perfect and have emotions just like anyone else, but I violated Practical Action #7 below. By choosing to end the discussion at this point, he left with the thought that 50/50 was a crock and I left puzzled why he didn't understand this brilliant revelation. We'd just opened the door to future potential problems that would have to be addressed again, inefficiently rehashing points already made that could have been wrapped up in a single meeting.

Practical Action #7
Don't disengage from a conversation if you're unclear or sense the other person is.

If you're really interested in Effective Communication, establish the Principle that no one leaves an interaction unless all parties express their understanding of the issues, believe that understanding is mutual, and confirm it with each other.

At Amazon, they have a list of fourteen (that's too many, but their heart's in the right place) "Leadership Principles" like Customer Obsession, Think Big, Bias for Action, and Frugality. Meetings at Amazon are not supposed to adjourn until the group has reviewed the content of their meeting relative to those fourteen Principles. People bring copies of the fourteen Principles to the meetings so that they can easily refer to them to make sure their meeting's productive relative to those Principles. Clearly not every meeting addresses all fourteen points, but keeping folks focused on the truly important is part of their culture.

The whole purpose of communication is to achieve a mutual understanding. Otherwise, you just have two people flapping their lips at each other. With some work, that could be turned into a Las Vegas variety show act, but it's not very practical in the real world.

Most people assume that what they say is what's understood. That's far from the case. As we've talked about, everyone has their own filters, their own interpretations of what they hear (and what they see, taste, smell, and feel). You need to understand that what you understand is not necessarily what the other person understands.

To drive home the point, here's one person's description of how they see math word problems (from the internet): If you have four pencils and I have seven apples, how many pancakes will fit on the roof? Purple, because aliens don't wear hats.

Too often when a miscommunication occurs, one party (say the sender, for discussion purposes) blames the other for the problem and fails to account for the fact that the sender may not have been clear or the receiver may have understood something different.

THE STUPID PENCIL MAKER
Some dummy built this pencil wrong,
The eraser's down here where the point belongs,
And the point's at the top - so it's no good to me,
It's amazing how stupid some people can be.
—Shel Silverstein

The lesson here is that whenever you talk to someone else, it takes a conscious effort from both parties to ensure clear communication. While you talk, you have to consciously think about and pay attention to the process of talking. Research indicates that we comprehend only 25% of what's said and, after two months, remember only half of that.

The brain's a marvelous multitasking thing. While you listen to me speak, you also think about how breakfast tasted, what you'll do when you get back to work, what you'll do after work, and a hundred other things. What I'm suggesting you do is train yourself to stop just one of those other distracting thoughts and replace it with concentrated attention towards making sure the message is mutually understood without question. True Prioritization. While the conversation takes place, take that 75% of unrelated stuff that's rattling around in your brain during the conversation and focus some of it on the process of communication. In the midst of all of the processing your brain does, what if you actively look for possible places where something could be misinterpreted and then ensure the message is explained more clearly?

You can most easily do this with paraphrasing. Paraphrasing is simply a restatement of someone's words, but stated in your own words, often to clarify meaning. It may be the most powerful tool to use to help ensure mutual understanding. Let me show you by paraphrasing what I just said. "Dan, did you mean that if I repeat back what someone said to me in my own words that I'll make sure I understood what the sender meant?"

Paraphrasing does three things that facilitate Effective Communication:

- The sender knows he/she is understood (or not).
- The sender's able to clarify their meaning of what was said.
- By paraphrasing, the receiver knows whether their interpretation is correct or incorrect.

The problem is that while paraphrasing may be the most powerful tool in the Effective Communication toolbox, people don't often use it. Before you go into any conversation, use part of that 75% capacity you have available and make a conscious, deliberate decision to use paraphrasing. Focus your brain on it.

Practical Action #8
Prioritize paraphrasing.

Part of the 50% that you bring to the conversation is around intent. In a coaching situation, the whole time you speak, the other person likely thinks about your ulterior motives. Defensive oriented people will always be on the lookout for any indication that you'll try to screw them somehow, that you'll try to blame them. Their brain filters will take whatever input you provide and twist it around to fit their preconceived notion of what they expected you to say versus what you did say. In a culture that deals with business issues instead of personal ones, that's less of a consideration, but those pure, ideal cultures seldom exist. You need to incorporate the lack of the ideal into whatever words come out of your mouth. What if, early in the conversation, you overtly stated that the goal here isn't to assign blame, but to address the business issue at hand? The goal is mutual understanding, not an assignment of blame.

I'm constantly amazed by how many people react not to what's said, but to what they *think* was implied by what was actually said. Negative political campaigns make their hay by deliberately taking an opponent's sound bite out of context, putting a spin on it never intended by the speaker, and then magnifying the spin. They tell you what they think is meant by the statement instead of actually asking the source what it is they meant.

Now to a large degree, I can't really blame people, because a common aspect of human communication involves a deliberate attempt at implication. We're trained that way in society. Yet, from my perhaps Pollyannaish perspective, wouldn't we all be able to get along better if we said what we actually meant? Maybe more to the point, wouldn't interaction with others be better if the receiver of the information tried to clarify their understanding of the information *before* having some knee-jerk, emotional response?

Many choose the route to be offended by a statement because of the implication they chose to attach to a statement. That's not bringing their 50% to the table. In fact, they almost turn it into a negative 50% effort. Now, emotions are by their very nature tough to control. However, don't you owe the other person the respect that would say that they've not deliberately tried to offend you? Communicate, don't react. Use your words.

The reality that you're likely to face is that most people don't understand how to Effectively Communicate. They simply don't have the tools or experience to bring their full 50% to the table. If you bring 50% and they bring 35%, then you've only got 85% Effective Communication. Therefore, as a manager who always seeks continuous improvement with your group, you'll often need to give more than 50% because it's likely that the other person isn't as attuned to their responsibilities in the whole Effective Communication process as you are. You'll have to have a keener awareness of when erroneous assumptions are present or could be present. You'll need to pick up the other person's slack by not only paraphrasing their comments more than usual, but also overtly asking them to paraphrase your comments, since they probably won't know about paraphrasing. Model the behavior you want in others.

Steven Covey provided one thought that falls into the category of bringing at least 51% to the table as the receiver so that Effective Communication can occur. In his seminal book *The 7 Habits of Highly Effective People*, he wrote "Seek first to understand, then to be understood." In practical terms, basically shut your mouth, listen for a change, understand or question, then say what you have to say. You might find that what you actually say will differ from what you initially planned.

~~~~~~

Assumptions

Before we dive too deeply into the problems with assumptions, I have this caveat. Assumptions are a necessary evil; we can't live without them. If we tried to follow each and every assumption made in any conversation back to its factual source, we'd spend all of our time tracing root causes instead of exchanging ideas. My message with assumptions is not that they're so bad that you should never use them because they'll kill you, but that you need to be aware of when assumptions are made and in play in the conversation. It's the lack of awareness that causes disagreements and misunderstandings, as bad assumptions unwittingly get incorporated into discussions and send people off on unintended tangents. Be aware.

Ineffective communication, miscommunication, bad communication, incomplete communication, and all other forms of the opposite of Effective Communication can often be traced to the root cause of assumptions.

There's a reason this old chestnut sticks around over the years: ASSUME means to make an ASS out of U and ME.

Assumptions are the silent assassins of Effective Communication.

Practical Action #9
Stop the argument and find the assumption.

If you find yourself in an argument or disagreement with someone, what if you treated that as a trigger for you to say to yourself, "Hey, there may be a bad assumption hiding in here somewhere?" Certainly not every disagreement has its roots in a bad assumption, but it's the best place to start when you want to reach a mutual understanding.

When you're in an argument with someone, as hard as it may be, take a timeout and stop talking. Just stop. The other person may also stop, since now you've disengaged from the interaction. If they don't, just say something a bit off base like, "Hey. Wait a minute. Can I have just a minute to think? How did this argument start in the first place?"

That's easier said than done, since both parties' emotions are probably at a fever pitch. If you can be the bigger person, step back, and take that logical, third person, objective view of the situation, you'll find your argument may go away. You'll suddenly be engaged in a calmer dialog as you both try to find the root cause of the disagreement. Not only have you both now drifted onto the same team with a common goal—find the root cause of the disagreement—but you'll likely find that the root cause is an assumption made by one or both of you. Often, identifying the root cause assumption will allow you to find common ground you previously thought didn't exist. The challenge for everyone is to be able to recognize an assumption involved in a discussion before that assumption can infect the rest of the conversation.

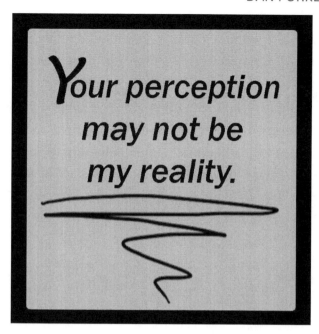

Your perception may not be my reality.

See if you can find the assumption in this joke before you get to the punch line.

> A man gets into the shower just as his wife dries herself after her shower, when the doorbell rings. The wife quickly wraps herself in the towel and runs downstairs. When she opens the door, there stands Bob, the next-door neighbor. Before she says a word, Bob says, "Oh, wow! Hey, I'll give you $800 to drop that towel." After a long moment in thought, the woman looks around, then drops her towel, and stands naked in front of Bob. After a several somewhat awkward seconds, Bob hands her $800 and leaves. The woman wraps back up in the towel and heads back upstairs. When she gets to the bathroom, her husband asks, "Who rang the doorbell?" "Only Bob, our next door neighbor," she replies. "Great!" the husband says, "Did he say anything about the $800 he owes me?"

Moral of the story: If you can recognize when assumptions are made, you won't get caught with your pants down.

Alternate moral of the story: If you're fully informed, you may be in a position to prevent unnecessary exposure.

The problem and challenge of assumptions is having the skill to recognize them when they occur and being able to call them out as assumptions in the heat of what may be a highly charged, emotional discussion. ***To become adept at it may well be the hardest thing you'll attempt in your career.*** I don't believe that's hyperbole, but more a statement of fact. It's a skill that must be (and can be) learned through a continuous, front-of-the-mind awareness that assumptions permeate every communication. It's not an inherent skill most possess because most people don't give any thought to the process of communication. Thinking about the process of communication while in the act of communication is counter-intuitive. It requires a force of will on your part to be able to break the cycle of assumption-conclusion-accusation.

That's offset by the fact that, if you can do it successfully, you'll have the most powerful tool there is at your command to generate Effective Communication, find root causes, and resolve interpersonal differences.

You've got to develop the skill to recognize when another person could legitimately have a different interpretation of what you say. Most of us think we're right and that's another root cause assumption of arguments. As I've said before, accept the reality that you may be wrong. As a matter of fact, and somewhat ironically, if you assume that you're wrong *before* a discussion, you'll be more open to find a common ground in any disagreement that may occur. It's the scientific method applied to communication.

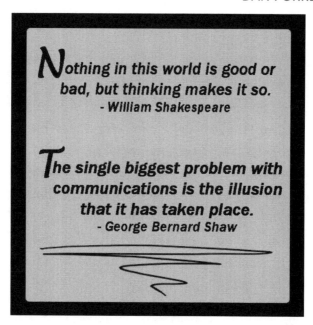

Nothing in this world is good or bad, but thinking makes it so.
- William Shakespeare

The single biggest problem with communications is the illusion that it has taken place.
- George Bernard Shaw

Look at this example of how easily assumptions can worm their way into otherwise innocuous statements that then lead to conflict. Robb's making dinner. Cindy tells Robb, "I'm going to run to the store and be right back." Sounds safe at first, but stop for a minute and see if you can come up with all of the various assumptions that might be made that could lead to a conflict. Let me warn you that you won't be able to come up with all of them, but here are a few and where they might lead.

Robb may assume:

- "Right back" means Cindy should be back in about thirty minutes. [Note: The first assumption made by someone often has underlying, foundational assumptions.]
- Cindy's driving, not walking or riding her bike. [Three assumptions in one.]
- There won't be any lines at the store.
- The store has what Cindy needs.
- Cindy's only going to one store.
- The car won't break down.
- The car has enough gas.

Cindy comes home two hours later, dinner's ruined, and an argument ensues. A valuable skill set many people don't have because they don't consistently exercise the skill is to Prioritize some key assumptions and state them to the other person. It takes mental discipline to get and maintain this awareness in the midst of a conversation, especially a routine one, but it only takes a little practice to become more adept. If Robb had been able to recognize his main assumption that Cindy would be back in thirty minutes, he could have stated it, which likely would have led to further clarification from Cindy about the factors/assumptions involved. They could have set mutual expectations more clearly before Cindy walked out of the door and avoided a future argument.

We had one simple example above. Consider the hundreds of relevant assumptions that float around on a daily basis, all of which could have an effect on Effective Communication. No wonder misunderstandings are such a common part of the human experience. You'll never get rid of assumptions entirely, but the more you can do to minimize them, the more Effective Communication you'll have. That, in turn, will free up time for you to spend on more productive activities.

~~~~~~

An Assumption Exercise

Here's an interesting exercise for you that relies on both assumptions and communication in order to verify the assumptions. The game's simple. It's kind of a detective game. I'll describe a situation and you need to figure out how the situation came about. You can only ask closed-ended questions and I can only answer "yes," "no," or "the answer's irrelevant."

What you'll find is that you'll be forced to make assumptions about certain things. Not knowing if the assumptions are true, you'll have to ask me if they are. It's really no different from what I advocate in everyday conversation—work to recognize the assumptions in play, put them on the table, and then verify them. However, for this game, you'll find there's one key assumption you'll make, but not recognize, that'll lead you to the solution. Much like when there's a disagreement between parties, there's usually one critical assumption made that prevents a mutual understanding and resolution.

Here's the situation: John and Mary lie dead on the floor. Around them is broken glass and water. How did this happen?

Since you're the reader and I'm the author and this is a book, we obviously can't have a dialog, so I'll fill in your parts. Trust me. I won't lead you astray. I'm a professional.

You: Were they shot with a gun? Me: No.

You: Did they die because they were cut by the glass? Me: No.

You: Were they drowned in the water? Me: No.

Me: Look, you're trying to come at it too directly. Focus on the surrounding clues, not the problem itself.

You: Were they inside or outside? Me: You can only ask yes or no questions.

You: Were they inside? Me: Yes. Now you're thinking on the right track.

You: Was there a lot of water? Me: No. [Note: A side assumption made with this question is that "a lot" means the same thing to both of us. Specificity using Names, Numbers, Dates, and Deadlines is an applicable concept we'll discuss in Chapter 9.]

You: Were John and Mary people? Me: No.

This exercise gets completed faster in a group environment, since you'll have more brains focused on the situation, but sooner or later, someone will stumble onto the key wrong, but unrecognized, assumption that John and Mary are people. With this knowledge, the questions usually become more targeted and you'll soon discover that John and Mary are goldfish. The solution is that the cat knocked over the goldfish bowl, which fell to the floor and broke. No, I don't know why the cat didn't eat the goldfish, but it just didn't. So there.

The point is it took some work, some conversation, to get to the root cause assumption that led to the mutual understanding.

Make sure you really, truly understand the impact of assumptions to produce Effective Communication and actively work to find those assumptions.

~~~~~~

Projecting You onto Others

The reason we usually miss seeing how a person could interpret something differently from what was intended is that we project ourselves onto others. If I'm logical, I'll usually assume you're logical, too. So, I'll take an assumption, turn it into action, and interact with you in a logical fashion. Works great if random chance happens to be that you're logical, but doesn't work so well if you operate from an emotional base. That's when the disconnects start to happen.

Projection is a well-known psychological concept. Classically, it's a defense mechanism in which the person denies their own negative attributes and ascribes (or projects) them onto others. More broadly, it takes *any* personal attribute and projects it onto others. If I like Italian food, you like Italian food. If I'm happy, you must be happy, too. Projection really starts with an assumption, puts it into action, and potentially takes a conversation down the wrong fork of the road.

Orson Scott Card has a great, enjoyable series of novels that started with his classic *Ender's Game* (a winner of both Nebula and Hugo awards for best novel). In the third of the series, *Xenocide,* he writes this interaction between two characters who grieve over the death of a mutual friend. It points out how projections impact communication.

> [Ender glared as Miro laughed. "I'm just trying to get you to laugh yourself out of your grief.] Didn't you ever think I needed somebody to jolly me out of it sometimes?" Miro asked.
>
> "Didn't you ever think that I don't need that?" responded Ender.

Miro laughed again, but it came a bit late, and it was gentler. "On target," he said. "You treated me the way you like to be treated when you grieve, and now I'm treating you the way I like to be treated. We prescribe our own medicine for each other."

Here's an interesting game challenge for you that'll bring home the reality of the ubiquitous nature of assumptions. Focus on assumptions for a day. Look for as many assumptions as you can as you communicate with others throughout the day. Don't worry so much about what you say or even what the other person says, just look for hidden assumptions that could be associated with any given statement. Count them. By the end of the day, you'll have a huge number. Because if you really look hard at assumptions, you'll find assumptions within assumptions.

Now you can take it to an extreme and continue on that path, much like mirrors facing each other create an infinite number of reflections, but try to stay grounded in reality and practicality. Keep your investigation to just the first one or two assumptions of a given incident you find and be happy with that. By the end of the day, you'll have a whole new appreciation for the impact that assumptions—those silent assassins—have on everyday communication. If you can apply that knowledge to help create Effective Communication on a regular basis, you'll be ahead of 95% of the people in the world.

Understand that it's not enough just to identify the assumption. You need to throw it out on the table for all to see and comment on. When you're in a conversation, it's often hard to stop it and take it in a slightly different direction, but it's what needs to be done to find the common ground. Talk about whether the assumption you just identified is true. You can always get back to your original discussion, but at least you'll know why you disagree.

Sometimes assumptions are true and identifying them won't be able to get you to agreement. Say we disagree on something and I, using the 75% of free time my brain has while you ramble on, am focused on finding underlying assumptions and think I've found one. "Hey," I say, "wait a minute. Can I have just a minute to think? I think that a basic assumption in our argument is that I assume you're a jerk. Is that the case?" "Why, yes," you reply, "I am." With that understanding, now you can go back to the disagreement with that as a basis. You've both Effectively Communicated.

Okay, admittedly a tongue-in-cheek example, but hopefully you get the point. Identify assumptions, let them see the light of day, and you'll give yourself a better opportunity to be understood for what you mean to be understood for.

The name of the tool used in the example above is the perception check. Its advantage is that it's straightforward, direct communication that uses a simple closed ended question that requires only a simple yes or no response. In the example above, you asked "Is that the case?" If you can ascertain that you made an assumption, just put it out there for comment. "Hey, Joe, I feel like you're angry. Are you?" Perception checks are quick ways to get out of the assumption mode. However, you've still got to recognize when an assumption influences the discussion in the first place before you can do something about it.

~~~~~~

Attitude and Effective Communication

If you go into a conversation looking for a fight, you'll likely find one. How you approach an imminent interaction makes all the difference in the outcome. Communication often just happens on the fly, as both parties make it up as they go. There's no thought to the how or why of the conversation. Purkey's Law of the 7 Ps (Proper Prior Planning Prevents Piss Poor Performance) isn't always practical when you enter a conversation, but to the extent that you know the fundamentals of communication and where it can go awry, you'll be ahead. Be proactive. Be ahead of the curve. Anticipate problems and consequences.

The attitude you come in with is an important component of communication. Earlier I mentioned that if you can accept the reality that you may be wrong before you even open your mouth, you'll be miles ahead. Do you seek to conquer and dominate your opponent to prove that you're right (my way or the highway) or do you seek to understand and include your teammate to find the best answer? If your attitude's one of acceptance and you come without preconceived notions of what the outcome's supposed to be, then your conversations will be more clear and productive.

Attitude extends to many situations. Annual evaluations are often dreaded by both givers and receivers. Receivers (in the subordinate role right off the bat) might mentally cower like a scolded puppy in anticipation of the pride crushing, humiliating conversation that's about to take place. Their attitude coming into the evaluation discussion may not be conducive to them learning anything. As a coach, it's important first to put the receiver into a safe zone at the very front end of the discussion. With some initial comments that address and dismiss or minimize what may be the employee's greatest fear (granted, an assumption), the employee will be more open to the instruction you provide.

For example: "You know, Jill, while we'll talk about how your performance can be improved in alignment with our Principle of continuous improvement, you should know that I think you're a valuable part of the team and I look forward to your contributions in the next year." Jill may or may not have been worried about job security, but taking that off the table right out of the gate sets the tone for the rest of the session. You've put Jill in a safe place where now she doesn't have to worry about her career path, but instead can focus on the more objective performance aspects of her last year. She'll be more willing to hear and internalize your coaching points.

~~~~~~

Judgments

If assumptions are the silent assassins of Effective Communication, then their more evil twin is judgments.

While assumptions can just exist inertly, hidden from conscious thought, judgments take those assumptions to the next level and turn them into actions. It's the actions, the overt behaviors that you exhibit to others, that become the problem when your inaccurate judgment is based on a false assumption. If you can realize when you've made a judgment and appropriately question that judgment, either with your conversation partner or internally, you'll make big gains in your Effective Communication.

Just like assumptions, the existence of judgments is a fact of life. Judgments are inescapable; you just need to be aware when you've made one. You don't necessarily need to question authority, but you do need to question yourself. When you communicate, you consciously need to examine what you say, what the other person says, and what judgments are invented. As with recognizing and naming assumptions, becoming adept at that with judgments is the same degree of difficulty—hard.

> "Let me dispel a few rumors so they don't fester
> into facts." —John Keating (Robin Williams) in
> the movie *Dead Poets Society*

There's a natural human tendency to rush to judgment, to categorize, to pigeonhole. That tendency has roots back to the dawn of humankind and has been ingrained in our psyche over tens of thousands of years. It's the basic fight or flight question, one that usually comes in the heat of the moment. When faced with survival, quick decisions are a requirement. That saber-tooth tiger won't wait for you to decide how to proceed before it acts; you need to make a decision (judgment) and do something fast before you become lunch.

The human condition hasn't really changed over the years to suppress this basic instinct. Once again, in yet another context, those brain filters we've talked about are in motion. By now, you should know that you've got to have an awareness of their impacts on your thinking. As you walk down the sidewalk, at a fundamental, autonomic level, your brain assesses everything you see as either safe or harmful. The safe stuff is simply filtered out from conscious action, while the harmful stuff is passed through your filters to a conscious level so that you can deal with it appropriately. It's instantaneous decision-making.

But instantaneous decision-making isn't limited to just safe or harmful. The process is a part of our being. As you scan your environment, you can't help but make judgments (always preceded by assumptions) about what you see. Thousands of things are processed by your brain in an almost infinitesimal amount of time. Pretty, ugly, like, don't like, obnoxious, fun, playful, stuck up, strong, weak, friendly, mad, disturbed, upset, prickly, threat, nervous, pleasant, etc.

Researchers from NYU found that we make eleven major decisions about one another in the first seven seconds of meeting. An article by Marina Krakovsky in *Scientific American* from January 27, 2010 says that most of those judgments are wrong because "they rely on crude stereotypes and other mental shortcuts."

Now that you're aware of how you work, what if you exerted your twenty-first century will to overcome your primitive human condition that still acts on you? What if you recognized a judgment you just made and pushed it to the front of your brain for further examination? Would that judgment stand up against reality? Is it true? Most of us assume our judgments are fact. If you can get past that phenomenon (back to accepting that you might be wrong), you'll find your ability to Effectively Communicate and get things done in an efficient manner will be greatly magnified. Judgments are not facts. They're simply the reptilian portion of your brain satisfying its need for an instantaneous categorization of a situation, regardless of the validity of the judgment. You're better than that.

Judgments don't need to be set in concrete. A judgment's something that can be changed based on additional input and thought. What if a judgment's something that's questioned as a matter of course? After further reflection, you still may come to the conclusion that the ugly piece of art you're staring at is in fact ugly, but you'll have at least given the art a fair shot. You'll have rational and assumptionless facts behind your judgment versus the almost thoughtless, instantaneous judgment you might otherwise make. Now you've become a rational, thinking human being.

A key communication skill is to be able to separate the behavior you see from the conclusions you make about the behavior. If you can *describe the behavior*, rather than place a judgment, you'll have made great strides in interpersonal communication. A description of the behavior often takes a conversation out of the accusatory, emotional tone it might have and puts it into a more logical, even-keel mode that allows for real dialog.

For example, as you respond to a comment, in the rush to judgment, you might say, "You're angry." You've made your judgment and now the action you've taken is to make an accusation. You've immediately put the other person on the defensive to justify their statement. Your accusation almost demands some sort of quick response. They'll want to either confirm your judgment or deny it. They'll want to either prove you right or prove you wrong. Now the conversation moves off on a tangent from the original topic to have one person justify or rationalize why they weren't really angry. You've just introduced an inefficiency into your busy day, since a discussion of anger won't make your customers satisfied.

Instead of the accusatory tack, what if you tried a more inquisitive, enlightened approach that puts you in a position of neutral observation and description versus attack? "Bob, I see your face is red, your voice is loud, you're pointing a finger at me, and your neck cords are strained. I can sense you're angry with me. Is that accurate?" Okay, this specific response might set Bob off even more if he judges you to be mocking him, but for illustrative purposes, it makes the point. Don't accuse; do describe. Don't judge without examining why you've judged as you have.

~~~~~~

Tips to Make Communication Effective

TIP # 1: Use "I" statements.

Good interpersonal communication (that leads to mutual understanding) has both parties respecting each other's experience. They don't try to ignore, discount, change, or rob the other person of their experience. On the other hand, poor interpersonal communication, either overtly or covertly, says "I don't care what you feel, intend, or experience. It's incorrect and wrong. What you really should feel, intend, value, or experience is . . ."

When you want to solve conflicts, look to the "I," not the "you."

We hide the "I" with judgments, accusations, sarcasm, and questions that really mask intended statements or commands. Once accusations start, your ability to Effectively Communicate diminishes rapidly. An accusation's simply a judgment that you project onto others and present as a fact. They often involve the word "you." You're ugly. You're mad. You're a jerk. You're late. With this approach, the person you talk to has a figurative finger pointed right in their face about an inch from their nose. What type of reaction would you expect, other than for that person to become defensive about whatever "fact" you've accused them of? After all, they make judgments as fast as you do.

A way to soften this perception of being under attack is to use "I" statements. That means to phrase your statements in terms of yourself instead of others. While the message may ultimately be the same, the ability to take the focus off the other person and put it on yourself, as one who controls what they can control, will help facilitate (not guarantee) productive, calm discussion.

"I" statements say what you think, how you feel, and why you feel that way. They most always begin with the word "I." Clever, huh? While in America we're generally taught that use of the word "I" is an indication of egotism and narcissism and something to be avoided, in this case it's the solution to Effectively Communicating because it takes away the accusatory tone that many conversations can have. An "I" statement generally takes the form of "I feel [insert your emotion] when you [describe the other's behavior] because [describe why you feel that way]." For example, "Pat, I feel frustrated when you arrive late to the meeting because we have limited time to get through some big topics."

Yes, it still involves pointing the finger at the other person to a certain degree, since the "I" statement does involve the word "you," but it's a two-way conversation involving two people, so it's hard totally to avoid a reference to the other person. The difference is that you name and take responsibility for your own thoughts and feelings versus make the other person feel baldly accused.

TIP #2: Suggest, don't command.

Use of the word "should" often sounds preachy and bossy to those who form judgments about what you say. The word regularly gets you lumped into the category of "do what I say, not what I do" right off the bat and can erode your credibility. Eliminating this word from your vocabulary would be a great boon to Effective Communication. (In fact, you should always try never to use these three words in conversation: should, always, never.)

"Should" comes with a number of implications that can derail a perfectly good suggestion as the other person attaches their own assumptions and judgments to the statement. It could imply "holier than thou." It could imply you won't help. Do you just find blame ("You should have . . .") or do you actively try to help someone or resolve an issue? Without further discussion, it could leave both parties unsatisfied.

Instead of saying "You should . . . ," what if you substituted the phrase "What if . . . ?" "What if" is less commanding, less threatening, and more inclusive, engaging the other person in a thought process to help answer the question. It invites the other person to take part in finding the solution by opening the door to have them extrapolate the concept to a logical conclusion and analyze problems that might be encountered along the way. "What if" simply puts out a hypothetical proposal that can be assessed objectively by both parties as a team. It doesn't say that you've already made up your mind, put your stake in the ground, and commanded them to do something. It's more like, "Here's an idea, let's explore it." That approach engenders discussion and critical analysis, things needed to arrive at a workable solution.

"What if" takes practice and a front-of-the-mind awareness of the opportunities as they present themselves. In an early draft of this book, I found with a word search that I'd used the word "should" 193 times. Now, there are many occasions where "should" is just the right word. But I looked at all 193 and rephrased as many sentences as I thought applicable to reflect "what if" instead of "should." You've probably noticed that phraseology already. Now there are 42 fewer instances of "should." When you see questions elsewhere in the book that start with "what if," that's why. It's a kinder, gentler way to ask another person to explore an idea instead of preaching to them.

TIP #3: Avoid extremes and absolutes.

Words like "always," "never," "none," and "all" express the extreme case and are seldom absolutely, literally true. They often incite an immediate, gut-level defensive response not related to the issue you're trying to resolve.

Suppose you want to coach Donna to be on time more often. To no surprise to you, Donna arrives to your meeting five minutes late. She walks through the doorway and you say, "Donna, you're *always* late and it's got to stop." Donna now starts to search for exceptions to your absolute statement to show that you're wrong. "Wait a minute. Just last week I arrived early for our meeting with Engineering. And I've been on time for most of our one-on-one sessions. On February 13, I made it to our potluck on time. On December 21, I showed up on time to my dentist." Now the conversation's off topic from what you wanted, as you move on to debate precisely what percentage of the time Donna's late with Donna also offended that you've mischaracterized her promptness.

Combining what you've learned about 'I' statements and avoiding extremes, what if you'd started the conversation with "Hi, Donna. I feel frustrated when you show up late to meetings because I think it contributes to our inefficiency around here, which I'd like to fix. What if today we talked about how to help you be on time more consistently and why that's important?" The issue is clearly presented as *consistency* in being on time versus *never* being on time. Now you've got a topic you can both more easily agree on and discuss intelligently without defensiveness.

TIP #4: Understand everyone has baggage and incorporate that knowledge into conversations. (The following is based on Ronald R. Short's example in *Leading Groups: Models, Concepts and Theory* (1988).)

When you're in a group, you can't help but communicate. You convey messages, knowingly or not, through body language, tone of voice, your verbal contributions (or lack of them—just because you're quiet doesn't mean you're not noticed), eye contact, your very presence, and hundreds of other silent ways that communication occurs.

At the same time you send messages, others receive them. The question is whether the receivers receive the same thing that you think you send. Those receivers who sit there in your meeting have their own filters that process the entire interaction. What those filters let through or prevent is unknown to you.

The things that affect those filters are called baggage. It would be great if, in a meeting, everyone's attention focused on just the topics of the meeting and the specific discussions that take place. But we know that it's not, since we only comprehend 25% of what's said. That other 75% is baggage. It's free time your brain has to provide its own twists on the 25%.

Let's go back to that coaching example we did with you and Donna where she arrived late. You started the meeting with certain expectations, primarily that you wanted to persuade Donna to be on time more often. What you may not realize is the fact that you came to the meeting with your own baggage—high motivation, high investment in success, expectations of fun, uneasiness as to whether Donna had equal investment and motivation, intentions, assumptions about Donna, emotional responses toward Donna, beliefs, values, past experience with people like Donna, your level of self-esteem, your level of confidence, skills, and a whole host of other things that can and do influence how the meeting will transpire.

Understand that Donna also came to the meeting with her own baggage. Her perception of you, her child has a cold, she didn't sleep well, snarled traffic, a recent argument with a colleague, beliefs, values, level of confidence, and on and on. When she arrived late, she might have been embarrassed and so might have been more defensive than normal for her.

It's impossible to account for all of the different types of baggage anyone comes with and you certainly can't take the time to go down the laundry list of how each one of them impacts the people you talk to on any given day. What you do need to recognize is that baggage exists, it affects people's filters, and their reactions may be determined not by a logical, cogent frame of reference, but by problems that aren't related to your current discussion. Here again, as we've discussed, if you find yourself in an argument, take a step back and look for the root causes that got you off track. Baggage is frequently the source.

Don't stress out over it, just be aware. Your characteristics will be liked or not liked based on the personal filters of each individual member of your audience. You can't control that, but you can influence it, if you have awareness and can adjust according to that awareness.

≈≈≈≈≈

Open and Honest Communication

"You can't handle the truth!"

—Col. Jessup (Jack Nicholson) in the movie *A Few Good Men*

Unfortunately in business today, many can't handle true open and honest communication. People who are worried about their jobs, the impressions they make on their managers, who keep their head down, and who are chameleons whose only real purpose is to adapt to whatever administration is in place have a hard time unless they shade the facts and spin messages.

In a culture that values transparency, open and honest communication's something to be revered. Imagine if people actually meant what they said and did what they said they would do. The concept scares many people because open and honest communication leaves no cover to hide behind. All operations and processes are out there for everyone to see and for everyone to comment on. Imagine the synergy that could exist in an environment where not just small working groups interact with ease, trust, and efficiency, but a much larger number of people get involved, including whole departments and the whole company. With larger numbers of engaged participants, synergies get magnified exponentially. (Understand I'm not talking about committees bloated with participants, but instead just having more people on board with the Principles.)

So why is open and honest communication so rare? Well, it gets back to the human factor again. Many people really can't handle the truth. They'd rather ignore problems or superficially attempt to solve them. Why, it might turn out that the actual problem involves those very people who don't want the truth told. It certainly wouldn't do to expose that truth, now would it? Nope, sure can't have that.

Ever have a boss or seen a movie in which the boss doesn't want to hear the word "no?" All they want is blind obedience. They only want to hear what they want to hear. They want to abdicate their responsibility to stay engaged in whatever project they started. They're the managers we talked about before that come in, make directives, go away for six months, and come back expecting results without any real effort on their part. That's not leadership; that's dictatorship.

This practice is common enough that you need to look at your own group and their interaction with you. What do your people think you want to hear? Do they hide inconvenient truths because they think you don't want to hear about them? If your folks don't positively know that you want to hear any and all problems in the interest of fixing them to drive customer satisfaction or employee efficiency, then you're missing the boat when it comes to great leadership.

At the XYZ Company, a new training program got rolled out. A month later in a group meeting of peer managers with their boss, the boss asked the loaded question, "Do the people in your groups have everything they need and understand the new processes sufficiently to implement the new training?" On the surface, the query seemed innocuous enough, but really she was cutting her people loose with minimal training and washing her hands of subsequent responsibility in an effort to deflect blame from her to them in the event of failure. Besides being antithetical to a teaching, nurturing management approach towards organizational improvement, the very concept is contrary to Steps 6, 7, and 8 to achieve operational brilliance (Chapter 9).

In an effort to be open and honest, one manager responded to the boss with, "Well, they certainly know enough to get started, but they'll need more support from me and others as they begin to use the training." The boss's response to his comment? "Wrong answer," delivered in a belittling, challenging tone.

There could be a whole separate chapter on personnel management techniques not to belittle people in a public forum, to incorporate the good management axiom of "praise in public, criticize in private," but that's for my next book. For our purposes here, the larger issue is that the boss simply didn't want to hear the true, complete answer, but instead wanted to hear, "Yes, they can do it and we can move on to other issues." The boss made up her mind before she even asked the question. She lacked the interest to evaluate the abilities of the group, communicate anything other than "this is solely your responsibility now," or adjust processes as necessary.

So, not liking the first answer, the boss immediately moved on to another manager and asked the same question about the readiness of his front line group. Taking the cue from his peer manager's *faux pas*, he responded with "Yes, they're ready." Now, his group was no more prepared than his peer's was, but that response met the boss's preconceived notion. The boss liked this answer, assumed all other managers would have that response, and moved on to a new topic without questioning any more managers.

In order for problems to get resolved and processes improved, management must want to hear the truth—the bad news and the good news. Simply willing the problems to go away by wanting to be told only the good news doesn't work in the real world. Managing like Scarlett O'Hara in *Gone with the Wind* isn't a formula for organizational success. ("I can't think about that right now. If I do, I'll go crazy. I'll think about that tomorrow.")

As unaddressed situations worsen over time, they ultimately take more of the organization's limited resources to resolve, which defines inefficiencies. These inefficiencies are often not even recognized in the chaotic rush to handle yet another fire drill. Management hasn't got the time to address problems early because they're too busy putting out all the fires, ignited by a failure to address problems early.

"Wrong answer," as succinctly stated by the boss in response to her subordinate's answer to the loaded question, only puts everyone else on guard so they don't get burned. Don't be a boss that asks a question whose answer you don't want to hear. If you ask it, be ready to assimilate an answer that's the opposite of what you expect. When leaders abrogate their responsibility to support their people, the group will fail. That support includes open and honest communication. Without it, the group's set up for failure and is set up to take the blame in case of failure.

So the right answer to the question "Do your people have enough information to implement this plan on their own?" is "No. However, my group has enough information to roll out the plan and I'll be there to support them as necessary to make it succeed."

~~~~~~~

Be Up Front (Open and Honest, cont'd.)

While some try to ignore the obvious, fortunately there are other personality types that want to put the obvious on the table. Hence the phrase "elephant in the room," devised to express the situation in which a huge assumption exists, but that few really want to address or put out on the table. What it points out is a human predilection to obscure, obfuscate, ignore the obvious, and sweep things under the rug. It describes a stereotypical condition in which people, would rather completely avoid a subject than be uncomfortable to discuss and resolve that subject. It happens often enough that someone came up with a phrase to describe it. The tale of *The Emperor's New Clothes* by Hans Christian Andersen could have been named *"The Elephant in the Room."*

"The elephant in the room" syndrome is the opposite of open and honest communication. It's often fueled by leaders who only want to hear what they want to hear, as we discussed earlier. In a culture that exhibits true open and honest communication, everyone plays the role of the boy who says that the emperor has no clothes. In that culture, there's no retribution to state the obvious or question any circumstance. In that culture, you'll hear more of "thanks for pointing that out" and less of "wrong answer."

How do you gracefully confront the obvious? One way is to incorporate the phrase "Let's address the elephant in the room" into the beginning of your remarks. That often softens the approach and will get heads nodding in agreement, even though those same people wouldn't broach the subject themselves.

Here's how I once confronted the obvious. It seemed to work, I think because of its slightly disarming nature, but mostly because I approached it up front, openly, and honestly.

At one time I was a subject matter expert witness who testified in regulatory hearings about my company's regulatory plans. That job description could include "answer questions under oath in the face of hostile cross examination by opposing attorneys and utilities commissioners." While that prospect terrified most, unfortunately including some of our other subject matter experts, I reveled in it. Why? Essentially because I had truth on my side. Mark Twain famously said, "If you tell the truth, you don't have to remember anything." I knew I had a foundation of fairness, openness, and honesty to back up the points I made and that gave me confidence that couldn't be shaken easily.

The schedule called for me to testify in back-to-back hearings in both Iowa and Wyoming starting on a Monday. On the Saturday before, I realized I needed to cut my hair in order to be presentable for the hearings. Now, being follicly challenged, for a long time I had cut my own hair with an electric trimmer with a spacer set to one-quarter inch of length and just buzzed my head uniformly. No muss, no fuss.

Unfortunately for me, my beloved University of Washington Huskies played a football game against Notre Dame on that Saturday. The Huskies had the lead in a tight, riveting game until an epic fourth quarter collapse cost them the win. During that fourth quarter, I realized I needed to cut my hair to be ready for the hearings. So as not to miss any of the game, I decided to cut my hair in stages during the commercials, stop when the game began, and go back to hair cutting during the breaks.

On one break, I decided I needed to trim my sideburns, so removed the spacer on the trimmer to take the end of my sideburns down to the skin. Then the game started again. Notre Dame scored to take the lead and left me, well, let's just say a bit distraught and distracted. But I had the mission to cut my hair, so proceeded back to the bathroom, picked up my hair trimmer (now without the spacer), placed it on the back of my neck, and cut a path in my hair down to the skin from the base of my neck up to my right ear. Now I had a cleanly shaved two-inch wide by four-inch long bare track in my otherwise one-quarter inch length head of hair. Oops. Not exactly the professional appearance I envisioned.

Once the game ended, I evaluated my options. There weren't many. First I thought I could just shave my whole head. But with the luminous, untanned, white skin that would be exposed, I'd look like a deranged convict being prepped for the electric chair. Not the first impression I wanted to create when I tried at least to appear competent as an expert.

I'd seen some stylish patterns cut into people's hair—somewhat of a fashion statement at the time—and decided on Plan B. I shaved an identical swath of bareness onto the left side of my head. At least my haircut would be symmetrical. After some fine-tuning with the help of my wife, I was ready to take the stand. Right.

Before any hearing, there's usually a bit of mingling and polite "helloing" among both friends and foes. Oh, I forgot to tell you. I'm six feet, five inches tall, and so generally stand out in a crowd, anyway. Add to that my new hairdo and, well, just imagine. Interestingly, no one commented on my new coiffure directly to me during all of the mingling and helloing, but an almost a palpable undercurrent of curiosity lingered, if not some covert glances in my direction.

I knew there were hundreds of assumptions made collectively by the group and I knew that Effective Communication means that assumptions need to be put on the table for all to see. I also knew that to succeed in getting across the points I needed to make, I needed Effective Communication. So, when called to the witness stand, I made the decision to confront the obvious—the elephant in the room. Before being sworn in, I turned, with some degree of trepidation I might add, to the audience and said, "You're probably all wondering about my haircut . . ." I then laid out the story for them just like I relayed it above.

Some smiled, some laughed, some shook their heads wryly, but all seemed sympathetic to my plight. Whew! Everyone, even the opposing attorneys and the commissioners, relaxed and we got on with business. Had I not addressed the issue forthrightly, my every answer would have been clouded by thoughts about my haircut and my points would have been missed.

Two days later in Wyoming, the scenario repeated itself, except this time I had less nervousness and proactively reached out to the minglers and helloers with the story before the hearing so that at least some of them knew before I gave my pre-swearing-in explanation.

We won both cases.

~~~~~

Leadership

As we'll see in Chapter 8, leadership is creating the page and then making sure that everyone's on that page. As a leader, the page you need to create from Day 1 is a culture of clear and continuous communication throughout the organization.

However, you can't just stop at the page creation and expect things to work right on their own. While the page creation may be fun, it's getting everyone to join you on that page that's the challenge and requires the work. It's why there's management. Sure, you have to step in as needed to put out fires, but in general, a leader's job is fire prevention. Management inherently means planning and, well . . . managing—thinking ahead to potential problems and avoiding them. I suppose you could attempt mostly to manage reactively and wait for something to happen before you actually stepped in and took action, but then you'd quickly become consumed by the fires. You'd not be in control, you'd be controlled. Prevention is the watchword of good management.

Communication's often the weakest link, the point of failure for many endeavors. People need clear directions, guidance, and unambiguous expectations. It's a scientific truism that nature abhors a vacuum and will work to fill any empty space. Absent communication, just like nature fills in gaps, people will create their own directions, guidance, and expectations, each according to their own personal tastes and comfort levels. What they create on their own may make their job more comfortable for them personally, but it likely won't help the rest of the company. Standards can't exist. Fair employee evaluations become impossible, since everyone has their own standards of what's good and what's bad. Without leadership providing continuous communication as to goals, progress, processes, and expectations, the team concept dissolves and the program fails.

A company's culture reflects the leadership style. The XYZ Company had a scattered, unfocused, chaotic, and reactionary owner. The company mirrored those characteristics—little discipline, an inability to stay on task, constantly changing Priorities, and actual, physical fights among technicians (who, surprisingly, were allowed to stay on with the company because they did "good work" . . . other than the fights, of course). The leader sets the stage for the success of the entire group, department, or company she or he leads. Don't believe anyone who tells you anything different. It's a heavy mantle to wear—leader—but never underestimate the impact you have on others in the realm that you lead.

There's a real and natural flow of attitude and approach from the top level all the way down to the front line. A leader is a parental figure, someone that others look up to and want to follow. A leader must clearly communicate or the followers won't be able to follow. A leader must be consistent in philosophy and in actions. Not to the point of refusal to change in the face of new information, just reliably consistent.

An effective leader will continually communicate, use a variety of methods with all departments and employees, discuss where things work and where they don't, and describe the customer benefits from an efficiently operating organization. An effective leader will have the core Principles, values, and goals of the company in mind at all times and link observed actions back to them at every opportunity.

The goal of an effective leader is to get the entire organization to understand the benefits of meeting customers' needs, get the individual employees to understand their respective roles to make (or not make) that happen, and then put processes in place to make the entire organization effectively serve customers. It does no good to have a great product (meeting a customer need) but not have the delivery system in place (the employees/organization) to get the product to the customer in such a way that pleases the customer.

An effective leader Prioritizes first creating the foundation of a strong organization in order to have a good mechanism to serve customers. Customers, in turn, will reward that organization by buying the products and generating profits.

Lead by example. Consciously model the culture you want to build.

Frequently management blames the front line when a process isn't executed as envisioned. Often, the front line just doesn't know what the process is. Back to the concept that communication is 50% sender and 50% receiver, as a leader, you need to provide more than your 50%. Take the extra step to verify that the front line knows the process and its intent. It's your company (or department or group); do all that you can to ensure that everyone's on the same page. It doesn't do anyone any good to assign blame; it does do good if you assign behavioral or process changes.

At the ABC Company, a vice president implemented a weekly, pre-recorded three-minute message that summarized events and results over the previous week that related to the stated goals of her team. Each supervisor group was required to listen to it as a team and individuals could listen independently if they couldn't attend the team meetings. When the VP saw team members in person, she dropped references to the messages to verify unscientifically whether people really listened. It helped keep both her and the team on point. Just by talking about the results and activities, it reinforced that these were important goals that everyone needed to focus on. Overt and subtle at the same time.

The first and second level managers started daily five-minute meetings at the beginning of the workday just as a chance to bring people together as a team. A chance to take a collective breath. A chance to decompress before the coming day. A chance to communicate directly about important issues, but briefly, as reminders, not long-winded speeches. The managers imposed very strict limits on the five minutes and the team members held them accountable to that. They assigned a time keeper (different for each meeting) to interrupt the speaker, whoever the speaker was regardless of management level, and stop the meeting (even in the middle of a sentence) at the end of the five minutes. Timekeeper became a position desired by the team members because they had friendly control of the situation, as they usually called time with a big grin on their faces.

These first and second line managers created a huge positive impact on their teams with the demonstration of alignment with some of the company's core values of integrity (five minutes only), respect (for their time), and accountability (running a tight ship).

~~~~~~

Pendulum Management

Consistency is an important quality of an effective leader. Consistency really should be fairly easy if you've got your Principles, values, and goals to fall back on. But you also have to be consistent in your willingness to change in the face of being "out-logicked."

Remember that it's the business issues that need to take your time during the day. Business issues generally don't involve emotions, but instead involve logic. The logic may be subjective in part, but because business issues are generally logical, you shouldn't get offended when one is surfaced and it involves you. It's not personal; it's business.

The challenge I make clear to my teams is that the process is what the process is and will remain the process until the champ's knocked out. If you want to change a process (i.e., a business issue), bring your A game and let's hear it. I always relish when someone comes to me (taking advantage of the open door policy) and presents a logical counter argument to whatever process is in question. Even if I came up with the original process, when someone can out-logic me as to why the process should change, I'm on board and grateful. I encourage you to follow that example. The approach shows consistency, but also flexibility. When an employee uses the open door, I also know that I've got engaged employees who care. Organizational success comes from such open and honest engagements.

At the other end of the spectrum, we have Pendulum Management, the opposite of consistency. It's maddeningly frustrating to work in an environment where management decrees swing wildly from one extreme to the other—Pendulum Management. It's as if management only has an on switch and an off switch; there's nothing in between. Unfortunately, that in-between state where the pendulum hangs straight down in the middle is where solutions are found and sanity lives.

At the XYZ Company, management feared the development of unions in the workforce. What I find ironic is that if workers are treated fairly and consistently in the first place in an environment of effective communication, there's no need for a union (whose ostensible purpose is to provide fairness and consistency for workers), but that's another chapter for another book. If you're a non-union shop and talk of unions creeps into conversations, look to management as the root cause for that union talk. At the XYZ company, unions became a wide topic of conversation.

Management, over time, had refused to hire more people even in the face of drastically increased workload. Extreme Policy #1: work them to death. Employees complained about too much overtime. If you work sixty hour weeks for a brief period, that might be okay, but not consistently over months. People burn out physically and emotionally, regardless of how much overtime pay they get. Finally, complaints mounted and management acted to change things.

Enter Extreme Policy #2: no overtime. None. Soon employees complained about not enough overtime, not only because of the dramatic pay cut, but also because customers didn't get served in a manner to produce satisfied customers. Management's response? "Employees are never satisfied." Employees' response? "Management doesn't know what they're doing." Welcome to Dysfunction World, breeding ground for unions.

At the ABC Company, they'd already implemented a solution that seemed to work for everyone. After discussions in team meetings with both front line and management, the company was able to reach a common ground solution. Employees signed up for the maximum amount of overtime they wanted and, as opportunities arose, management assigned shifts according to those desires. Management instituted and communicated to all a baseline policy of no overtime guarantees and limited overtime, subject to customer needs. ABC also had a good handle on how customers perceived the service they got and hired additional people when they saw a need for more resources to satisfy customers and still be consistent with the common ground overtime policy.

As a leader, give people respect, responsibility, and help and you'll have a loyal, engaged workforce that'll boost profits beyond imagination.

~~~~~~

Failure to Communicate Example

Sometimes the failure to communicate combines with Pendulum Management to make for some curious results. In any company, Effective Communication between operations and marketing is a requirement. It doesn't do any good to sell a product if you've got no way to deliver it. Similarly, if operations is ready to deliver, but marketing doesn't do anything to sell, then you've got unused capacity as operations folks just sit and wait for an order.

At the XYZ Company, accounts receivable got out of control. Customers, in record numbers, didn't pay their bills on time or at all. Now the good news here for XYZ is that it had metrics and goals relative to accounts receivable, which it had appropriately Prioritized and tracked. But then Finance management chose to go the Pendulum Management route.

They needed to clamp down on receivables, so they put in a new policy that told customer service reps not to accept new customers with poor credit and to proactively go after delinquent customers. They drew a hard line in the sand for a minimum credit score, below which new customers wouldn't be accepted. No exceptions. After all, what's the point in getting a new customer if the customer ultimately didn't pay their bill? Directionally, the actions made financial sense on the surface (although they attacked a financial problem with a financial solution, the fallacy of which we'll talk about in Chapter 8), but problems began to appear with the no exceptions policy.

Finance expected that sales would take somewhat of a hit because of the tighter credit policy. Sales plummeted below expectations when they closed off communication with customers and didn't give them the opportunity to explain, for example, their low credit scores.

Unbeknownst to Finance, Marketing worked hard on a parallel path to attempt to increase sales. They aptly named the idea that emerged Summer Frenzy. Marketing would attempt by any and all means to get as many customers as possible, regardless of credit or payment issues. Prices would be slashed and bad credit customers would be proactively encouraged to sign up. Not two weeks after Finance had instituted its draconian credit policy with the customer service reps, Marketing rolled out Summer Frenzy that gave those same customer service reps the exact opposite instructions from Finance. "Frenzy" was right.

XYZ had taken the classic Pendulum Management approach and gone from no credit required to full credit required and then back to no credit again.

CHAPTER 6—TOP DOG

How to Know Where to Focus

B efore you jump into any solution (and remember that this book's about creating the solution to bad management, both individually and organizationally), it's important to have a firm foundation from which to jump. A pogo stick doesn't work so well on the beach. That strong foundation is created with a vision, a strategy, a view of the big picture about what the business wants to be when it grows up. In short, Principles. Then, actions are taken within the context of and in alignment with the big picture. In a good, efficient business, actions that aren't congruent with the established big picture are stopped and redirected. The managerial challenge is to make the practice—the actions—be in alignment with the theory.

Here's another way to look at the foundation for this book in the form of a hierarchy of business components:

Profit feeds Management;
Management feeds Employees;
Employees feed Customers;
Customers feed Profit.

Let's expand on this concept so you can really understand it and internalize it. "Understand it viscerally," as a boss of mine used to say. If you understand this circular hierarchy and can keep it in mind in the face of the urgent needs of the day, then you're halfway there. It'll guide you on where to spend your limited resources and energy when you come up against issues that affect your profitability.

Look closely at the order. In the hierarchy of business components that involve humans, it starts with management. Here's an example of why:

> An Administrative Assistant, a Sales Rep, and their Manager are on their way to lunch when they find an antique oil lamp. They rub it and a Genie comes out. The Genie says, "I'll grant each of you just one wish." "Me first! Me first!" says the Admin. "I want to be in the Bahamas, driving a speedboat on the ocean, without a care in the world." Poof! He's gone. "Me next! Me next!" says the Sales Rep. "I want to be in Hawaii, relaxing on the beach with my personal masseuse, an endless supply of Piña Coladas, and the love of my life." Poof! She's gone. "OK, you're up," the Genie says to the Manager. The Manager says, "I want those two back in the office after lunch!"

Moral of the story: Always let your boss have the first say.

Kidding aside, management is the most important component of business success. Are you screaming incredulously (hopefully with your "inside" voice), "Profit's on the bottom? Are you nuts? If a business doesn't have profit, you don't have a business, at least for long." Okay, granted. I'll give you that. Actually, I gave you that in Chapter 1. But, let's look at the hierarchy logically and start from the bottom, with two concepts in mind: *dependencies* and *finding root causes*.

Profit depends on customers. No customers, no profit. A logical certainty with which I don't think anyone can rationally disagree. Somebody external to your company (that'd be customers) better give you money, do it consistently, and do it in sufficient quantities if you want to stay in business. Pretty easy to see that if a business wants profit, it had better have some focus on customers.

Okay, if you're a hair-splitter, yes, I know that profit is revenue minus expenses, so expenses play an equal role in profit creation. However, in a simplified view, management controls expenses and customers control revenue. Therefore, "no customers, no profit" is accurate.

Move up to the next point on the hierarchy—**customers depend on employees**. Employees are the delivery system for the products that customers buy. In short, if you can't get the products and services to the customers, customers won't give you any money. So, if a business wants profit, it had better have a good delivery system in place. That means employees need to be efficient and productive. Still with me on the irrefutable logic track?

Next, **employees depend on management**. Management creates the framework in which the employees do their jobs. Management establishes the culture, the environment. Management provides (or doesn't) the proper tools and support for employees to do their jobs effectively. So, if a business wants profit, it had better have the right management team and philosophy in place. You need strong leaders with the right skill sets to mold the employees and the organization that'll ultimately drive that profit.

Finally, **management's wholly dependent on profit** to survive. Probably the number one reason for management layoffs (in whatever form they may take, like wholesale downsizing) is a lack of profit. Basically, only managers, and even at that, generally just upper level managers, are really measured on and directly held accountable to profit. No one has a more vested interest to obtain a positive P&L than management. Logically, you'd think that management would do everything in its power to obtain that profit, but the reality says otherwise. Maybe it's just that management doesn't know how to obtain that profit other than cut expenses or attempt to raise revenue somehow. Management's often just a two-trick pony.

While some, like Stephen Covey, distinguish leadership separately from management ("Effective leadership is putting first things first. Effective management is discipline, carrying it out."), in the real world, there are no job titles called "Leader." Managers, whether they're C-level managers (CEO, COO, CFO, etc.) or line supervisors, need to have inherent leadership qualities. So, while leadership is necessary, it's an intangible characteristic that requires a real person—a manager—to make it happen. You can have management without leadership (that would fall into the "bad management" category), but you can't have leadership without management. As William Butler Yeats asked (popularized by The Eagles in their album *Desperado*), "Who can tell the dancer from the dance?" For the purposes of this book, management—at least good management—is indistinguishable from leadership and I'll frequently use the terms interchangeably.

You'll see in this hierarchy of business components that each does something active except for profit. Profit just sits there passively, dependent most directly on customers to live, but also indirectly dependent on employees and management to thrive. So, if you want profit to grow, you can't just yell at it and hope it'll respond.

Ironically, you can't address profit with financial solutions, either. If inventory's too high, it does little good to cut inventory to the bone (a financial solution) if that negatively impacts your ability to deliver your products to customers. The only way to make profit grow is to focus on management, employees, and customers.

Despite some managers' desperate attempts to alter the laws of physics, there really are only twenty-four hours in a day. There's a limited, finite amount of time available in which to accomplish tasks. Time is precious. As a manager, where will you spend your time? What will you focus on in order to drive increased profit? From the hierarchy, your most direct and effective fulcrum to leverage greater profits is employees because employees are the closest thing to generating profit that you can control (at least relative to controlling customers and assuming it's even possible to control employees),. By controlling employees, I don't mean to use one of the two tricks (mentioned above) in most managers' bags—cut expenses via employee cuts. I mean make your employees better at what they do. Spend your time on them.

But, who teaches the teacher? While profit feeds management, profit's certainly no teacher of how to manage effectively. Profit only sits there dependent on management, employees, and customers to keep it happy. Therefore, management has to pick up the slack and teach itself.

Management has a dual role—not only to coach employees, but also to increase its own knowledge of effective management techniques. That means making a Priority of making you, management, better at what you do. If you aren't the best you can be, then how can you teach your employees or set up systems and processes to be the best they can be? If you're a bad manager, it's likely you'll influence your employees to produce bad results. The apple doesn't fall far from the tree. Get good at what you do first, then turn your attentions to employees. It's like the airline instruction that, in the event oxygen masks are deployed, put your own on first before you help others. The logic is that you won't help others for very long if you pass out from lack of oxygen.

Once you've fixed yourself (and just a caution here that you should never believe you've been completely fixed—that's what continuous improvement's about), that doesn't mean you should focus on employees exclusively. Multi-skilled is an important attribute of an effective manager and you really need to be able to improve yourself and your employees simultaneously. Employees can't sit around and wait for the perfect you to appear. It's really more a question of the percentage of your day you'll devote to employee improvement.

As a manager, you play many different roles in the business. In the role of manager, if you have a choice between working on an employee issue that directly affects customer satisfaction or working on the P&L, you'd be better served to work with employees, since that'll help fix the P&L at the same time. Make reasoned decisions about where you'll spend your valuable time, in the context of trying to create greater profit. See Chapter 2 on Prioritization.

In the role of an employee, your fulcrum to leverage profits is customers. Interestingly enough, you also are limited to twenty-four hours in a day. Go figure. Your time must be used wisely, just as a manager's must be. You're faced with choices every day about how your time will be spent. What do you do that affects how customers perceive the business and its products? How can you make that customer experience better? Do you understand how you fit into the big picture and how you impact that big picture? If you know that employees provide a key lever for profit and know that management establishes the framework and environment for success, do you spend your time to look for direct, customer affecting process improvements that make you and your co-workers more efficient and that can be implemented throughout the business? Any employee needs to have the bigger picture in mind, as well as the smaller picture of the task at hand.

In the role of profit, how can you spend your time to improve the situation? Well, the answer is you can't. All you can do is hope to hell that everyone else does their respective parts, because you, in your role as profit, are totally dependent on them for your existence. Good luck.

~~~~~~

Okay, so now the stage is set. With a little more theory under your belt, let's get back to some practical things you can do to improve your lot in life for both you and your business.

CHAPTER 7—GOALS
How to Achieve Goals in 5 Steps

Achieving goals sounds easy. Much like the term "Priority," the goal to achieve goals is often stated, but also often not accomplished. This chapter breaks down what it takes to achieve and, perhaps more importantly, sustain goals. In business, you can't be satisfied to simply achieve a goal and stop there. If the goal isn't sustainable over time, then you've achieved nothing. What if employees were so engaged in the processes needed to achieve the goal that you (individually) aren't needed? If you get hit by a bus, the goal would continue to be met by the business long after you're gone. That's the true measure of success (without the getting hit by a bus part).

The five steps needed to achieve goals are:
1. Prioritization
2. Simplification
3. Standardization
4. Execution
5. Verification

Don't just read that list of five and say, "Yeah, okay, I've got it. What's next?" I know you're busy. Part of the message of this book is to slow down a bit and resist knee-jerk reactions to everything.

The CEO at the XYZ Company attended a large-sized meeting and asked Joe, an operations manager who happened to be standing nearby, to point out all of the sales managers in the room and name them. Joe, a bit flustered by the random question out of the blue from the CEO who had never said a word to him before, started to scan the audience.

Unknown to the CEO, however, the sales department had just gone through a series of downsizings and also had new players in place. The CEO also didn't know that Joe's boss had previously instructed Joe to stick to his own knitting in the operations department and not involve himself with other departments. Naturally, Joe couldn't come up with the names fast enough to suit the CEO. Ever try to name the seven dwarfs? Most people, even though they're very familiar with the story, miss at least one or two. Now put yourself in Joe's position—under scrutiny from a CEO known for knee-jerk reactions without a view of the whole picture and demanding answers.

Joe's inability to name the seven dwarfs immediately was career impacting, maybe more of a statement of the CEO's management capabilities and his predilection for quick, judgmental reactions, but career impacting nonetheless. So, slow down a little, unlike the CEO. Take a look at those five steps again. Each step takes some understanding in order to be able to put it into practice effectively. So let's start.

~~~~~~

Step 1: Prioritization

In order to *achieve* goals, you've got to *have* goals. Whether you realize it or not, the Prioritization exercise you did in Chapter 2 actually set up your goals. We just called them Priorities. You've already accomplished Step 1 on the ladder to success. Congratulations.

Chapter 2 covered a lot about how to Prioritize, but let me interject a few new and refresher thoughts about the topic, since it's such a key component to make your job less stressful and provide efficiencies for the business as a whole.

A failure to properly Prioritize is a significant step towards business failure. As we discussed, Priorities are easy to talk about, but actually sticking to them is one of the biggest challenges that managers face. So often the emergency of the moment casts a True Priority into the shadows. One business owner I worked with literally shopped at Costco for office supplies while his company struggled to find its identity with quality and customer service. He'd Prioritized office supplies and coffee over the work needed with his employees to improve their performance. He'd Prioritized the easy and mindless over the health of his business, probably because dealing with the many tough issues to make his organization better extracted too much of a toll from him. Wrong choice. Because of limited resources, he gave the excuse of, "Well, who else will do this?" My answer was, "Anyone."

A director once told me, "Dan, with me, everything's a number one Priority." Sounds great, doesn't it? A real go-getter attitude, like this person was really, really engaged in his work, juggled multiple projects at once, and did so with success. My reaction was, *"If everything is a priority, then nothing is a priority."* (You may have heard that one before.) The director's statement really said that he was a bad manager, unable to figure out the important from the unimportant.

A leader in an organization should be like the natural filters in the brain. A leader's capable of discerning what's truly essential from that which is merely important. That's True Prioritization. Then, the leader will rally the company, department, or team around those essential items, even at times to the exclusion of the important, if necessary, until the essentials are well in hand and under control.

~~~~~~

Step 2: Simplification

The good news is you've also already got a head start on Step 2 from the work on your earlier exercise to Prioritize and your commitment to let stuff fall off your plate. See? This stuff isn't so hard if you really apply yourself to it.

Unfortunately, Simplification can get complex, especially if you fall off the True Prioritization bandwagon. Yes, you've got a list of Prioritized actions to take, but it's probably long. Just that visual of an arm-long list will likely inhibit you from taking action if you constantly look at the whole list. It can be overwhelming. A natural reaction would be to jump to the conclusion that it will never all get done, so why try?

In alignment with letting stuff fall off your plate, construct a separate list that contains only the top five items and work only with that. Tape it to your desk in a very visible place where both you and others can see it. Seriously. To repeat myself (and education's largely about repetition), we all only have limited time and resources. It's better to under commit and achieve some things than it is to over commit and achieve nothing.

While reducing the size of your Priority list to only a few visible items is Simplification in one form, Simplification's more than that. It's also about a philosophy to gain efficiency and understanding for as many people as possible. The less complex something is, the higher the chance that a larger percentage of people will be able to execute that something successfully. Basically, make it easily understandable.

A successful process is one that's executed by the highest percentage of people who use the process in the way envisioned by management. If employees don't understand the process, then the ability to execute it is compromised. Simplification's the key to successful process execution.

Here's where our earlier discussion about Strategic, Tactical, and Task Priorities comes into play.

REAL WORLD EXAMPLE: At the ABC Company, the quality of their installations reached unacceptable levels, as determined by customer feedback and their own quality control inspections. As a management team, they decided to make improvement of installation quality the number one Priority so that customers would be more satisfied and therefore generate more profit. That became the Strategic Priority because it depended on other Priorities that needed to be completed first.

Both regular and ad hoc meetings needed to be put in place to move the project forward. Since those meetings hadn't existed before, something had to give, because time's a finite quantity and they already had other Priorities in place. They Truly Prioritized. The team identified some lower importance items and got the approval of their VP to allow those to fall off the plate. They redirected their time to the Strategic Priority. With everyone in the loop on the Strategic Priority and making appropriate accommodations, they moved forward.

One of the Tactical Priorities (in alignment with and support of the Strategic Priority) became to find out what inhibited techs from quality work. They were puzzled, because they'd written documentation in the form of an installation manual that spelled out exactly how any given installation should be performed. The techs only had to follow the manual. How hard could it be?

They talked to the techs (novel concept, eh?) and discovered that very few of the techs did things by the book. Over time and through the exchange of tribal knowledge, each tech had developed his own way to do an installation—what worked for him according to him. In fact, the techs hardly ever referred to the manual because of its over 200 pages of information.

Techs are under tremendous time pressure during the day to get through all of their scheduled installations. For some reason, customers actually expect them to show up when promised. A delay on one job affects the tech's ability to show up on time for subsequent appointments for that day. How could they possibly haul a 200-page manual into the customer's house and then be expected to start at page one and work through the manual until completed? Management had naïvely set an unrealistic expectation. The framework built for technicians to work within had some flaws. (See, I warned you about those management guys.)

The team decided to Prioritize the steps in the manual. They brought in key techs to be a part of the evaluation team, they eliminated those outdated or rarely used steps, and consolidated other steps so that the procedures became simpler. The bottom line? The team reduced the 200-page installation manual to sixteen pages.

The results? First and maybe foremost, happier techs. They now had clear, understandable guidelines to follow for the first time. They finally understood that no one really expected them to follow all 200 pages on each installation and the removal of that burden alone led to better morale. Before, they carried a secret around with some degree of guilt. After, everyone worked from the same sheet music in the spirit of open and honest communication. Because they participated in the development, they easily bought in to the relaunch of the installation manual and followed it more closely. From a metrics standpoint, quality (based on Quality Control inspections passed) jumped from the mid-70% range to the 95% range. Because following the manual more closely created more efficiencies and allowed the techs to complete jobs faster, a side result manifested that the percentage of jobs completed for any given day jumped also from the mid-70% range to the 95% range. Customer complaints dropped correspondingly.

In fairness, other factors also entered into the metrics improvements, but Simplification of the installation manual drove the bus. Just the process of Simplification increased the awareness of everyone that quality was Job One (Thanks, Ford marketing department.) and the techs responded. From the management team's perspective, Simplification of the Priorities list down to a single Priority to increase quality allowed them to concentrate energy on that and complete it instead of only talk about it.

Simplification leads to action and action's the engine that drives improvement.

~~~~~

Step 3: Standardization

Standardization is the core process that'll decrease the nonstop external interferences that get in the way of you doing your job. The more you can drive your team to understand and execute standardized processes as designed and intended, the fewer problems you'll have. The more you can work with your peers inside or outside of your department to do the same, those departments that used to always bug you for clarification or help or escalations will find that they can solve it themselves just fine. You'll find your management by crisis greatly diminished, which frees up your time and decreases stress levels for everyone.

Standardization is simply getting everyone to do a given task in the same way every time. This is the essence of Lean Management. For now, remember standardization's a key.

There are two primary components that comprise standardization—processes and metrics. This assumes that you've already

Prioritized and Simplified, because if you don't have clarity about what and why you're standardizing, you'll be headed down the wrong track. Practice doesn't make perfect; perfect practice makes perfect.

The goal of standardization is to get people to follow processes without even thinking about it. The ideal would be that they perform the processes every day in the same way almost by rote habit. What that does is free them up to spend some of their intellect to discover other things that can be improved upon that otherwise would never come to the surface because they're too busy to do their jobs. We want to create space in people's heads and time in their days to think and contribute ideas to make things better. Standardization provides that foundation.

We often hear about people overthinking things. They get so focused on the minute details of how to do something that they no longer can do that something they try so hard to do. Golfers are notorious for this affliction. The more they try, the less able they are to hit the ball consistently straight. When the swing motion becomes natural (i.e., they don't think about it), all of a sudden their game improves. Standardization helps people get to the point where their tasks become just like breathing. Breathing is absolutely necessary, but if you had to think about it all the time, you'd certainly be less efficient in your daily life.

There's a joke that illustrates the point.

> A woman never went anywhere or did anything without her headphones jammed in her ears. Walking, showering, sleeping, working—she always listened to something on her headphones. One day she went to the dentist for a root canal and had to be put under anesthesia. "Doctor, even though I'll be asleep, please don't take the headphones out of my ears. It's important, okay?" she said. The dentist agreed, but the more he got into the procedure, the more he found that the headphones got in the way of the root canal. Finally he

couldn't stand it anymore, took the headphones off, and set them aside. He continued his work, but soon his patient started to gasp for air. He tried to give her oxygen, but she didn't respond. As she continued to have problems, he realized the seriousness of the situation and tried everything he could to get her breathing again. Unfortunately, nothing worked and she died. The room grew silent as everyone sat in stunned disbelief at what had just transpired. Then, the dentist heard a small, tinny sound and realized that the noise came from the headphones he'd taken off her earlier. Curious, he put the headphones in his ears and heard this: "Breathe in, breathe out. Breathe in, breathe out. Breathe in, breathe out."

So, ***learn to breathe the processes.*** You'll have more time to direct towards ways to improve you and the business.

≈≈≈≈≈

Processes (Standardization)

One of the reasons you're too busy to do your job is that the processes the company has in place don't work or, worse, you simply don't have any processes.

Processes are a double-edged sword. Too few of them and people gravitate to whatever procedure's most comfortable for them individually. That may not necessarily result in the most efficient execution of the task. Too many of them (i.e., too detailed, like the 200-page installation manual) and people will be stifled and unable to think on the fly when something comes up that's out of process.

Think of a frustrated customer standing at a return counter "helped" by a customer service rep who refuses the return due to company policy. The customer sees an easy solution to the problem, if only reason and common sense could prevail. However, the rep, frozen into one way of thinking, keeps referring back to, "I'm sorry, it's our process and I can't do anything about it." It's a fine balancing line that's a challenge for managers to find.

Unfortunately, the only way to find that balance point is through trial and error. You can make all of the plans and preparations you want (and you should) in process development, but you'll only know for sure that you have the right plans and preparations when the processes are used by frontline employees. Yes, do the best job you can to construct logical, smooth-flowing processes, but don't get locked into a rigid adherence to them when customers or employees uncover process holes. Be ready to modify them based on feedback you get.

As you're no doubt discovering, all of the concepts we've talked about so far are intertwined and sometimes tough to separate. Nothing stands alone without an influence by or an interaction with something else. The Simplification exercise to go from 200 pages of an installation manual to sixteen also required that the sixteen pages that stayed contained the "right" processes. Prioritizing which processes would stay that would keep us in alignment with the Principle to produce better quality also played a role.

Practical Action #10
Involve both management and frontline personnel in the development of processes to make them more useful and successful.

Frontline employees, for the purposes of this discussion, can be defined as any level of employee who will actually use the processes in their work. The traditional frontline, those who don't manage people, may have procedures they work with directly every day to input an order into the system, complete store inventory, etc. However, executive managers also could be considered frontline if they're the ones using a given process.

There are two primary reasons to involve the frontline in process development. First, you want the people who use the processes actually to believe in them. You need buy-in. A great way to get that buy-in is to have the affected employees themselves have a hand in the creation. If you build your own house, you're likely to take great pride in that effort and more likely to live in it.

Second, the affected employees are most likely to have the best understanding of what works in the pursuit of the larger goal (e.g., improved installation quality). They're the ones who deal on a daily basis with the frustrated customers, with the department upstream from them that never seems to get the right information to them, or with their own inability to do their job because there are no effective processes in place.

≈≈≈≈≈≈

Keeping on Track (Standardization)

So, you've identified a Prioritized issue to fix and want to set up a process team. The first thing you need is to clearly state the reason why you even want a process team. Specifically, what do you want to accomplish? You need some form of a brief charter or a mission statement, some guiding light that'll keep the team on task. The charter helps narrow the scope of a process team to counteract the natural tendencies of groups to veer off course. Make that mission abundantly clear from the outset and that in itself will drive efficiencies into the group.

Ever been in a group of people mindlessly watching some bad movie on TV when someone finally speaks up and asks, "Why are we watching this?" You need those types of people to bring the group back to reality and redirect them to something more productive. You want to encourage that type of open and honest communication so participants can freely question why the team's going down the path that it is. With a clear charter in place, when the team begins to digress to a tangential topic (as groups are wont to do), the foundation's there for someone to ask, for example, "How does that directly impact [fill in overall goal]?" Encourage your team to act with a "question authority" outlook.

≈≈≈≈≈≈

Process Clarity (Standardization)

Processes need to be written in understandable terms. In plain English. With clarity. Without industry jargon and acronyms, to the greatest degree possible. While not always possible, the standard to shoot for is to have your process so understandable that you could bring in an intern off the street and have them perform a task simply by reading the process. Remember the 200-page installation manual reduced to sixteen pages? A large portion of that simply changed gobbledygook into a guidebook anyone could understand and eliminated steps/instructions that had no relationship to the reason for the process.

The purpose of the process has to be in alignment with the Priority that's addressed. If the Priority is to improve on-time performance, any time spent to develop a process that keeps better track of luggage at the airline is time wasted, regardless of the noble idea not to lose luggage. Now maybe reducing lost luggage is a Priority worthy of addressing, but there's a time and a place for that and your Prioritization list will show where that should fall.

Make sure you allocate enough time to develop a given process fully. Sometimes managers get so impatient that unrealistic and artificial deadlines get imposed. That then drives the team to be less engaged in the process development or start to take shortcuts in order to meet the deadline. You won't develop the process for world peace in thirty minutes, so don't expect to.

~~~~~~

Step 4: Execution

Execution's where the rubber meets the road. The most critical component of the whole endeavor is also the hardest to implement successfully. For all of the planning and development meetings that generally occur before actions are actually taken, you'd think that execution would be easy. That's not to say that good execution's impossible—far from it. If Prioritization, Simplification, and Standardization are handled thoughtfully, Execution can be a relative cakewalk. It exemplifies Purkey's Law of the Seven Ps: Proper Prior Planning Prevents Piss Poor Performance.

Unfortunately, there are a lot of gremlins in the path of proper execution that need to be recognized ahead of time in order to smooth out that execution path (and I don't mean an execution path as in Stephen King's book and movie *The Green Mile*). As a manager, if you understand them, you can avoid them. Among the gremlins are:

- Failure to communicate
- Lack of employee buy-in
- Lack of employee understanding
- Lack of management follow through
- Lack of measurable tracking

Let's take them one at a time.

Failure to Communicate (Execution)

"What we have here is failure to communicate."
—The Captain (Strother Martin) in *Cool Hand Luke*
(Heard that one before?)

Effective Communication is the very first building block in the foundation for business success to help you have time to do your job. It's also probably the most overlooked factor to make things work smoothly. We talked more extensively about the importance of Effective Communication in Chapter 5, but let's take a quick look specifically at how communication affects good execution.

Frequently a new process is simply thrown out into the ether and people are expected to follow it. There's no formal announcement (or, ironically, a process) to make its existence widely known. Often it's only tribal knowledge that gets the word out, with its attendant misinformation. How often have you been at a customer service counter and had the representative struggle with your transaction, when a co-worker comes over and says, "Oh, we don't do it that way anymore. Here's what you need to do."

One of the basic management job functions is to ensure—
really ensure—that every employee who uses a process understands
the process. However, there's often a lack of communication and the
appropriate information isn't incorporated into the employee's actions. What happens when employees don't know the process? They
either make it up or they come to you for answers, but you're too
busy to help them because people always bug you for answers they
should already know.

The XYZ Company set up a Microsoft SharePoint site to
house all of the processes that had been developed. Very ABC Com-
pany-like, to start with, anyway. Management assumed that people
would check the site proactively and regularly for any new processes
or to verify how current processes should work. Management failed
to understand that people were too busy doing their jobs and so
didn't proactively check anything. They just tried reactively to keep
their heads above water. Therefore, few followed the processes that
management put in place since Effective Communication of their
existence didn't take place.

Further, management posted many draft processes on the
same site. Although they labeled the processes as drafts, the few who
actually checked the site utilized them as gospel. Inevitably conflicts
occurred. The process authors feebly tried to rationalize that if the
processes appeared on the site, then they were official. Besides, they
further rationalized, all processes are subject to change, so labeling
them as drafts caused no harm. I wish I made this up, but I didn't.

If you, as a manager, want to make sure your direct reports
actually work a process as it's intended (and reduce your workload at
the same time), there are two actions you can take. 1) Make sure
you've reached out (i.e., directly communicated) to your people
about the new process and had at least one group discussion about
the hows and whys, with an opportunity for folks to ask questions. 2)
Soon after the process has been deemed "in effect," periodically
walk the floor and ask your team directly how well the process
works. Not just a perfunctory surface question, though, because the
answer you'll get is probably "Fine." Ask more detailed questions

about specific steps in the process, if they make sense, and how they really work. Don't rely on second or third hand information. This direct feedback will be invaluable as you make any tweaks to improve the process and to understand if people use it correctly and effectively.

Lack of Employee Buy-in (Execution)

Regardless of how well a process is constructed, if people don't believe it'll work or it has no applicability to them, they won't use it correctly or at all. This is frequently how processes are sabotaged. Remember that in the absence of direction to the contrary, people will formulate their own ways to do things that are most comfortable for them. Therefore, your mission as a manager is not only to lead the horse to water, but also to make the horse drink. The most effective way to do that is to explain what's in it for the employee. What are the benefits to the employee to do the job this particular way? How will they have their stress level reduced? How will they be able to do their job better and/or faster?

Of course, sometimes it just comes down to forcing the issue, if there's a particular reluctance to use the process. Will their evaluation be impacted by how well they implement the process? Make this tie-in and it often nudges people into compliance, which, after all, is one of your jobs as a manager. A true open door policy [Note: See Chapter 13 for more on what a true open door policy means.] with your team will help facilitate your understanding of whether they use the process and use it correctly. If they really struggle with it, what if it was okay for them to come to you for coaching or to provide feedback without feeling that doing so would be a career-impacting move?

The great side benefit from your perspective, though, is that with everyone in compliance, with buy-in, fewer interruptions and fewer questions will come your way about issues, which frees up your time so you're not so busy. Then you'll have more time to do your job. It's really in your self-interest to ensure the processes are effectively communicated and implemented. Self-interest can have negative connotations, but from my view, it's all to the good. My theory is that all inventions, from the wheel to the computer, were generated out of some person's selfish interest to improve their own personal circumstances. The guy who invented the wheel probably got tired of the effort needed to drag stuff across the ground all the time and thought that there must be an easier way.

Lack of Employee Understanding (Execution)

The biggest culprits in the lack of employee understanding are that the process is too complicated or there hasn't been sufficient training. Many managers fail to account for the fact that people learn in different ways and at different paces. What if you didn't assume that just because everyone's gone through training once that the information's actually learned? Repetition's a key component in any educational process. (You may have read that earlier. I try to practice what I preach.) While some won't need remedial training, others will. As a manager, you'll need to remain patient in the early stages of a process rollout as you'll likely explain things multiple times to some folks. To the degree possible, try to vary the way you present the explanation in order to hit on the one learning style that may resonate with whatever individual you coach.

Everyone has a mix of learning styles, but most have a preferred method. While there are a number of different learning style models, most generally they're described as auditory (people who learn best from listening), visual (they learn best by reading or being shown), and kinesthetic (they prefer to be hands-on). The better you know your team's individual styles, the better you'll be able to generate understanding. So, with the person who doesn't quite get it, mix up your coaching efforts with the three basic learning styles and you'll likely get the breakthrough you need.

Lack of Management Follow Through (Execution)

We've already talked about some management related reasons for process failure and here's another one. The biggest problem is the assumption that the process is implemented in the fashion that you anticipated. We talked just above (in the Failure to Communicate section) about how to walk the floor and ask some detailed questions about how the process works for individuals. This simple act sends the message to your folks that you're engaged in this new process and are there to support them. When they see your involvement, they'll know that you think it's important enough for you to follow through. That'll help with their buy-in

Many managers spend too much time in their office (because they're too busy). A conscious effort needs to be made to get up out of your chair and circulate. Be visible. It'll give people one additional path to talk with you, if they're not proactively coming to you through your open door.

As a manager, what if you were skeptical that any new process is well executed? Generally assumptions should be avoided, but if you assume things aren't going according to plan, then your questions will be more directed to uncover any problems. For example, if you ask a closed-ended question like "Does this process work well for you?" you'll likely get a "Yes," regardless of how things really are, particularly from people who don't want to rock the boat or are insecure. If you phrase an open-ended question in the negative at the outset, you'll more likely get some true feedback that can lead to process improvements. Try something like "What about this process doesn't work well for you?"

Lack of Measurable Tracking (Execution)

You can work all day long and execute a process forever, but how do you know your process is executed effectively? The answer, of course, is metrics—those numbers used to track progress towards goals. If people are held accountable to achieve clearly stated goals, they'll be more apt to achieve them. What gets measured gets improved is a truism. However, it's true only so long as the measurement is applicable to the desired outcome and is just one of a few, limited quantity of metrics.

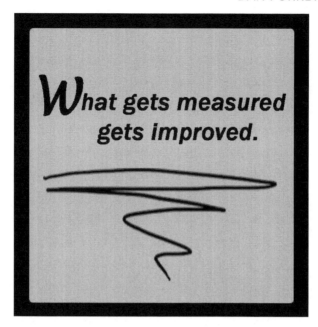

It's important to understand that the root cause reason things improve when they're measured isn't because they're measured. It's because management is actually paying attention to the issue and has prioritized the issue enough to assign a metric to it and create some focus around it.

Just the fact that there are metrics out there is enough to motivate many people to try to achieve them, given intrinsic competitiveness and pride. However, the real benefit of metrics is not seen in the Execution phase of goal achievement, but in the Verification phase. Let's get to that.

~~~~~~

Step 5: Verification

While Execution's in the main purview of the frontline, Verification's clearly in management's court. The problem is that many managers are too busy putting out fires to implement measurements to determine whether their people execute processes per the plan. Consequently, the frontline's left with little direction, implements what they individually think they should do, and customer satisfaction suffers. Now maybe the very fact that the managers are too busy putting out fires should tell them the process execution isn't going well, since the processes should be designed to minimize the fire drills, but that's beside the point (sort of).

A number (i.e., a metric) provides proof positive as to how well execution is done. If your goal is 100 and you only produce 50, you can't deny that something's wrong somewhere in the execution of your process, including that the process itself may be flawed.

You also have to consider that maybe the goal is set incorrectly. It may be unattainable regardless of how good the processes are. Sometimes managers get so wrapped up trying to reach a goal that they fail to recognize the goal is wrong and blindly push their people to achieve something that can't be obtained. Remember that goals, as necessary as they are, are simply made up numbers based on some manager's wish. To repeat for emphasis—goals are made up. It's important to remember that. You need to maintain some flexibility based on the situation at hand instead of continuing a slavish devotion to established goals.

On the other hand, keep in mind that the reasons a given goal isn't met fall into these Prioritized likelihoods:

1) improper execution
2) improper processes
3) incorrect goals

Managers are paid for and to use their experience. Most managers have good experience as to what their groups can actually do, so while a goal is made up, it usually isn't without some respectable managerial judgment. If a goal isn't met, first focus on execution to see whether current processes are carried out according to plan.

Metrics have gotten a bad reputation over the years, probably from those who underachieve (editorially speaking). "Oh, all you want is the end number. You don't care about the customer or the employee" is a common refrain. Another's that "You just want to use the number to justify firing me." Well, if the metric's set appropriately, then it'll automatically incorporate its desired effect on customers and employees. What if metrics were primary components in employee evaluations (e.g., this is what we pay you to do) and they were used to reward people when they demonstrate they can exceed expectations?

~~~~~

A Proper Metric (Verification)

So how do metrics contribute to you being or not being too busy to do your job? If they're well-considered metrics backed by good processes with good execution, they'll give you extra time, since things will run smoothly. If they're misapplied or pie-in-the-sky metrics, you'll spend an inordinate amount of your valuable time to continually answer questions and deal with problems associated with the bad metrics, including dealing with customer and employee complaints as a result of bad processes, execution, or metrics themselves.

For a metric to be considered useful and proper, it needs to be in alignment with these four Principles:

1. Directly applicable to the behavior desired and used to coach that behavior—a behavioral metric
2. Largely in control of the person measured
3. Administratively simple
4. Used to uncover and correct process or efficiency issues

Let's take a look at the rationale behind these four metric Principles.

1. Directly applicable to the behavior desired. Metrics need to have a defined purpose, other than just to exist or be there for show. They need to drive action and behaviors of both employees and departments.

Keep in mind the Prioritization discussion from earlier. If you have a million metrics, that doesn't mean that customers or employees will be happier or that work life will be easier. Before you construct a metric, make sure it's associated with something that you really want to accomplish (i.e., Prioritized) that'll be of the highest impact to improve customer or employee satisfaction. It should be an incentive for people to try to excel at that particular task. It should feed into people's natural competitive instincts and sense of pride to cause them to act (behave) in the way that you, as a manager, would like.

At the XYZ Company, metrics were a relatively new concept and some departments didn't have any. Chaos ruled the work environment, but no one really knew why. Everyone did their job without any real thought as to why the situation existed. Upper management finally came to understand that metrics would help reduce the chaos.

In order for the metrics to become a reality, however, they needed IT resources to compile the necessary data. Naturally, IT was also too busy to do their job and competition was fierce among departments that wanted reports developed. Finally, one department's VP negotiated some time for IT to devote to develop metrics for his department, ostensibly driven and backed by the president. Funny how a little executive involvement can make things happen that were stalled before. But I digress.

The VP decided that the metrics should be along the lines of the total number of installations, the total number of repairs, and the total number of incomplete jobs done per month. Pretty basic, you might think, but remember that the XYZ Company had no metrics at all before. Certainly from an executive manager standpoint, understanding the number of installations done per month is nice-to-know information, since it's indicative of the revenue that could be expected. However, the actual revenue's more directly what the executive needs to know. It's the revenue (more particularly, profit) that determines the executive's success as well as the success of the Board of Directors. So why deem the number of installations per month to be the number one Priority when a different measure (actual revenue per the accounting department) gave the executive what she really needed?

In the same vein, the number of incomplete jobs per month is purely a reactive number, a trailing metric that doesn't predict anything; it only describes what has happened in the past. It doesn't allow you as a manager to do anything different from what you did before because it doesn't give you any actionable information that you can effectively use tomorrow. So you had 1000 incomplete jobs in March and 1200 in April and 800 in May. So what? If you attempted a million jobs in each of those months, maybe it's reasonable to be satisfied with the number of incomplete jobs and nothing needs to change. However, if you attempted only 4000 installations each month, then it's reasonable to believe that level of performance leaves both customers and employees unsatisfied and something does need to change. The total incomplete job number only becomes significant when compared to the total number of jobs attempted (i.e., a percentage).

What if most metrics could be expressed in terms of percentages instead of total numbers? That allows you realistically to compare performance from month to month without the variability of volume differences. Percentages get you closer to understanding what behavior change is needed to improve things. In the above example, an average of 1000 incomplete jobs for every 4000 attempted jobs is a 25% incomplete job rate. That, combined with the level of customer complaints that consistently flowed into the customer service department, gave the XYZ Company actionable information. With this realization, the VP instructed IT to incorporate percentages into the reports.

However, even this percentage metric didn't relate to a specific behavior that could be changed. Sure, you could tell your installers not to leave until the job's complete, but if you don't understand why they can't complete the jobs, no management directive will help them.

But now the VP had some meat to work with and could drill down and ask penetrating questions about why the percentage of incomplete jobs stood so high. Remember earlier when we talked about the 200-page manual and the fact that installers have tight schedules to abide by and that if they get behind on one job, that delays all jobs after that? That domino effect is magnified when techs show up late for their very first job. If techs arrive at their first job on time, that gives all of the day's jobs a better chance of completion.

With some manual tracking, management discovered that techs only showed up to their first job on time about 75% of the time. If the behavior of the techs could be changed to show up on time for their first jobs, that would improve the percentage of incomplete jobs and result in more customer and employee satisfaction. The proper, corresponding behavioral metric that could be implemented established a goal of 95% on time to the first job. Now the techs had a clear expectation on which they could be measured and evaluated. Essentially, their behavior could be measured—a behavioral metric.

However, this being the XYZ Company, things didn't get executed according to the theory, regardless of the logic. While the department manager manually tracked the first-job-on-time percentage and moved the needle from 75% to around 92%, it took considerable time to construct the reports. With this added burden on a manager already too busy to do his job, ultimately the reports became sporadic. The first-job-on-time percentage dropped correspondingly. The VP, who still wanted IT to produce total volume metrics, never tried to automate this key behavioral metric to improve the customer and employee experience—"a Priority" that everyone had agreed on.

Meanwhile, the ABC Company, faced with virtually the same situation, automated behavioral metrics and demonstrated their success with improved profits. More jobs completed in less time produced more satisfied customers and fulfilled employees.

2.   Largely in control of the person measured. For this behavioral metric of first-job-on-time percentage, the beauty is that techs are in sole control of getting to the first job on time. There's no one else to point the finger at—no scapegoat—when a tech shows up late. Personal responsibility and pride take over in those situations and that drives improvement. In addition, accountability, a value desired in most companies, is clearly established.

While a minority of techs felt under the microscope (relative to what they were able to get away with before), it's fair that they should be. They're paid to be on time and the company should get its money's worth. It becomes an easy coaching session for managers when they have to call in a tech for not meeting the metric. Your conversation might go like this:

Manager: "Tech, you only get to 60% of your first jobs on time. Why is that?"

Tech: "Well, traffic's always a problem for me early in the morning and it often makes me late."

Manager: "I can relate to that. Traffic here is terrible. Our company standard is that you be on time to your first jobs 95% of the time. What do you think you could do to get to that level?"

Tech: "Well, I guess I could leave my house a little earlier than I have been."

Manager: "That sounds like a great idea. It's certainly something you can control. What if you started that program tomorrow and we'll see what happens to your percentage?"

Tech: "Okay, I'll give it a shot."

The more control over a metric that an individual has, the better chance you have as a manager to have that metric met or exceeded to drive the result you want (e.g., better customer satisfaction). The less control over a metric that an individual has, like with the total number of installations, the less chance you have as a manager to move the needle.

3. Administratively simple. As seen in the example above with manual tracking at the XYZ Company, if a metric becomes administratively burdensome, it will simply fade away. It's really a cost/benefit equation. A manager only has forty hours a week to work. (Humor me.) If ten of those hours are needed just to produce a reported metric, the manager becomes too busy to do their job and performance in other areas suffers. We find ourselves back to the Prioritization question. Is it more important to produce this single number or is it more important to have time to coach your people? Only you as the manager can make that call, but make the call based on a complete understanding of the tradeoffs.

Sometimes metrics are easily trackable via manual methods, but for the most part automated processes are best. You may need to call in favors from IT to develop them or maybe do some extra up front work to develop a spreadsheet that can be easily populated. If the behavioral metric you want is important enough, a high enough Priority, then you need to find a way to make it happen.

The Principle of Simplification (as described in Step 2 of this chapter) can also come in handy with some metrics you need to help you manage. Don't get hung up with analysis paralysis. You don't always need to have complete data in order to drive different behaviors or uncover root causes to problems.

I once asked a manager to track the number of escalations that came to her on a daily basis in order to quantify why she was too busy to do her job. She immediately believed she needed to construct a master Excel spreadsheet that included the reason for the escalation, the name of the person, the time of day, how long it took to resolve, etc. She worried about this now becoming a permanent part of her job. In short, she was too busy to take on this task.

I provided a simple solution: Simplify. First, we needed to reset the expectation. Before we got into the reasons for the escalations, we needed to understand the order of magnitude of the problem. In essence, we just needed to know how many escalations per day. That could be tracked with a pencil and paper with a stroke tally throughout the day when someone came to her with an issue. Second, we decided we really only needed a sample size, not a complete study that would continue until the end of the earth. We needed to determine if it was a real problem or just a perception of a problem. We agreed she could undertake this for a two-week period and then we'd see if we needed more data or if we could come to a reasonable conclusion based on the sample size we had.

It turned out that she, in fact, did have too many escalations. From there we took the next step—tracking the reasons for the requests. However, based on our previous Simplification to get only a sample, we agreed she could do that for the reasons, too. This step-by-step, Simplified approach got us the data we needed eventually to attack the major root causes for the escalations. Yes, it took a little longer, but through Prioritization and Simplification, we ultimately accomplished something that improved her ability to do her job (more time because of fewer escalations) and improved customer and employee (other departments) satisfaction.

Now, how about an example of the opposite of metrics Simplification (perhaps called *metricus maximus*)? At the XYZ Company, the owner created a master spreadsheet of 75 steps needed to process an order from the initial customer contact to the first bill delivery and assigned metrics to each step. Now, that's really not a bad exercise to understand how the business works, in that it could help get to the root cause of any particular issue. The master spreadsheet detailed (albeit in a really wide format with 75 columns) all upstream and downstream departmental relationships so you could see where gaps presented themselves.

However, the owner didn't create the tracking for an overview understanding of the business, but instead to manage the daily business using primarily just the metrics. He operated on the theory that he could eliminate many manager positions if the frontline personnel simply input their individual actions (like start time and stop time of the first customer contact) for each activity they did throughout the day. The spreadsheet would get populated with data, he could just sit in his office, easily call up the spreadsheet, and know the status on any given order for any given customer. He could then ask questions of the people who were out of compliance with the metric established for a given step. Nice theory, at least.

The theory crashed up against practicality pretty quickly, primarily because it violated the third law of a proper metric. It would be a stretch to call this 75-step process administratively simple. First, salespeople had to proactively log into the system to input their information about customer contacts and status. While it's a stereotype, it's also largely true that salespeople abhor paperwork.

They just want to sell, not take their time away from customers. They possess a natural resistance to the imposition of an additional administrative burden.

Second, no handoff occurred between departments to monitor an order's progress. Assuming that a salesperson would actually input the necessary data, no process existed to let the next department in line know that the salesperson had completed their portion. Therefore, delays formed in the progress of the order until the next department just happened to find out that they were next up to bat.

Third, no one defined when the data had to be input. Did they have to fill in their portions immediately after executing the step or could they do it maybe a few days later or maybe a couple of weeks later? After all, everyone was too busy to do their job to find the time to fulfill this new administrative burden.

The major problem developed, however, when the owner only checked the spreadsheet sporadically and, even then, not in detail. He was too busy to do the job that he created and, at least in his mind, had more important "owner stuff" to take care of. He didn't follow up to coach those who fell behind schedule. In short, he didn't verify that the required activity actually took place. He assumed because he had this wonderful system in place that it would be used and that people would use it out of fear that at any time the owner—the guy who writes the paychecks—could check up on them.

After everyone's initial flurry to comply with the owner's new system, the frontline soon began to understand that essentially no enforcement (i.e., no verification) existed. In short order, people began conveniently to forget to input their project status data or they put it in only occasionally to keep up appearances. The whole system collapsed. Customers became disenchanted as installations didn't happen in the time promised by the sales people. This led to an increased sales cycle (the exact opposite of the intention).

With a Simplification of the 75-step process down to about 15 steps and the insertion of departmental managers to monitor the 15 steps, the sales cycle shortened from 50 days to about 30. Sales people had always promised customers an installation in about 30 days even when that time frame couldn't realistically be met, so now the salespeople and operations aligned. The result? Not only happy customers who saw promises fulfilled, but increased cash flow as dollars flowed in faster than before, since bills arrived at the customers earlier. All due to Simplification—a powerful ally in the search to find time to do your job.

4.   Used to uncover and correct process or efficiency issues. This is the main reason for metrics. Metrics shouldn't be just idle information that's nice to know. You need to actively do something operationally with a metric or get rid of it. Metrics aren't really there to punish people for failure or even reward them for success. Certainly they can be used for those things, but the purpose is more to find out what doesn't work to expectations. Metrics provide a lever to activate the Bat Signal, bring managers into the fray, find out what's wrong, and fix it. Metrics are the fire alarm switches in buildings. Pull in case of an emergency and help will come.

The real power in metrics is for managers to see what doesn't work so they can begin to fix it. They allow managers to Prioritize their work to focus on the truly important, since, by definition, a proper metric wouldn't exist unless managers wanted a particular important behavior executed. Certainly sometimes the problem comes down to an individual, but then you can ask questions like "Does the employee have enough training or the right training?" or "Is the employee motivated and why?" or "Does the employee understand what their job is?"

Most often, though, the problems are departmental in nature. If a goal isn't met departmentally, mathematically some individuals may be over the goal, but most individuals won't be. If a high percentage of people have problems achieving the goal, the problem likely is an organizational process issue, not an individual problem.

A properly constructed and tracked metric simply allows the manager to ask intelligent, insightful questions based on facts. It's a wakeup call to take action.

In the course of your verification of process compliance, once you've found a problem, you've usually got to dig deep to find the root cause. For example, if the missed metric is the average time taken to complete an installation, don't be satisfied with a surface answer, like "Well, the techs missed the goal because they work too slowly." That response initially focuses you on developing a change with the techs to make them faster. You might assume they need more training, so you implement a big program to get them trained up when lack of training isn't the root cause.

Instead, ask *why* they're too slow and you'll get a different answer that'll lead you down a different path. "Well, they take too long on their jobs because their information (like address, phone number, appointment time, equipment needed, etc.) is inaccurate." That should lead you to ask why the information's inaccurate. Now the focus should get redirected off the techs and on to the department that provides them the information. But don't stop there. Ask why that department provides inaccurate information. The answer might be that the department relies on yet another upstream department for the information. Now your focus for a solution may shift yet again.

The process is commonly called the Five Whys and is a key to discover root causes. You almost have to be like a bothersome little kid who asks "Why?" over and over and over. Whenever someone gives you an answer to a question, follow that with "Thanks, but why is that?" Continue that process five times in a row and you'll likely end up at the root cause of the problem, or at least pretty close to it. It takes some perseverance because you may have to go to several people along the way to get your answers, as one person likely won't know it all. If they did, the problem probably wouldn't exist in the first place. As Thomas Edison said when asked why he had a team of twenty-one assistants, "If I could solve all the problems myself, I would."

So, when you get an "I don't know" response to a "Why," a great follow up question is "Well, who do you think might know the answer?" Channel Sherlock Holmes in your quest to discover the root cause and you'll be well on your way.

Metrics often have a bad frontline reputation not because they're innately evil, but because managers have misused them. Metrics are great when it comes to evaluation time, since they're a black or white assessment of performance versus expectations. However, many managers don't look at the metrics at any time other than the annual evaluation and miss great coaching opportunities throughout the year. Ironically, if metrics were used to help coach up the poor performers throughout the year, managers wouldn't have to deal with all of the problems created by the poor performers, thus freeing up more time for the managers to do their jobs.

Metrics are also great reward tools. For an organization that performs, they can instill a sense of pride in the workforce, as accomplishments of goals are there for all to see. They can inspire people to work even harder in the mission to blow away the goal. Want to see the phrase "what gets measured gets improved" in action? Pick an important behavior that you want to see everyone in your group do. Attach a metric goal to it (that contains all of the four points of a proper metric) and promise a reward, say a lunchtime barbeque paid for by you personally, if they achieve the goal inside of a certain, limited period. Publish the results publicly and daily. Drop not-so-subtle hints about the barbeque during the defined period. Get people focused on achieving the goal with Effective Communication.

My advice is not to do this too often, as you'll find your wallet empty from all of the barbeques you'll pay for. You can get creative in your rewards so they don't necessarily require a heavy monetary investment. Maybe the reward is the boss shaves his/her head. Maybe three people get chosen to throw cream pies in the boss's face. Potlucks are good team builders. Whatever reward you choose, make sure that the people in your group believe that it's a worthwhile reward commensurate with the value of the goal or there won't be the appropriate motivation to succeed.

~~~~~

Choose Metrics Carefully (Verification)

Choose your metrics carefully and judiciously. They're a powerful force for good and shouldn't be overused. Make sure whatever issue you want to fix is important enough to warrant the creation of a behavioral metric. At the ABC Company, they're infused with the concept of metrics. While certainly not perfect, they run so smoothly and efficiently that, although everyone's busy, they're not so busy as to lose sight of the concept of continuous improvement. Their major metrics are well under control for the Prioritized, high-impact goals they've set, so they have the time to work on the second tier Priorities. Those are Priorities that are on the list to get to someday, that would be nice to do, but which most businesses never actually seem to find the time to work on.

EXAMPLE: A manager at the ABC Company noticed in his group, indeed in the whole company, that written documents—from emails to formal process documents—had frequent incorrect grammar usage. Whether filled with misspellings, punctuation, or verb tense, the image projected to employees, customers, and investors was less than professional.

A professional image is important to a company for many reasons, but ultimately to increase profitability. Grammar's like personal hygiene. You can ignore them both, but don't be surprised at the judgments people form as a result.

This manager decided to tackle improvement of the company's professional image. Since everyone at the ABC Company firmly believed in the concept of continuous improvement, they felt almost obligated to improve their grammar to be in alignment with that Principle.

As an aside and to contrast this situation, managers at the XYZ Company took the stance to ignore grammar and professional image, since they, in their minds, had bigger fish to fry. "Besides," one manager said, "this isn't high school where we teach grammar." My response? "You're right, it's not high school. But to the extent that people didn't learn this in high school and professional image is important and in alignment with continuous improvement, maybe we should step up to the plate and solve the problem." Disturbingly, this manager couldn't make the connection between the larger issue of professional image and profitability.

It's the ability to understand the difference between knowing *your* [fill in the blank] and knowing *you're* [fill in the blank].

Back to the ABC Company manager. He decided to take on the task of improving grammar. But where to begin? To drive the desired behavior of no grammatical mistakes, what metric do you use? As discussed earlier in this chapter, ***the involvement (i.e., buy-in) of the people who will be measured by the metric is an important aspect in the development of metrics.*** After he reviewed a recently submitted report filled with errors and discussed the basic challenge with the team, the manager decided to send a memo to his team. Here's an excerpt from it:

"The definition of a given metric is key to drive the desired outcome (behavioral metrics). We need to figure out what the right metric is for us to improve our grammar. I found 26 grammatical mistakes in the report, again mostly commas and apostrophes, but also verb tenses and some misapplied words. According to Word, there are 22,908 characters in the document, so there's an accuracy rate of 99.89%, based on character accuracy as our metric. That seems pretty good on the surface, although ironically short of the Six Sigma goal dream. (Six Sigma is 3.4 defects per million instances, or 99.9997% accuracy.) There are 4096 words in the document, so we have an accuracy of 99.37% based on words. Still pretty good. There are 546 lines, for an accuracy per line rate of 96.5%. Falling a bit. There are 192 paragraphs, for a paragraph accuracy of 86.5%. Seems a low accuracy achievement. There are 18 pages, for a page accuracy average of -144% (meaning there's more than one error per page). Okay, lots of metrics, but which metric is most in alignment with the Principle to improve the customer experience (one of our three main goals)? For that, we need to ask the customers. Once we do that, we can pick the right metric and then determine if we satisfy them. Beauty's in the eye of the beholder."

Now you might think that this manager should attend a twelve-step program through Metrics Anonymous, but the point is that the whole department already had bought in to the concept of metrics. At the XYZ Company, this memo would have been received like a three-headed, fire-breathing dragon crashing through the door. People at the ABC Company took the memo in the somewhat light-hearted vein intended, but also with the more serious, underlying understanding that, "Yes, we do have a problem and we need to turn our professional attention to it."

The ABC team decided that tracking any grammar metric on a consistent basis was not administratively simple. No one had budget for a proofreader to be added to the headcount. They decided to compile a Simplified list of ten common grammar mistakes (and correct usage) and place visible, offbeat posters around the office to remind people to pay attention to the issue. They made brief mention of the initiative in team meetings, but managers basically left it up to individuals to use their own initiative to improve their writing.

However, managers also understood the concept of verification. If the issue was important enough to create some posters and take meeting time (however limited) to drive improvement, then it was also important enough to actually make and verify improvements. They selected a manager to infrequently and randomly choose documents (again, from emails to official reports) and proofread and grade them. He then provided feedback on those random audits. This more informal approach still used the concept of metrics, but minimized the time involved in the interests of administrative simplicity.

In addition, the team instituted their own quasi-audit. They agreed that they could point out an error to a colleague without fear of being perceived as having "pointed the finger" or placing blame for blame's sake. While they didn't establish a "quarter jar" for each error found, it did become like a game to them. In effect, with the focus on the business issue of correct grammar instead of blame, they helped each other improve over time and did it in the spirit of help, not blame. A great example of teamwork.

~~~~~

Finger-Pointing Versus Raising Business Issues (Verification)

A quick word here about finger-pointing versus business issues. The cry of "finger-pointing" is usually an emotional, defensive reaction from the person at whom the finger is pointed when accountability comes home to roost. Frequently the root cause person or department gets offended and tries to deflect accountability. Then you end up with a whole different set of problems to deal with and lose sight of the original issue that needs to be fixed. Often the result is that the person at the center of the problem gets away with whatever behavior originally caused the problem and nothing's fixed.

In contrast, business issues are expressed in terms of how the company or department is affected by particular actions, generally associated with customer satisfaction.

Let's go back to one of those key Principles—continuous improvement. Are you more interested in continuous improvement or not being held accountable for mistakes? What's your True Priority? In a culture that stays in Alignment with Principles, the answer's clear. What if it were no big deal in this culture to say, "My fault, let's figure out how to not have it happen again and move on?" The person shouldn't be raked over the coals for a mistake. Fix it and move on is the right attitude.

The problem is that finger-pointing has likely been long accepted by management, which uses a witch hunt philosophy more intent on finding out whom to blame rather than fix the problem. A culture of fear gets ingrained in people. They worry more that they'll lose their jobs if they make a mistake rather than make the effort to fix the mistake, learn from it, and move on. In this culture of fear, people won't raise their hands when they see a business issue. All this leads to inefficient or ineffective processes that stay in place longer than they would in a well-run business.

Accountability's critical to a business's success. True accountability, in which names of responsible people are named (whether for good or bad actions), is a part of any well-managed business. Identification of a root cause is not finger-pointing; it's integral to fixing a business issue.

When the culture is one of fear that the slightest mistake results in being humiliated or worse, fired, no one wants to be accountable. The culture adopts a finger-pointing attitude as the norm. As the leader, change that attitude from one of fearful finger-pointing to one of raising hidden (either deliberately or innocently) business issues to drive improvement. It's the lessons learned that are the important things, not who screwed up. If a person continually screws up, then that's another coaching challenge, but make it safe for people to raise business issues without the perception that they're a fink. (Note: Sorry, just had to use that word. When was the last time you saw "fink" in a book published since 1950?)

The attitude demonstrated by all employees is the main thing. What if everyone led by example? Departmental and company attitude starts at the top, so as a leader, get past the finger being pointed at you. Don't take it personally; don't make it personal. Either you did it or you didn't. Own it. If you need to clarify in the interests of Effective Communication, that's perfectly acceptable, but time is wasted to find excuses. Time's not wasted to find reasons. Get to the business issue; fix the business issue; move on.

~~~~~~

Follow Up (Verification)

A final thought about Verification. While metrics are the best verification, there's also the non-numerical part of verification that often gets overlooked by managers—engagement and follow up in the process by the manager and particularly the executive. Do you know the most dreaded words in business? "Hi, I'm from corporate and I'm here to help."

Dilbert By Scott Adams

Too often a manager steps into a process, gets it all set up, generates some dust to kick off the process, and then walks away, assuming that since he'd made his directives clear, there would be absolute compliance. Wrong. Six months later he shows up and wonders why things didn't work. Hand the man a mirror so he can look at himself. The processes didn't work because he lacked engagement in the very processes he set up.

He demonstrated a failure of leadership, clear because if no one follows, whom do you lead? The owner with the 75-step plan is only one example of how an absence of upper management's active engagement in Prioritized actions leads to the downfall of objectives. Don't be one of those disengaged managers who are opposed to staying involved with the problems of the frontline. As I've said, if it's important enough to measure, then it's important enough to follow up on. It takes dedication on the part of the leader with a constant and unrelenting engagement in the process until it's fixed. Don't get carried away and think that it will take one hundred percent of the time of the leader. It won't. But keeping a hand in the action is critical. Even the simple act to ask (verify) people how the new process works for them says volumes and motivates people by having them know that we're all in this together.

CHAPTER 8—PARTS
How to Work the Components of Business

Practical Action #11
Allocate your corporate energy in direct proportion to the Priority level of the component.

L et's circle back to the model discussed earlier in Chapter 6 that Profit feeds Management, Management feeds Employees, Employees feed Customers, and Customers feed Profit. Let's Simplify it. (Hmmm . . . that sounds familiar.) Really, it boils down to four components: Management, Employees, Customers, and Profit. Some models would add the components of Community and Product/Service, but Community's really composed of Customers and Product/Service is really a component of Employees—the thing that customers rely on. For our purposes, let's stick to the four we've already discussed.

Is each of the four components equal in importance? If you paid attention, clearly they aren't. Everything rests on management. So why don't organizations spend more time to improve their managers? Many managers, if not the majority, are promoted up through the ranks. The theory, for example, is that if you're a good sales person, you must make a great sales manager; if you're a good technician, you must make a great manager of technicians. As discredited as that theory is, it's still in common practice.

The reality is that people at all levels need continuous training to get better at what they do. Management practices and techniques aren't learned in the womb or by osmosis. They have to be taught, including through the school of hard knocks. For many businesses, the only management training is via that school and it's the most inefficient way to learn. In that hard knocks school, learning can only take place as random situations pop up and they're dealt with, either successfully or not. There's no structure to the learning, so some topics may get skipped over and never covered at all. As an overall approach, trial and error isn't a good methodology to train managers.

Let's see how this philosophy impacts businesses.

Say you believe that each of the four components above is equal in importance. Say you just can't possibly Prioritize them one over the other, despite what you've learned from Chapter 2. There are operational implications that depend on your belief. If all were equal, then from the Prioritization theory in Chapter 2, it would imply that you should spend 25% of your organizational time on each of the four. The fallacy in this is easily seen by supposing you spent 25% of your organizational energy on profit. You'd need an army of accountants to run your business and accountants would play a huge role in your business decisions. Sorry to disappoint you accountants out there, but I don't want accountants to run my business. I want accountants to help me and provide information to me, but I don't want to devote my limited energies to manage finances. Let the other 75% represented by the other three components drive the decisions and the profit will take care of itself, so I can spend more time on the other three.

If we Prioritized the four business components in order, based on the amount of impact they have to create a smoothly functioning business, they'd be listed as management, employees, customers, and profit. If the four components of business aren't equal, then the amount of time you spend on each should also be unequal. For example, just to throw out numbers, you should spend 35% of your time on management, 30% on employees, 20% on customers, and 15% on profit (finances).

Circling back to Chapter 2 and flexibility in Prioritization, the beauty of the unequal approach is that you can more quickly fix the biggest problem (management) because you focus the most energy on it. Once that biggest problem's fixed, you've freed up 35% of your time to devote to the next biggest issue—employees. Now moving all 35% to the next item is impractical, since maintenance still needs to be done, but maybe you could move 25% or 20% from management to employees. Once you've fixed a problem, it's logical that it won't take as much time as it used to. No component should be entirely ignored, but energy and resources are limited commodities and you need to know how to focus them for maximum effect by understanding where the biggest lever is to drive profit.

In a business that's struggling, many focus on the finances and spend the bulk of their energy to study the numbers. After all, if there's no profit, then the business can't survive. Their energy gets directed to those two tricks of cutting expenses and/or increasing revenue. They erroneously concentrate on finances *per se*, not what *drives* the finances. Management of Profit and Loss (P&L) statements is a concentration on finances. However, if P&Ls are used properly, they can be thought of as metrics. If you remember the four characteristics of metrics, the fourth and primary one is to use the metrics to uncover problems and start to ask questions.

Often, though, P&Ls are used in a cursory fashion. For example, if labor's over budget, why then, let's just cut headcount. If overtime's over budget, why then, let's just mandate no more overtime, regardless of the root causes for the overtime or customer impacts from the cuts. Financial problems are not resolved with financial solutions; they're solved by operations solutions that make the business run more smoothly and efficiently.

Certainly P&L management is important, but frequently management gets distracted by items on the P&L of less importance. If a P&L line item's over budget by 200%, but the line item accounts for only 1% of total expenses, an effective leader will ignore that line. Instead, an effective leader will focus the team on those P&L line items that are, as an example, over budget by 20%, but that account for 15% of the total expenses. A cutback on pencils and paper has never led a business to profitability, yet I've been in executive meetings where we spent valuable time to discuss how to reduce the number of pens we purchased. Seriously.

What if leaders focused on what feeds the finances, not necessarily the finances themselves? It's a basic root cause situation—a theme that you've already seen and one that'll be repeated throughout this book. The focus on root causes instead of the extraneous stuff that masks the real problems is the difference between a true leader and one who only has the title. When met with a problem that appears as a financial force, typical management says to meet that financial force with a greater financial force; attack the problem head-on; two titans locked in a great wrestling match.

My philosophy, analogous to the practice of tai chi, says to take the force of the problem and redirect it back on itself in a different way. In essence, address a finance problem with a customer solution. A leader truly understands that without customers, there's no business. Leadership actions in harmony with that simple truth are a strength of the best leaders. Finances don't feed finances; customers feed finances. Therefore, effective leaders will direct their energies to meet customers' needs, primarily via employees.

~~~~~~

Leaders' Actions

That being said, how do customers' needs get met? Employees meet those customers' needs, not finances. Prioritizing employees over finances doesn't mean to pay exorbitant wages or coddle every whim of the employees. It does mean that employees need to be developed to understand the customers' needs and how to meet them. It means that departments must be developed to work cooperatively for the common good, with a minimization of turf issues. It means employees must have the job knowledge and management support to be able to meet those customer needs most efficiently. The overall organization must effectively work together, as a unit, towards this goal. An effective leader will continually communicate with a variety of methods, with all departments and employees about where things work well, where they don't, and what the customer benefits are from an efficiently operating organization.

The main goal of an effective leader is to get the entire organization to understand the benefits of meeting customers' needs, get the individual employees to understand their respective roles to make (or not make) that happen, and then put processes in place to make the entire organization effectively serve customers. It does no good to have a great product (meeting a customer need) if you don't have the delivery system in place (the employees/organization) to get the product to the customer in such a way that pleases the customer. An effective leader Prioritizes the creation of the foundation for a strong organization first. That provides the best mechanism to serve customers, who will in turn reward that organization with product purchases and, ultimately, profits.

~~~~~

The Operations Hierarchy

Maslow's Hierarchy of Needs, proposed as a psychological hypothesis by Abraham Maslow in the mid-twentieth century, is a model that says, for the human condition, if certain basic needs are not met first, then a given person cannot advance emotionally or intellectually to higher levels of function. For example, if you don't have basic physiological components like air, food, and water, you won't be worried about the next level of the human condition up from that, which is safety (concern for health, employment, security, etc.). If you don't have a level of safety, then you won't be worried about love/belonging aspects like friendship and family. Ultimately, this hierarchy reaches its peak at self-actualization that deals with morality, creativity, and acceptance of facts.

Similarly, there's a Purkey Hierarchy of Business Operations that shows you how to Prioritize your limited time when you want to move an organization forward. It's really a road map of how to build a successful business from scratch. An effective leader understands that a focus on management and employees pays the greatest dividends to maximize profit. That leader puts the energies of the organization to work in proportion to these levels in Priority order, realizing that if the base level doesn't run effectively or efficiently, then all other levels above it suffer. Here's that model.

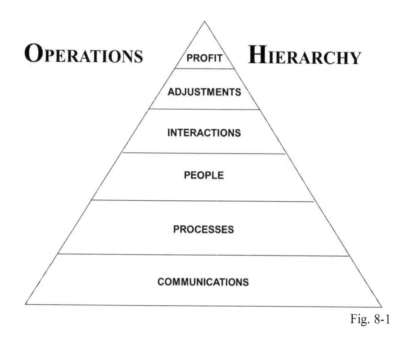

Fig. 8-1

This hierarchy is really nothing more than a root cause analysis that shows how each level is dependent on the previous one. If you understand this broad concept of dependencies, then it's easier to figure out where inputs of one department are the outputs of another department—the upstream/downstream relationships. This in turn leads you to the knowledge of what the True Priorities are to put fixes into place.

This exercise of understanding relationships among departments or among levels in a model isn't done enough in business. Without it, the Priorities become what you feel in your gut (or whatever crisis crosses your desk) versus determined through any sort of logical analysis. You may see hundreds of unused pencils on people's desks and it might really bother you at a gut level, but the real question is: Do you try to save money on pencils or do you look for the expenses with the biggest impact on the bottom line? When you put things in terms of hierarchies or process flows, that can be a big factor ultimately to make the business run better.

As a leader, you need to know the key lever points in order to move all employees to success. Let's look at the various levels of Purkey's Hierarchy of Business Operations one by one in more detail and see how and why they are what they are. This'll help guide you to more improvements more quickly. It's really another Prioritization exercise, which by now you should understand is a key to your success and to gain the time you need to do your job.

1. Effective Communication

Note that this title is not just "communication" but "Effective Communication." Too often people delude themselves into thinking that because one person talks and one person listens that Effective Communication takes place. We explored this in more detail in Chapter 5, but for now just know that the issue's not whether communication takes place, but whether that communication takes place in such a fashion that both (or all) parties have the same internal understanding of what's said. You can talk all day long, and many do, but if the parties on the receiving end of the talk don't understand it in the same way that you intended it, you don't have Effective Communication.

It's hard to argue that Effective Communication is not THE most important factor to create a successful business. Here's the fundamental truth of the matter: without ideas exchanged from one person or one department to another (i.e., Effective Communication), nothing can happen. It's one hand clapping. Effective Communication to a business is like breathing to a person. You can survive a while without the critical component, but ultimately without it, you'll die.

With business, however, it takes much longer for death to arrive. That's because a business is made up of multiple people, sometimes hundreds of thousands of multiple people, so there's endless communication that takes place at all times. Even without overall Effective Communication, businesses can take a long time to die because they get lucky enough times in the course of a million conversations that some degree of actual knowledge is passed on. Like a drunk negotiating a long hallway, the business will bounce from side to side off the hallway walls, stumbling and tripping along in ignorant bliss as it makes its way to the destination at the end of the hall. The business may get there or not, but it won't be a pretty sight along the way. What separates a quality company from an also-ran company is that a much higher percentage of those daily human interactions are truly effective. Thoughts are conveyed accurately from one person to another, so those thoughts can be executed according to plan.

If you can't effectively communicate then it's not possible to design effective processes, since the concept of a process will remain stuck inside one person, unable to be fully expressed to others. That person may talk to others, but if the talk's in Swahili and the listening's in English, the process will never see the light of day. Talk and Effective Communication are wildly different and a good manager knows the difference. Grasp that concept and you'll be miles ahead of others. Actively work to bridge the gap between the two and you'll be in an elite category of management.

Everything depends on the ability of an organization to Communicate Effectively.

2. Processes

Once you're able to incorporate Effective Communication routinely, you'll have the ability to coach and pass knowledge along to others. One of the first things you'll want to do is organize people such that they do things in an efficient manner that'll produce the results you want. Processes allow that organization. They're the tools that employees use, like training, procedures, manuals, strategies, tactics, desks, chairs, etc. They're the visible indications of a dynamic business—the operations.

At this point or level in the hierarchy, it doesn't make any difference who the people are. The processes are the framework within which people work. People can come and go (and they do), but if the processes in place are tested, sound, and effective, then the processes will stay in place regardless of the personnel involved. People can always be trained to run the processes as designed.

3. People

Great. Now you've got an ability to communicate effectively and a framework of processes that'll allow you to produce what customers desire. The house is built. Now you need to move in. That means hiring people. This is the most complicated portion of the hierarchy and can require the most attention. Other people are one of the main reasons why you're too busy to do your job.

The reason is that people are human. They come in all varieties of capabilities and motivations. One person may see a process as infinitely complex and incomprehensible while another may think the same process is right on target and easy to implement. As a manager, you need to find the right people who have the necessary capabilities and motivations to execute the processes efficiently.

The first step in that is for you to know intimately the processes, procedures, position functions, and the results you want to achieve relative to your line of direct reports (and maybe even the next level down). Easy to say, hard to execute. The second step is to be able to Effectively Communicate those necessary attributes to the candidates and set clear expectations up front. The third step is to find those people whose work ethics are in alignment with your needs and to make sure those people will do what they say they'll do (i.e., accountability).

Leadership is about creating the page and then making sure that everyone's on that same page.

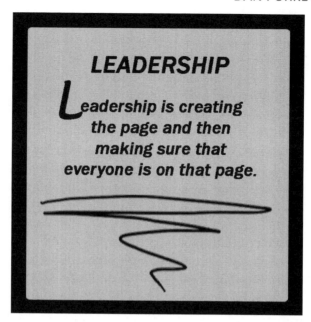

LEADERSHIP

Leadership is creating the page and then making sure that everyone is on that page.

Effective Communication and processes are the more mechanical aspects of the page. In theory, they can be created out of whole cloth by a single person with a vision. The more difficult, esoteric aspect of the endeavor is to get the people in alignment with that plan, because people are variables that can't be controlled, only managed. Think herding cats.

4. Interactions

So, we've added people to the equation. Now the going gets tough. We have a community, a larger collection of individuals in which, since people are people, they necessarily interact with one another. This is where a foundation of Effective Communication can make or break an organization.

While it may seem patently obvious, it bears repeating that people are different. Few really, truly, internally, intimately understand that people are different, since few take the time to take that concept and put it into action. There's a lot more energy put into lip service than deeds. If people are different, what if you *treated* them differently? A characteristic of Effective Communication (dealt with in more detail in Chapter 5) is to find what method works to help the person you're talking to understand the thoughts you have in the same way that you intend them. In short, how do you get to a meeting of the minds?

Each person has their own comfort zones and own preferences for how they learn, whether they know it or not. If one person's quiet, then talk to them in calm tones. If another likes to debate, then maybe the way to get through to them with your concept is to lay out extremely logical arguments and be prepared to defend them. If another's an emotional type, then the best way to get you both on the same page is to talk in terms of feelings instead of logic.

Where it all breaks down is when the individuals in the organization don't understand the impacts they have on others. They treat everyone all the same and, in fact, generally treat others in the same fashion that they want to be treated. (Remember the interaction between Miro and Ender from the book *Ender's Game* in Chapter 5.) That sounds good on the surface, but there are problems with that approach. This is a prime reason why Effective Communication is so elusive. With the infinite varieties of personalities, degrees of sensitivity to being offended, different agendas, and other dissimilarities among people, it's a wonder that anything gets done at work or in life.

Your ability to manage yourself and others through all of the various interactions that occur throughout the day will determine whether you're able get less busy. Predictably, Effective Communication and Simplification are the keys to success.

First, how can you Simplify the infinite possibilities? It's a question that you should ask yourself when faced with virtually any problem that confronts you, but it's particularly helpful when you try to get people interactions smoothed out. To Simplify, set some communication ground rules—some Principles that everyone can refer to when (or before) the interactions start to turn ugly and nonproductive. The first ground rule is to talk in terms of business issues, not personalities.

Practical Action #12
When dealing with problems, talk in terms of business issues, not personalities.

In a culture where everyone plays by the same rules, this Practical Action takes blame out of the equation. People aren't personally threatened. You're not out to get Alice because she's a royal screw-up, you're out to fix the business issue of an unacceptable level of errors seen in work results. (Note that this fits in with metrics, so you have something to refer back to and support the discussion.)

While the cultural norm to talk in terms of business issues is an ideal, you can control this at least on a personal level by walking the talk. Establish yourself as one who deals in business issues, not blame. Make your actions and words congruent. Create a reputation for yourself based on how you deal with situations. People will come to admire your stance and begin to emulate it when they see that it works. Thus spreads the culture.

If you manage a group of people, explicitly set (yes, dictate—to control what you can control) the ground rule that this group will deal with problems in terms of the effect that actions have on the business. Require the group to perform in that fashion and hold the individuals accountable to act in that fashion, either by you or by their peers. Sometimes Effective Communication takes the form of dictating in environments where you have that ability, but don't overuse the power. Absolute power corrupts absolutely, according to Lord Acton—like Roman emperors who declared themselves gods.

Instead of accusing another manager of being turf proprietary (and hurting her feelings in the process, which then may become the issue you need to fix and that distracts you from the initial concern), talk to that manager about how her team's performance affects the ability of your team to perform well and how that affects the customer experience. Discuss the bigger picture and help them understand their impact on that bigger picture. It's a non-threatening way to explain the business issues, which everyone should want to solve. (Notice the assumption in there?)

5. Adjustments

Just because you got the interactions to run smoothly, that doesn't mean that things will run perfectly or even to plan. Again, if the proper metrics have been put in place, they'll tell you how things really work. A vital part of any manager's responsibilities is to keep the organization in alignment with established strategies and tactics. You've got to be able to effectively assess your group's performance relative to the Priorities you've established, but not get so locked into a previously defined way of doing things that you keep going down the same unproductive path if things don't work according to plan.

Flexibility's an inherent attribute of a great manager. Make whatever adjustments are necessary to get the group's performance to drive customer satisfaction. Adjustments are really a representation of an attitude of continuous improvement.

In football, coaches often say, "Keep running that play until you get it right." What that really means is that while the overall play may be sound, if you don't tweak the various components in the execution of the play, then you'll never get it right. You may need to adjust how the blocking assignments are done or adjust the snap count or modify any number of the hundreds of components that go into a play. This approach is not only desirable, it's necessary. It's why coaches (i.e., managers) get paid. Adjustments are *not* a sign of weakness or a cause to put a label of failure on something; they *are* a sign of strength, an indication that the managers have an ability to recognize changing situations and act accordingly in alignment with providing better customer satisfaction.

Here's a little test to see what your predilection is towards flexibility and making adjustments. This certainly isn't a be-all, end-all sort of test, but one that is designed just to point out how it's usually possible to see things from different perspectives if you try. That's a characteristic necessary for flexibility.

Look at Figure 8-2. Most people see a cube—a solid block like a brick. The center point of the figure (the star) appears to be on the exterior.

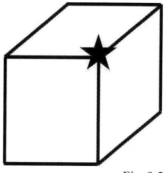

Fig. 8-2

However, if you look at the star and adjust your mind, you can see a different object. Instead of thinking about the star as in the foreground corner projecting out, imagine it as in the background distance, as if you were looking into a box at the far corner. Now your vision is one of the inside of a box instead of the outside of a box.

If you can recognize when you're locked into one way of doing things, then you can be flexible. When you want to make a change, remember the box exercise to help you realize that it is possible with the right approach.

6. Profit

At the top of the pyramid is profit. Let's not delude ourselves that a business exists for anything else other than to produce profit. Everything else, customer satisfaction included, is only a side effect of the drive to produce profit. The relevant question is how does that profit get most effectively produced. Profit relies on all of the other levels below it, which collectively provide the foundation for success. If your business is not profitable, start to assess honestly how well you and the business pay attention to the foundational layers of this Hierarchy of Business Operations model.

~~~~~~

A Focus on the Employees

You'll notice in the Hierarchy of Business Operations that every level except Profit has a direct relationship to employees. Let's set aside management as a group for now and take a closer look at the consequences of having the focus on employees at the top of your attention list. This doesn't mean disregard other components. It just means that at the end of the day, the largest amount of your time should have been spent on employees—whether it's to improve or design processes to gain more efficiencies, train, coach, bolster workplace environment, increase safety, deal with personnel issues, create more and better tools, hold communication meetings, conduct evaluations, define metrics, or whatever other tasks would make employees' work lives easier, smoother, and more efficient. Before you go home at the end of the day, what if you could say that you made an employee or group of employees better off than they were before the day started?

Don't interpret that focus to mean that you cave-in to every employee desire. We talked about pendulum management—the wild swings from one extreme mandate to another—in Chapter 5, but essentially you need to make sure you don't go overboard to satisfy every little thing every little employee comes up with that might satisfy their current whim. Ultimately, employees get paid to do what management asks, no matter how you might want to spin it politically. Sometimes you have to ask things of employees that they don't necessarily like, but that in the bigger picture provide improved customer satisfaction.

Your mission as a manager is to make sure that your employees have all of the necessary tools (both literally and figuratively) to generate that improved level of customer satisfaction and to make sure that they use those tools in the most efficient manner possible. Develop your employees always with an eye towards the impacts on customer satisfaction. Develop departments to work cooperatively. The more the overall organization works together—as a unit—the better off you'll be. Your ability to incorporate these Principles into a work atmosphere that's a positive one for your teams is what separates success from failure. If you never lose sight of customer satisfaction and act in alignment with that, it's hard to go too wrong.

Another way to look at this employee focus is that you can't control your customers, you can only influence them. If we could command customers to come in and buy our products, we wouldn't need marketing and we'd all be madly profitable. Spend your efforts to control what you can control.

In theory, you can control your employees. They work for you, after all. The practical reality of the level of actual control may be a point for discussion, but work with me on this one. It's at least fair to say you have more control over your employees than you do your customers. If that's the case, then logically the largest portion of your limited time should be spent on employees. Why spend time on something you can't control, since whatever that something is will simply do what it wants, anyway? You shouldn't try to teach a pig how to sing. Pigs can't sing and you just annoy the pig.

~~~~~~

Here's a special note for you readers who are C-level managers (e.g., CEO, COO, CIO, CFO, etc.) or those managers who are a few levels removed from frontline employees. This focus on employees we're talking about isn't just meant to focus on frontline employees. For anyone who has direct reports, your main focus should be your direct reports, but you also have to consider your influence on employee levels below you.

Often at this level, an assumption's made that your direct reports already have their act together, so they don't need assistance. That would be a bad assumption. They may need less assistance than the average person, but keep in mind that the blame for the ills of the organization is management (see Chapter 1). What if you were always a coach, regardless of your organizational level?

It's easy to get distracted by your "important" duties, like to develop and present reports to the Board of Directors. If you're not careful, soon your "important" duties will overwhelm the basic management functions you should do. Remember your True Priorities.

You'll need to conduct skip level meetings—those in which you meet directly with your direct reports' direct reports. You'll also need to engage regularly with all employees to reinforce the company's Principles with specific actions people can take to make sure they're in alignment.

At the ABC Company, the CEO had a monthly all-employee conference call of thirty minutes or less. They generally started with financial results, but people's eyes quickly glaze over if an entire meeting is devoted to financials, particularly if the meeting contains nothing but that month after month after month. Remember that the financials will take care of themselves if your leadership keeps everyone on the same page with their actions. Provide specific examples of interdepartmental cooperation and teamwork in alignment with the Principles and that goes a long way to motivate people to stay in alignment, which drives profit.

~~~~~~

Turf

Turf is the concept of staking out your department's figurative territory to ensure that no one infringes on it. It manifests itself in the Interaction phase of the Purkey Hierarchy of Business Operations. It's a very proprietary and protective approach to management that says "I'm perfect; I know more about my work than anyone else, so keep your nose out of the way I run my department."

Certainly there needs to be some amount of pride in a department, but taken to an extreme, it leads to an independent, walled-off (siloed) department that doesn't understand how it impacts other departments downstream from it in the process flow, nor does it care. Turf maximizes what you have, even if it minimizes what others have. It's an uncooperative, self-centered approach that leads to failure of the overall organization to achieve all that it otherwise could. It's the antithesis of open and honest communication. If every department acts in the same insulated manner, soon turf wars break out as each department attempts to expand its realm of influence and takes responsibilities from others. Over time, you have a dysfunctional organization with every man for himself. Don't participate in this destructive behavior.

There's a management theory called "dynamic tension" that was the buzz in the 1990s and actively pursued by "progressive" managers at the time. Basically, it says that if departments or individuals compete in a controlled fashion, then the competitive tension among them sparks more creativity and produces better results. It builds on most people's natural, competitive natures, in theory to bring out the best in them. It relies on Department A to look over its shoulder at Department B's performance and, if B does better than A, conclude that A had better step up its game.

A friend of mine once told me, "Some chaos is good when you're undergoing change." Kind of like my old fishing skipper's line about a certain amount of pollution being good for the environment that I mentioned in Chapter 1. (As an aside, they're both from Sitka, Alaska. Maybe that's the root cause for that outlook. Leave no stone unturned in the quest for root causes, however idiotic it may first appear.) I disagree with both. While they (chaos and pollution) may be inevitable, they shouldn't be introduced deliberately into the equation.

The intent behind these ideas is good—create urgency and a sense of immediacy to improve performance. The result, however, ultimately leads to dysfunctional organizations. Too much chaos in a work environment causes employees to lose focus on the essentials and choose their own Priorities according to their individual preferences. Anarchy ensues.

You want to create *some* pressure in an organization. People need to feel that they're there to perform and produce results, that they have expectations of them that need to be met. But, there's a fine line between pressure and stress. Make sure you don't push your people over the edge.

The problem's that in the real world, this dynamic tension can't be controlled. There are emotions and real people with all of their differences involved. Jealousies and envy naturally develop and escalate, which lead to turf wars and dysfunction. Teamwork, except within the department, is thrown out the window, so cooperation among different groups and the associated synergies that come with that cooperation are lost.

It's ironic that dynamic tension really says that cooperation among individuals within a given team should be maximized for the best benefit of that team, but when it comes to interdepartmental interactions, cooperation should be minimized. Employees and departments that are pitted against one another with dynamic tension will perform to enhance their own individual fiefdoms, but at the cost of not maximizing overall company performance. Management may have had good intentions with this plan, but come on. If the theory had considered how humans actually function in the real world (e.g., envy, jealousy, greed, selfishness, etc.), it never would have seen the light of day.

Here's an example. The XYZ Company had separate Installation and Repair departments. People in the Installation department only did new installations at customer premises, while people in the Repair department only did repairs on what had already been installed. Not too bad of a system, since it allowed technicians to specialize and become proficient in their field of work. However, if we look at the other side of the coin, those installers had no real incentive to do quality work. They got measured on how many jobs they finished in a day. So what if the jobs required subsequent repairs as a result of their work? That's why the Repair department existed.

Similarly, the Repair department got measured on how many repairs they could do in a day. (It needs to be pointed out here that neither of these metrics tied directly to customer satisfaction, only to internal expectations of the company for its Installation and Repair technicians. Bad dog.) The XYZ Company didn't understand that Repair could be a most effective Quality Control organization. After all, they only sprang into action when customers called to report something wrong. When they repaired the problem, they usually could pinpoint the root cause, which was often simply a lack of quality. All they lacked was to document the root cause to pass on the lesson to the installation tech.

The problem was turf, both at the management level and the technician level. Repair techs didn't want to "rat out" their installation buddies and get them in trouble. Repair techs could have improved the installers' job performance and helped them get better, but feared management would figuratively beat the installation techs about the head and shoulders versus using feedback as a coaching/improvement opportunity.

The manager of Installation didn't want the manager of Repair to stick his nose in how Installation worked. They created a classic turf situation because of the culture fostered by management, which caused customer care to pay the price. From both an employee and manager standpoint, this created extra work (inefficiency) that's yet another contributor to cause people to think they're too busy to do their jobs.

The solution to turf wars is found in Alignment with Principles. You've got to show the other party how their actions aren't in alignment with a Principle that the company has agreed on for everyone and how your request is in alignment. You'll also need to dig into what the benefits are for the other party to get into alignment. That'll require some discussion with Effective Communication. You'll talk about their Priorities and probably the need to reprioritize to get into alignment. It's likely that since they set their Priorities initially, they'll want to maintain those. Consistently come back to alignment with the Principle at stake. If you maintain respect in the discussion, logic should eventually win the day.

~~~~~

Employee Job Knowledge

Remember that your mission as a manager is to make sure that your employees have all of the necessary tools to do their jobs effectively. Job knowledge is one of those tools. It's a function in the People phase of the Purkey Hierarchy of Business Operations.

Have you ever dealt with an ill-prepared customer service rep, like with the phone company, the cable company, an insurance company, a bank, a vendor, an internet provider, or any of the other thousands of companies out there who profess world class customer satisfaction but actually fail to deliver it? How frustrating is it to be forced into an online chat session in order to get any semblance of customer service when it takes thirty minutes to get to a rep, then takes forty-five minutes of so-called help, and yet you still can't get the issue resolved? We've all been there. What if your company provided this irritating level of customer non-satisfaction? Employees must know the company and its services and this only comes with training. You, as management, need to provide that support.

Training's one of the tools absolutely necessary to employees. However, it's usually among the first things cut in a slash and burn mentality of bad management hell-bent to improve the financials. "In the first place," the slash and burn mentality manager rationalizes, "our people are too busy for us to pull any of them away from frontline activity in order to train. Sure, training's a Priority for us, but there are practical realities that make it impossible. Second, training costs money. There's not only the cost of the class itself, but also the travel expenses involved if we have to send people offsite. Make no mistake that training's a Priority, but we just can't afford it. And think of the poor, poor customers who would suffer so if people get taken off the front line to get trained."

This management style, commonly seen in all industries, is a short-term, shortsighted style. In effect, they'd rather continue to provide lousy customer service in volume than take steps to improve the quality of the customer experience. Probably not contained in their initial business model, but it evolves over time as the company embraces the easy way out or what's expedient in the moment. It's a result of a failure to properly plan staffing needs to build training time into the equation for the number of Full Time Equivalent (FTE) employees needed to operate the business successfully.

Similar impacts are seen when management fails to account for sick days and paid time off in the calculus to determine how many employees are needed for a given function. This approach puts employees into a "too busy to do my job" scenario right out of the gate, as management scrambles to put extra work on those employees who did come to work. This in turn causes managers to be extra busy as they try to fill the holes. It's a wasteful process.

As a general proposition, training that'll improve an employee's performance should comprise 5% to 10% of their total hours worked. That means one to two days per month dedicated only to training. For example, say you've figured out you need 100 people in order to provide a given service. If 10% of them are in training, then you'll only have 90 workers—ten short of your need. Now you'll have 90 people who will be too busy to do their jobs in an effort to make up for poor management. Therefore, you need to hire 111 people so that when 10% of them are in training, you'll have your necessary 100 people to produce something. Naturally, you'll also need to account for sick and paid time off, but the point of this section is to emphasize the need for training and the need to accommodate training.

An extreme example of the need for training is seen in the Information Technology industry. It undergoes exponential changes in technology/software advances measured in months. It seems a new iPhone version comes out about every six months. In an IT environment, if you're not constantly learning about the new innovations that are developed, you're dead on arrival. Imagine a company that still operated with Windows 1.0.

Training needs to cover more than just company products, processes, and procedures, however. Job knowledge is not only knowing the company's products, but also knowing how to effectively communicate, how to speak and write clearly and professionally, how to time manage, and a hundred other things that'll allow employees to be more efficient in their jobs in order to satisfy customers. You'll never run out of pertinent training topics if you're truly focused on customer satisfaction, so build in the hours necessary to create stellar employees.

CHAPTER 9—BRILLIANCE

How to Achieve Operational Brilliance in 8 Steps

T hese eight steps to Operational Brilliance are like fly-ing an airplane. If you're not a pilot and I gave you the basic flying instructions to 1) start the plane, 2) take-off, 3) fly around, and 4) land, I'm sure I'd not want to be your passenger based on your level of knowledge. Nor would I think you'd want to be your own pilot.

These eight steps incorporate all of the topics we've dis-cussed so far, but are put into a format that allows you almost to check the box with each step in order to achieve success.

Accordingly, you may hit some sections where you think to yourself, "Hey, he already said that." There are a number of points to be made that you should understand if that phrase pops into your head. The first one is that it's good to have that thought. It means you've paid enough attention to what's been said so far that you rec-ognize that particular concept. It's been incorporated into your brain. That makes you more likely to turn the idea into action.

Second, while the concept may be the same, generally the contexts or examples are different. As I said in the Introduction, inef-fective communication takes many, many forms to the untrained eye. ("Hey, didn't he say that already?") The more forms/examples you're exposed to that have the same concept, the better the chances that you'll be able to associate that concept to whatever issue you happen to address.

Third, slow down, chew, and digest this book. ("Hey, didn't he say that already?") One of the reasons that the problems in business persist is that people never put into action the things they read in management books. There are two reasons for that. 1) Management books generally are constructed to move from one new topic to the next new topic without describing how all the topics interact or without even a summary of what you were supposed to learn. 2) People look for one silver bullet to fix all their ills and flit indiscriminately from topic to topic like bees around a flowering bush. They're in such a hurry to find the perfect answer because they're too busy to do their jobs. They often don't recognize when they've found a solution as they buzz on to the next topic. "Yeah, yeah, I've got it" is their reaction. Well, if they've got it, why is it so rarely implemented? They've got so many good ideas (i.e., Priorities) that they can't effectively manage them all and nothing changes.

Fourth, a key to effective learning is repetition. You may have heard that before. Don't get annoyed when you read the same concept in a new context. Think of it as practice.

All that being said, this chapter isn't about repetition; it's about pulling together what you've learned so far in a more organized and summarized fashion. There are also some new, important concepts introduced for you to chew and digest.

Warning: This is powerful stuff. Do not operate heavy machinery while under the influence of these instructions.

1. Establish a Principle of clear, continuous, open, and honest communication with and among all levels of employees.
2. Establish a business culture of unrelenting customer satisfaction with key Principles with which to align actions.
3. Initiate departmental performance assessments—what works and what doesn't.
4. Prioritize issues that most significantly affect customer satisfaction.
5. Establish measurable goals and deadlines (i.e., metrics) for the tactics at both group and individual levels.
6. Execute and track progress towards goals and deadlines.

7. Continually communicate clear expectations and results in various forms to all levels.

8. Adjust as necessary. Maintain constant, unrelenting pressure to achieve strategic and tactical goals.

Okay, I lied. I need to be up front about that. There are many more steps to operational brilliance than just eight. Many, many, many more. But these are the big, overall strategic steps you'll need. You might even say they're Simplified. I've provided details and specifics in earlier chapters that build to this chapter and I'll provide more after this chapter in order to round out the lessons to enable you to succeed.

My goal is to spark some thought in your mind about what *could be* versus *what does* happen in your organization. If they're one and the same, great. If not, well then, hopefully you'll find ideas that you can explore in more detail later.

Let's take a look at these eight steps and begin to flesh out some important concepts.

~~~~~~

Step 1 (Establish a strategy of clear, continuous, open, and honest communication . . .)

There are three key words in this step: establish, communication, and employees. Each has a lot of implications that need to be understood in order to get them implemented correctly.

The first of the three key words—"Establish"—means that someone has to take charge. Someone has to lead. This gets back to the concept that Management Feeds Employees. Management creates the framework in which employees work. "Establish" also carries a connotation of sustainability. Why establish something if it won't last? The Pilgrims established a colony that grew into the United States (with apologies to St. Augustine, Florida).

Beyond sustainability is also the concept of perseverance. The Pilgrim leaders didn't just come ashore, plant a stake in the ground, go back to England, and then return a year later to see how their colony had progressed. Executive leadership, indeed leadership at all levels, needs to engage continuously in not only modeling Effective Communication, but also encouraging others to jump on the bandwagon. When things go wrong, what if the first thought of a great leader was "What haven't I Effectively Communicated and how can I turn that around?"

Maybe a lack of Effective Communication isn't the root cause of a given issue (however unlikely that possibility is), but if the leader doesn't have the thought process at the front of her/his mind to start with an examination of communication related reasons, then the organization's set up for failure. "Establish" not only means begin, but follow through. Too often businesses are plagued by management's flavor of the day (consider the stereotypical classic "The Customer Is King"), as Priorities shift like the wind on a spring day and don't allow the organization sufficient time to assimilate the new program before a newer one comes along. Put a stake in the ground and cling to it for dear life as forces around you conspire to pull it from the ground.

The second of the three key words—"Communication," more particularly Effective Communication—is easy to talk about, but maybe the most difficult thing in business to do well. Unfortunately, most people take communication for granted, but it's probably the single most impactful issue that affects business efficiency, productivity, and profitability.

It constantly amazes me that the most impactful issue that affects businesses is often given so little regard. Consequently, businesses run at less than optimum output. How often have you heard a CEO say, "You know, we need to make a concerted effort around here to improve our communication because that ultimately affects our profitability, morale, and efficiency. We'll invest both time and money to ensure that we effectively communicate consistently with both employees and customers." I hesitate to say you've probably never heard that statement because it's a big world, but "never" probably comes closer than any other ballpark number. It's a sad commentary on the state of business. Take another look at Chapter 5 on the necessity of Effective Communication.

The third of the three key words—"Employees"—means real people are involved to keep your business alive. As a manager, you always need to remember you deal with real people with real emotions and real lives. You don't simply manage a faceless organization in which you can make impersonal decisions and pawn it off on "the business." You shouldn't assign blame for bad decisions (or good ones, for that matter) to some faceless entity that lacks a physical existence. A "business" is not God. A business is composed of real people and decisions are made by real people. So, while "business decisions" must be made, make them with an understanding of the ramifications to people and that people make the decisions.

While this paragraph may belabor the point above, it's a point worth belaboring so we're certain we have a mutual understanding (i.e., Effective Communication). Take responsibility and accountability. Personalize the business. "The needs of the business" may be a true statement when it comes to layoffs, but it always ultimately comes down to a person somewhere in the chain of command who says which individuals stay and which go. Words must be spoken and, with limited exceptions, only humans make words. There's a body and a thought process behind any decision that's made in a business. It's not the processes, it's not the policies, and it's not the needs of the business. It's people. Be accountable for your actions.

Leadership establishes the Principles with which the organization needs to align. Principle #1 is to have a culture of Effective Communication. You need to be a leader for Effective Communication.

It's great to call yourself a leader, but if no one follows you (and I'm sorry to be the one to break the news to you), you're not a leader. Employees must buy in to the whole endeavor or all will be lost. You'd think this would be almost a no-brainer, since not only do these Eight Steps to Operational Brilliance make common sense, this whole book does. Yet, in any population of more than one, opinions may vary. As a leader, you need to accept this reality and work within it. You don't have to be happy with it, but do accept it. It'll take time and energy (largely in the form of communication, somewhat ironically) to gain the critical mass of employee buy-in (i.e., believers) to get the organization as a whole to move forward.

Employees aren't just the key to get the Principle of Step 1 into action, they're the only way it can happen. All levels must agree this is the way the business will operate and it has to be constantly reinforced that this is the expectation. If you have departments or a significant number of employees who don't buy in, that'll take down the whole system.

Let me provide you a real-life example. Two companies wanted to establish a sales culture outside of just the sales department. Both faced firm resistance to the "sales approach" from some front line departments (e.g., Engineering, Operations, Finance, etc.), since those employees had not traditionally been asked to sell anything to customers, even though they often interacted directly with customers.

In the ABC Company, the second level managers understood the ultimate value to customer satisfaction gained with an attitude to understand and meet customer needs instead of thinking they were forcing unwanted products on customers (i.e., the stereotypical negative view of sales). They held meetings with somewhat sales-averse first level managers, who eventually saw the wisdom of the effort. They all agreed that customer satisfaction stood as the common denominator of why they had a business. They built buy-in over the course of several meetings, not with a snap of the fingers.

The first level managers then took the message to the very sales-resistant front line. Over time, with unrelenting communication from the entire management team about the "why" of the effort, the front line saw the wisdom, as well. The entire company fell into alignment with a main Principle to provide customer satisfaction.

Frontline people were asked to talk to customers, identify what customers needed to be better satisfied (relative to the services provided by the company), and present options in the context of helping satisfy those customer needs instead of "selling." All levels bought in and the ABC Company saw quantum leaps in sales results (an actual ten times increase over previous sales levels in some departments that had never seen themselves in a sales role).

At the XYZ Company, however, the first level managers never got to the buy-in stage. These managers remained out of alignment with the Principle of customer satisfaction because they felt their people were too busy to take additional time to sell stuff. They played a good game and told the second line managers what the bosses wanted to hear, but when they dealt with the front line employees, first level managers sent decidedly different messages.

Without the necessary buy-in to the company's goals, the first level managers embarked on a program to "protect" the front line from the evils of sales and undercut the direction of the company. Since the front line wasn't naturally inclined towards sales in the first place, the new processes never gained traction. The front line didn't lack the capability for sales, they just didn't see it as part of their job (despite the fact that their job function ultimately was to provide customer satisfaction). The real culprits, though? Management. Management failed to Effectively Communicate the necessity of total customer satisfaction and how those front line employees contributed to it.

The XYZ Company had a logjam. In an ideal world, logic and Effective Communication would have prevailed and the first levels would have eventually seen the light. However, the emotional tie they had to their own view of what the company needed could not be broken. Or maybe it was that they couldn't be moved out of their comfort zone of what they'd always done before.

In this case, they needed a fresh perspective and the non-believing first levels simply had to be removed from the equation, to be replaced with those who shared the company's vision. After the change in personnel, another attempt to engage the front line employees occurred, this time with the desired results. Of course, a few individual front line employees still couldn't get themselves to buy in, for whatever reasons. Here again, if it's determined that buy-in will never come even after extensive coaching has been provided, then changes need to be made to find employees who are the right fit for the vision of the company.

You may conclude that the moral of this story is to eliminate all dissention and begin a program to clear-cut. Far from it. The investment of companies in their tenured employees is almost incalculable. It's always better to take a current employee and coach them up versus throw out the baby with the bathwater, hire new, and start over. But it's also important to recognize when coaching has no effect and selectively cut the dead wood.

Employee buy-in is a non-negotiable requirement for success. You need to spend the time necessary to become an advocate for culture change and work tirelessly to gain employee buy-in.

~~~~~~

Step 2 (Establish a culture of unrelenting customer satisfaction focus with key Principles . . .)

We talked extensively about establishing key Principles in Chapter 4, but it's important to reiterate that those Principles are what drive your business both strategically and tactically. Make sure they're ones you believe in and can act on.

Textbook Lean Six Sigma management teaches that value is something a customer purchases. If there are activities that don't directly lead to something a customer will spend money on or are not associated with a critical business function (e.g., finance), then those activities are defined as waste. Waste needs to be eliminated.

With a company-wide focus on producing value—essentially customer satisfaction—everyone's eye is on the same ball at all times. Employees start to breathe customer satisfaction. (Refer back to Chapter 7, Step 3: Standardize and breathe the processes.) Everything, and I mean *everything*—every action, every process, every meeting—is related back to customer satisfaction. Waste will rear its ugly head almost without effort in a culture that has everyone ask "Yeah, but how does [fill in the blank] lead to customer satisfaction?" Everyone's steeped in the concept that if you can't answer that question, regardless of which department asked it, then you've got a potential candidate for waste reduction. Note that waste reduction's just a form of Simplification, one of the Big Four Principles.

Two concepts stand out here: customer satisfaction and employee engagement. Customers feed profit. If you have dissatisfied customers, how much profit do you think you can generate? Maybe at first you can fool some customers, but as word gets out about consistently unhappy customers, the death knell will have sounded. Remember that people are more likely to share unsatisfactory experiences about your company than convey good interactions.

The best way to understand how your customers feel about your performance is to ask them. What if all businesses had some process to get timely feedback directly from customers in a form that's directly translatable into operational processes? It doesn't need to be a complicated questionnaire with tons of questions that'll make customers irritated about the survey. However, you need some way to gauge the pulse of the people who give you money to make sure they continue to give you money.

The XYZ Company fielded customer complaints as a dominant, consistent way of life, almost to the point that employees became jaded. Another complaint? Just part of the daily grind. Management, however, wouldn't take the step to catalog the real reasons for the complaints. They needed to understand the range of both positive and negative comments with which to start some Prioritization exercises as a prelude to change. However, no systems existed to make it easy to question customers directly, other than in a reactive mode. Without systems, management basically decided to throw up their hands because—say it with me now—they were too busy to talk to customers. In their minds, no spare resources could be found to take on such an effort. Consequently, no one could change anything because they didn't know what to change.

Fortunately, one manager broke the code. This manager understood the Priority to provide customer satisfaction. The manager also understood that any data's better than no data. You don't need elaborate IT systems with Pareto charts and statistical analyses that incorporate every single customer transaction in order to accomplish the mission to find out what customers really think. If you take a random sample of customers, that'll do just fine if you've got limited resources. All you need is a pencil and paper and keep a stroke tally of responses.

With this Simplified approach, she acted. She went to other departments to find someone, anyone, who could take a few minutes each day and call customers with a Simplified script of questions about the customers' experience with the XYZ Company. She found a department who could spare a person for thirty minutes a day for a couple of weeks. She made her pitch to the manager of the other department that this would be a temporary situation for a short duration period. Negotiation skills, using customer satisfaction as a lever, and understanding and incorporating the other person's needs, are invaluable to a manager (or anyone, for that matter) to get a larger team effort started.

The manager designed the questions to draw very explicit responses from customers, associated with specific actions that could be taken to improve the customer experience. For example, if the customer had made the appointment but didn't show up, the question became what the *XYZ Company* could have done better to help the customer show up next time. If the customer couldn't come up with anything, the survey taker referred to a list of prompts (like, "If we had a reminder call, would that have helped?") based on some ideas the manager had about how to change the scheduling of appointments.

Contrast this with a question that could have asked the customer what the *customer* could have done better to show up. By having the company take responsibility for the interaction versus implicitly blaming the customer, the customers felt more inclined to help and respond instead of getting defensive and closing up like a clam at low tide. Note that this method was a practical application of the use of "I" statements, discussed in Chapter 5. After interviewing fifty customers, the manager had the data she needed to make changes to ensure customers showed up for appointments so that installers could do their jobs.

~~~~~~

Employee Buy-in

Step 2 has the precondition of Step 1 that all employees and departments are fully engaged in this master strategy. That means employees need to understand how customers feel about your business—the customers' level of satisfaction. It means everyone needs a direction to success, a path down which they can proceed to a destination. If employees understand exactly how they fit into the process to satisfy customers, that provides them some significance to their jobs. With a purpose, employees should be able to leave the job at the end of the day with a sense of satisfaction and the knowledge of what they did to contribute directly to the greater good. On the other side of the coin, it also provides a platform for employees to leave at day's end with some dissatisfaction if they couldn't deliver that positive customer experience. If Step 1 has been correctly implemented and buy-in exists, that'll lead to suggestions for improvement from employees—always a plus. In short, employees become more engaged in their work if management sets up the right conditions. An engaged person will perform better than one who's not.

At the ABC Company, an employee once sent me an email— proactively and without any prompts—that apologized for not having all of the information in an order, which had led to a customer complaint. He took accountability for his actions and vowed not let it happen again. In addition, he suggested a procedure to help others not make the same mistake. What a great, engaged employee working in alignment with customer satisfaction and continuous improvement with an eye to improve the overall business.

Engagement leads to buy-in. Engagement's evidenced by consistent performance of an action, whereas buy-in's more about a belief in the philosophy or vision. Employees who buy in can become emissaries of the mission and enlist others to the cause. Once a critical mass of employees with buy-in is reached (granted that precise level of critical mass is unknown, but it's less than the majority of employees), the company will walk on its own towards success.

When you hear people use the language of whatever the Principles are and the way the Principles are achieved, you'll know you're on the right path. When you overhear employees talk in terms of customer satisfaction of their own volition in casual conversations, you've made it. Of course, buy-in will also be reflected in the metrics you've chosen to measure. If your metrics trend in the right direction, it's another indication you've got buy-in from that critical mass, if not more.

~~~~~~

Step 3 (Initiate departmental performance assessments . . .)

One of management's functions is to take a step back from the workaday world and evaluate what goes on within the company or department and why. Think of it as an out-of-body experience so you can take an objective, third party, neutral view from above. You become your own consultant (at a significant cost savings). The self-assessment exercise will also get departmental leads more engaged in their work. This will include both inter- and intra-departmental interactions and P&L analysis.

However, caution needs to be used with these assessments. "Simplified" is the operative word. The business shouldn't be paralyzed by managers who ignore other job functions in order to turn their departments inside out to produce a hundred-page white paper on what's wrong. I call this the AT&Tization approach. Now, don't get me wrong. AT&T has been around in one form or another for well over a hundred years. They must be doing something right. And this approach to "complexify" things isn't limited to just AT&T. However, they have a tendency to examine things in painful detail to the point of "you've got to be kidding." They'll throw tons of resources at an issue that sometimes isn't even worth as much money as the company spends to examine the issue.

Your assessments should be one page (okay, maybe two, if you feel particularly bureaucratic), bullet points, and a combination of things that work (so they knowingly can be continued) and things that don't (so they can be modified or eliminated). What are the pain points of the department? What drives people crazy? Compiling this information is the first step to implement change.

In larger companies, there may be more than one of a given type of department. Look for commonalities across the peer departments. However, just because a given pain point's listed by one department and none of the others doesn't mean that the issue should be skipped over.

In group discussions among peer departmental managers over whether to Prioritize a given pain point for resolution, it's tempting just to take a vote to make it a Priority for action. Avoid that temptation. For example, if there are five small departments and one big department and the big department's the only one with the problem, the issue might be associated with the size and volume unique to the big department. If the group votes not to address the issue, then when the small departments grow big, they'll likely encounter the same issue. If the big department is 40% of the transactions of the company, fixing a 40% problem from the company perspective is a good thing, even though the vote might be five to one against fixing it. The general philosophy should be for smaller departments to adopt the procedures of the larger departments, not vice versa.

Common processes are all well and good and are something to set up as an ideal, but variations may be acceptable. Just be sure to document when and why the variations are needed. Managerial judgment comes into play and you should expect healthy discussions among the departmental managers as to local differences and the rationale behind those differences.

In a culture that honors open and honest communication, you'll find that questioning others (not in a Spanish Inquisition sort of way) is not only an accepted part of everyday business, it's expected. People don't take offense at being probed (not in an alien sort of way). Questions like "How do you know that?" and "How does that directly impact customer satisfaction?" are common. Everyone understands that the questions aren't personal or asked to assign blame or to embarrass others; they're asked in the spirit of making the business better and dealing with business issues instead of psychological ones.

While as a manager you need to maintain a positive outlook and pump up morale, at the same time you need to approach your job as a bit of a skeptic. If you run the group, it's hard to separate your personal investment and feelings from a truly objective view, but that's your task. Many managers take a false sense of pride about their groups. They simply declare their groups the best, without any support for that statement. ("How do you know that?" is an appropriate question to ask of that manager here.) To go a step further, some managers assume that because their group's the best, their teams need less supervision and can run on their own without much coaching effort. As a result, group performance actually declines while the manager deludes himself to believe just the opposite. Metrics play a key role to prevent that delusional belief.

The more dispassionate you are about your group's performance, the better you'll be at uncovering more opportunities for improvement. The more passionate you are to improve the well-being of your group, the more respected as a leader you'll be.

~~~~~~

Assessments

If you want to form a team to accomplish a goal and if you understand the expertise required, you need to assess yourself, potential team members, and departments for their abilities to fill the expertise gaps. Self-assessment is a key to improvement, but it's also one of those areas that's hard to teach. By definition, self-assessment's a personal thing, influenced by your own internal filters and how you see or would like to see life. It's slightly easier to assess others, but you've still got those pesky internal filters that can fog true objectivity. See Chapters 3 and 5. All I can tell you is to do your level best to be objective, to look at yourself through the eyes of others, and try to see what they see without your pride getting in the way. That's a tall order, but doable with the right attitude and practice.

It's easier to show you what not to do. The XYZ Company did a survey of its employees that showed how hard it is to be objective.

Question 1A: *When I disagree with another member of my work team, I always (or frequently) go directly to that person to resolve it.* This is both the best theoretical and practical action to resolve disagreements—go to the source and talk it out. The vast majority of employees, likely in tune with that theory, answered "Strongly Agree."

Question 1B: *At work, I always (or frequently) hear things about me indirectly, rather than directly, face-to-face.* The vast majority of employees answered "Strongly Agree."

Now we've uncovered a bit of a logical quandary. If the majority of the people go directly to others when they have a problem, how could it also be that the majority of people only hear things about themselves indirectly? What's happened is that the majority of people have ascribed the good attribute (talking directly) to themselves and ascribed the bad attribute (essentially, gossip) to others.

To move this survey out of the realm of the individual, the survey asked similar questions of employees about their work groups.

Question 2A: *Our work group knows what other groups need from us and we always (or frequently) get it to them.* The vast majority of employees answered "Strongly Agree." XYZ apparently has a great, communicative, responsive organization, at least according to XYZ. Would that we were all so fortunate.

Question 2B: *Our work group can never (or seldom) get what we need from other groups to do our job well.* The vast majority of employees answered "Strongly Agree."

Oops. Again, we have a logical inconsistency. If everyone gives everyone else everything they need, how is it that no one gets anything from anyone? At the XYZ Company, all of the teams had learned that all of the other teams were not cooperative. Hmmm . . . objectivity has clearly been compromised in this survey. XYZ employees may have understood the theory of the best practices, but they fell far short of turning the theory into action.

Make sure you're both logical and objective with your assessments.

~~~~~~

Conducting Departmental Assessments

Here are some high level points to include in the departmental work assessments you'll need to undertake (or verify, in the unlikely event they've already been done).

➢ Look at each group, defined by the existence of a management lead. Include all levels of management.

➢ Create high-level work flow charts that show the upstream and downstream relationships of the departments—functional, nothing fancy. Where does the output of one department become the input of another department?

A structured way to conduct an inter-departmental assessment is to follow an order through the system from start to finish. Be the order and experience what it experiences in the process. The starting point's when the salesperson walks through the door of the customer or the customer walks through your door. Depending on the problem you're trying to address, you can extend this starting point even earlier to when the salesperson plans a customer contact. The stopping point's when a customer uses the product. Here again, you may want to extend the time frame to after that point because of service and support issues involved after the product is used.

> ➤ Include interdepartmental interaction summary descriptions. How is the information transferred from one department to another?

> ➤ What works and what doesn't—objectively. These are best shown as bullet points, one to two pages max. Why are they important relative to the company's strategies/Principles/goals?

The departmental assessments provide additional benefits if they include others in the data gathering.

- Tactics are easier to develop if the management team understands how their respective departments interact with other departments.

- Managers gain a perspective on the business as a whole. It prepares them for further advancement in the company.

- Others walk in your shoes; they feel your pain. And you theirs. This engenders Effective Communication.

- Others learn how they can help you.

- Team building on a peer level is accomplished, as well as helping establish a culture of continuous improvement.

- The front line's impressed when they see engagement from management in their arenas. They'll know that management doesn't just sit idly in the corner office and make proclamations.

~~~~~

Step 4 (Prioritize issues . . .)

Prioritization has been covered at length already. See Chapter 2 primarily. It's one of the Big Four Principles. However, you need to understand that Prioritization has its place and relies on both upstream and downstream steps for it to be effective. In order not to Prioritize things that shouldn't be Prioritized, you need that foundation of Effective Communication in place. That means a collaborative environment exists with your team, your peers, and your upper management, along with an unrelenting customer satisfaction focus and an accurate assessment of departmental performance.

Logistically, assign accountable leads to resolve a limited number of the top Priorities. Address lower Priorities in due time. You can't solve everything at once and if you attempt to do so, it creates chaos and backlash.

~~~~~~~~~

Step 5 (Establish measurable goals and deadlines for the tactics . . .)

What gets measured gets improved. If you don't know where you're headed, you'll never get there. These two statements mean that measurable goals are imperative to success. But the goals need to be realistic and achievable. Some managers pride themselves on "stretch goals," but they set the bar so high they can never be reached. All they do is set themselves and their teams up for failure and disappointment. They might save some money by not paying out bonuses when they miss the stretch goal, but the increased frustration and resentment from employees is a high price to pay for that savings.

Taken to extremes, employees then begin to believe that they can never succeed and simply don't try, which leads to performance declines. Employee engagement is diminished. Some managers respond by getting tougher, setting the bar even higher in an effort to drive the slackers to achieve. This makes about as much sense as the dictate mentioned earlier that "The beatings will continue until morale improves."

The very concept of stretch goals seems to me to be antithetical to good management. They're really of no value except to try to impress the boss. They're akin to giving 150% effort—meaningless. They say, "Well, if we get wildly lucky and everything goes perfectly, this is where the results should be." Good management isn't about luck; it's about a disciplined, consistent implementation of proven techniques. If a goal is well considered, then there's always room to exceed the goal. That's a given. A proper goal incorporates the fact that some will exceed it, some will make it, and others won't. If you think you'll make a stretch goal, then why wouldn't that be the actual goal? If you think you'll only make a stretch goal under perfect conditions, who cares? Perfection over time isn't realistic. A stretch goal minimizes the importance of the actual goal to which you'll hold people accountable. A stretch goal's a hedge bet from a manager not confident of success or one who just wants to kiss up to the boss.

A better path is to go back to Step 3 and take that dispassionate approach to examine the situation. Again, limit the number of goals to True Priorities to make them manageable. Sure, you set the goal, but did you set it correctly? Or are you so infallible that because you decreed the goal, it's automatically the right goal? For some perspective, remember that at the goal's core, it's just a made up number or ideal. A little humility's required to set any goal.

"Deadlines" is the often-overlooked aspect of this step. It's great to have some limited, targeted, measurable goals, but if you don't have time frames around them, there's no point. Deadlines are the best way to create a sense of urgency. Attach deadlines to goals and you really bring the Prioritization of the issues home. It's an easy way to manage how people at all levels spend their time and keep them focused on what's essential.

When deadlines are documented, managers are less likely to make willy-nilly changes in a Dilbert-esque boss fashion. Deadlines are an important component to allow you to take control of your life and become less busy so that you can do your job. Deadlines need to be treated with respect.

A manager who continually, habitually reprioritizes and sets new deadlines lacks integrity (and, probably, competence, but that's a different issue)—integrity defined as doing what you say you will do. Most everyone agrees that integrity's a big component in any interaction among humans. The ability to maintain that integrity in the face of competing demands on a person is one thing that separates a good manager from a bad one.

Documentation of goals doesn't need to be an elaborate system, just something that's easy to update and monitor. Simplification. Usually a simple Excel spreadsheet can be constructed that, when regularly reviewed in team meetings, can keep people on track. Here's an example (Fig. 9-1) of all that's needed:

ACTION ITEM	ASSIGNED DATE	DUE DATE	OWNER	COMMENTS
Reduce time for contract signature to average 30 days	04/01/13	05/13/13	Michael Lee	4/1 – Current avg is 50 days 4/3 – Jean Benevento notified of new goal.
Increase QCs per tech to 15% of jobs	03/01/13	~~04/30/13~~ 06/30/13	Dennis Roth	4/1 – Need budget approval for headcount from Mark Reynolds by 5/1.
Complete inspection of all trucks	04/15/13	04/30/13	Keith Scandora	4/25 – On track. Next step is scheduling inspections.

Fig. 9-1

Certainly more extensive projects may need more formal project plans to keep track of everything, which is why Microsoft and others have made a bunch of money with project planning software. But at a work group level, the example above is usually all that's required to keep the team on point. Individual owners of an action item will need to develop their own deadline matrix for the sub-steps involved to complete their action item. Put that in their control to help them meet the overall master deadline shown in the above example.

Let's take a look at the thought process behind each category of a deadline matrix.

Action Item: The impacts the action items will have on the business and customer satisfaction need to be well considered. There needs to be a clear understanding between you and the action item owner that the owner is to allocate sufficient time in the day to move the project forward. It's the same concept we discussed in Chapter 8 to match the time you spend throughout the day to the relative importance of the goals. The fact that the action item even appears on the list means that it's a Priority and needs to be treated as such.

This is an obvious use of one of the Big Four—Prioritization. This is not a wish list. Don't put every little nitzy item that you'd like to have done on here. There's limited time in the day, so the action items assigned to people also need to be limited. The deadline matrix (i.e., the action items that make it onto the list) is a tool for you to keep track of what your team members do relative to bigger tasks, not to understand when and where they go to lunch or take their breaks.

Be aware that a natural tendency is to "complexify" project plans. I've seen supposedly professional project managers put so many steps into a project plan that the administration of the project plan became more time consuming than the actual project work. Ironically, deadlines started to be missed because of so much time spent to make the project plan as accurate as inhumanly possible.

One project manager in particular at the XYZ Company worked nights and weekends to develop a system of various colored symbols and macros that indicated certain levels of progress for each action item. He used so many colors and symbols that we needed a Rosetta Stone to figure out what they all meant. When we pointed out to him the unwieldy nature of his plan, he went back to the drawing board and came back with an entirely new set of colors, symbols, and macros equally incomprehensible. In his mind, and this is almost a direct quote, "It's the old 80/20 rule. We should spend 80% of our time planning and 20% of our time doing."

Granted, planning's important to most tasks (remember Purkey's Law of the 7 Ps is Proper Prior Planning Prevents Piss Poor Performance), but if your company spends only 20% of its time actually doing things, you're doomed. Now, if you want to spend 20% planning and 80% doing, that might be a better rule of thumb. Don't worry, this particular project manager was a contractor (apparently with a sales pitch better than his capabilities) and when it became apparent he was the impediment to progress, his contract was terminated. We then Simplified action items, and the project finished to everyone's satisfaction, late though it was due to the rocky start.

Assigned Date: The project start time's important to track how efficient the owner is with the task. A project may seem like it takes a long time, but without that start date to reference, it's only a perception without any basis in reality.

Due Date: This is the meat of the matrix. This is the deadline, clearly and explicitly stated for all to see. How that deadline gets established, however, is maybe more important than the deadline itself. At the XYZ Company, a boss established deadlines by decree—basically because she said so. Just like goals, though, deadlines are also essentially just made up. The more you can incorporate rationality and reality into a deadline, the better the chance that the deadline will be met.

What if deadline setting was a negotiation between the action item owner and the boss? Questions like "Well, how busy are you now?" and "What would need to fall off your plate of current duties in order to get this item addressed?" would be part of the discussion. A shorter deadline may mean the owner would need to drop everything and work the item, while a longer deadline might mean the owner could work the item into his regular day without any major disruption and still get it done. Seems obvious, but over commitment to multiple, short deadlines is a major contributor to being too busy to do your job. Negotiate something reasonable that works for all parties. Find the common ground.

Many people don't give the deadline much thought or discussion, pluck a date out of thin air (or some part of their anatomy), and consequently set themselves up for failure. If you set some off-the-cuff deadline to satisfy whatever pressure's applied (or perceived as applied) to accomplish the task in order to get someone off your back, you shoot yourself in the foot in the long run. That method needs to be avoided at all costs. A good deadline needs to have thought behind it.

More on the Form's Due Date Section: What if we considered a deadline a sacred contract, not to be messed with, something to be honored? It gets back to integrity and doing what you say you'll do. People want to work with people with integrity and those they can trust.

Due dates are commitments. Due dates are promises. Promises are sacred. It's your word, your bond, your reputation, your reliability, your integrity, and your trustworthiness that's at stake. What if all efforts got expended to meet the deadline?

At the same time, reality does intervene on occasion. To adhere rigidly to a given deadline in the face of changed circumstances is bad management. If, after some discussion and negotiation, a persuasive case can be made to change the deadline, then the deadline needs to be changed. Notice that the second Action Item in Figure 9-1 has a changed due date from 4/30 to 6/30. Just like it's important to document the *start* date of the whole project, it's equally important to document the original *due* date. If you treat the due date like the sacred contract it is, you won't have many projects with due date changes. But if the date changes after a compelling case is made, you can see the history in the Due Date section. If the newly assigned due date gets changed again, then, as a manager attuned to Priorities, you can begin to question the project's degree of importance. Maybe the Action Item shouldn't be a Priority in the first place.

If after further study you decide the project warrants an appearance on the Priority list, then you can begin to look at the root causes of why the date needed to be changed. It might be time to implement something different to get the project back on track. Maybe you've got the wrong owner, so what if you put someone else on the task? Maybe a more thorough examination of the owner's other responsibilities needs to occur in order to take something off the owner's plate. Maybe another department's a roadblock to completion and a management escalation needs to happen. If you track due date changes, that'll allow you to make those assessments at the appropriate time.

Even More on the Form's Due Date Section: A word about the timing of due date changes. Few things are more frustrating than this set of circumstances: 1) You have an agreement with LaVerne that she'll have a task done by a date certain. 2) You depend on that date certain to schedule your work output. 3) Others downstream from you depend on you to meet your date certain with them. 4) On the due date, LaVerne tells you, "Whoops. I won't make that deadline that we had for today." This method of "day-of" notification that a due date will be missed naturally creates some fire drills, as people and departments scramble to make up for planned activity and adjust their own deadlines. The "day-of" notification is inefficient on an organizational level and inconsiderate on a personal level. It shows a lack of respect for others' time and responsibilities.

Yet, "day-of" notifications are commonplace. The victims may even try to play nice, so as not to offend, and say, "Hey, I know we're all busy. Hopefully you can get it to me soon." The perpetrator will then say, "Oh, absolutely. I'll get it to you as soon as I can." The parties then go their separate ways with no new due date set, with one person left with a faint hope they can get the information at some point. Hope's not a strategy. (Well, it actually is, but just not a good one.) "Soon" is not a number or a date.

Perpetrators get away with and victims allow perpetrators to get away with these vagaries every day. Maybe the supposed victims are actually contributors to the problem (enablers) and let the perpetrators skate by. All that leads to is more wasted time and more stress in your life. As a responsible employee, you've got an obligation to nail down a mutually agreed to specific time and hold people to it.

Train yourself and others to speak about topics, whatever the topic may be, with the language of Names, Numbers, Dates, and Deadlines. The culture will change to one of directed action and accomplishment instead of chaos and dysfunction.

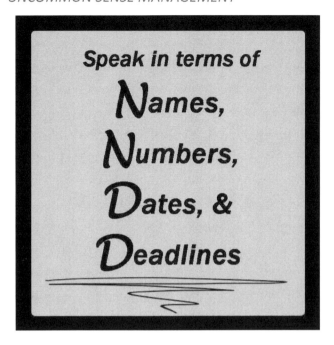

The Principle above banishes the word "soon" to the nether regions of everyone's vocabulary, never to be heard from again. What if you heard the word "soon" in a statement, politely interrupted the speaker, and asked "When does 'soon' mean?" *In a culture of Names, Numbers, Dates, and Deadlines, no one will take offense and a real, accountable deadline will get set.*

Without that culture, however, you're likely to be met with some hems and haws in response to your inquiry. The perpetrator may feel under pressure to set a new deadline sooner than they can actually deliver, particularly since they've already missed the original deadline. Ask anyway.

Emotions, particularly embarrassment, are likely a factor in this type of interaction. What you don't want is for them to throw out yet another off-the-cuff deadline just to please you and get you off their back. Show some sympathy to their plight, but also be clear this information's important—it's been Truly Prioritized. If appropriate, talk about other departments that are also involved and that we're all reliant on the perpetrator (FYI, I wouldn't use that word in your discussion, but it certainly creates an image, doesn't it?) to deliver. Ask what you or others might be able to do to help the perpetrator meet the new deadline.

After some negotiation and they give you a potential new date, provide some wiggle room for the perpetrator. Hey, they already missed one date, so maybe a few days more delay could be beneficial. Reemphasize the importance of the task and let them know that if they need another day or two beyond the potential new date, that's okay, simply set the new deadline out a couple of additional days. But, the date needs to be met. Be firm, but make sure that they're comfortable that they can easily meet the new deadline they agree to.

These can be prickly discussions, but as an excellent manager, they're ones that you need to drive. With consideration for the perpetrator's emotions, mutual accommodations can be made that leave both parties satisfied.

Yet Even More on the Form's Due Date Section: Why are missed deadlines commonplace? One of the reasons is that the organization likely doesn't have a set of values as their guidepost. Let's assume everyone shares the overtly stated company values of respect and integrity in the culture of daily work. In that case, when you say you'll miss a deadline, it really means, "I'm sorry, but I don't respect your time and I haven't got the integrity to do what I said I would do, so I'll miss this deadline." In such a values-based culture, ideally it would be okay for the victim to say, "Well, we already know that a missed deadline is out of alignment with our values of respect and integrity, so how can we make this right?" Ideally. Probably not practically. But shoot for the stars and maybe you'll hit the moon.

The bottom line on making deadlines is "do." The bottom line on missing deadlines is "don't." Make them meaningful and achievable in the first place. Under promise and over deliver.

If, for example, you know a task will take you two days, promise the other person three days and deliver in two. Everybody wins. If you know you'll miss a deadline, let the affected parties know well in advance of the deadline versus dumping the surprise on them on the exact due date when they expected results instead of excuses.

Owner (the next section on the form, finally): You need to have the right tool for the right job. Just as you shouldn't use a hammer to cut a board in two (you can, you just shouldn't), you shouldn't assign an owner with sales experience to solve a problem with order input accuracy. Select the owner based on expertise, including the soft skills (e.g., Effective Communication, ability to Prioritize) in addition to the more technical expertise directly applicable to whatever problem you face. Set expectations with the owner clearly and up front. The owner must understand that they make a solemn oath to get the project done within the agreed to time frame. They must understand their integrity's on the line and that this project's a True Priority. You'll need a person who believes they can get the task accomplished and is able to communicate progress as well as obstacles effectively.

Remember Names, Numbers, Dates, and Deadlines? This is the Names part. Be specific as to who has accountability for the success of the task. Name a name. Don't make the owner a department or a group of any sort. Even naming dual owners should be avoided versus designating a single owner.

Comments: This section can really be anything you want that's related to the progress of the task or obstacles to be overcome. Identify the next step(s) to be taken in this section before the next meeting to keep things on track. Update this section at regularly scheduled meetings. Track progress and record agreed upon adjustments.

Practical Action #13
Never leave a meeting/conversation about someone doing something without exact clarity about . . .
  - ➢ **Who will do**
  - ➢ **What**
  - ➢ **and When**

It's especially easy to part company without a When—a committed due date. Remembering "When" requires vigilance. Remember that.

Don't tell me what you WANT to do; tell me what you WILL do and WHEN you'll do it.

Figure 9-1 from earlier is an easy way to put Practical Action #13 into effect when you're in a meeting environment. The hard part is to remember that same Who/What/When process when you're in an actual conversation in more informal discussions. It takes practice (i.e., repeated action).

~~~~~~

Step 6 (Track progress towards goals and deadlines . . .)
How could you possibly know if you improved if you had no way to verify your progress? You could always claim to be better, and many often do, but where's the proof? Remember, as an excel-

lent manager you also need to be somewhat of a skeptic. What's the point in having a goal if you never know if you achieve it?

Verification takes resources, so for this reason alone, you're better off if you can minimize the number of things you try to verify. Whether those resources are taken from your own group for manual tracking or they're from IT, time must be used to verify. Perhaps I'm beating a dead horse to death some more, but the minimization (i.e., Simplification) of goals helps keep people focused on the things that are truly important.

Metrics are useful for more than just understanding outcomes. Remember from Chapter 6 that a proper metric is used to uncover and correct process or efficiency issues, as well. They help you manage the process by seeing trends on progress towards the goal over time. A simple graph in Excel that shows the level of achievement at various points in time is a visual indication of the progress. If you know that you're 25% of the way towards the goal but that 75% of the time has passed toward the deadline to achieve the goal, you can adjust resources or methods to get back on track.

≈≈≈≈≈

Celebrate: Goals and metrics are necessary to measure success and you also need to celebrate that success. Rewards are generally expected, although the type of reward may vary. Moderate the expectations of your group. Handing out a Mercedes to everyone may be a great reward, but financially irresponsible. Meaningful recognition's often enough of a reward to satisfy folks. Ask your group what they expect as a result of achieving a goal and come to a team consensus.

The ABC Company instituted a Tech of the Month program and gave recognition in company-wide reports to the top ten techs based on six objective behavioral metrics directly related to Prioritized actions that drove customer satisfaction. The tangible rewards fell into the category of "trash and trinkets"—a term used by marketing folks to describe things like company or vendor logoed hats, coffee mugs, and t-shirts. Techs loved the stuff, not for the intrinsic value, but for the recognition. While all ten of the top techs got rewards, the higher up they finished, the more rewards they got. The marketing department used their contacts to get free stuff from suppliers to keep costs down. Movie tickets and popcorn for two bought much more in appreciation than the movie and popcorn actually cost. For an extremely low cost, ABC got an extremely high positive impact with employees.

I think people easily forget to say "thank you" or acknowledge somebody else's contribution for the smaller efforts made, but which took time. Some can feel slighted without some degree of appreciation. Small recognitions go a long way towards building loyalty and they can act as an incentive to produce more work or more effort.

~~~~~~~

Goals and metrics also allow you the opportunity to improve performance by giving you something specific with which to coach employees. You can avoid vague generalities and the perception of subjectivity if your coaching's backed by an ability to point to a number and question why the associated goal achievement fell short. In an evaluation, it's much better to say, "Alice, you had a goal of 95% accuracy on order input, but you achieved only 83%. That puts you into the needs improvement category" instead of "Alice, I just don't think you do good work and it needs to be improved."

You have to remain open to the possibility that you may have set the goal incorrectly, without consideration of events that couldn't be or weren't anticipated at the time the goal was set. Remember, all goals are made up by fallible humans. At a minimum, however, even a bad goal provides an opportunity for meaningful dialog about how the employee does the job, what's involved, and what can be done differently.

~~~~~~~

Step 7 (Continually communicate clear expectations and results . . .)

It's great to have these goals and deadlines and track them, but it's of no use if no one knows what the goals are or if those goals are on plan. That's the reason Effective Communication's the foundation for the Hierarchy of Business Operations model seen in Chapter 8. Your goals can't be deep, dark secrets. Everyone needs to know what's expected of them individually and the organization collectively—essentially, the goals. Everyone needs to know how well the expectations are met. With a factual basis, a leader can rally people to do better if the results lag (with specifics, not just a general "we need to do better") or can inspire people to continue to work hard if the goals are on track to be met.

Effective Communication (one of the Big Four Principles) is so important that we spent all of Chapter 5 on it. The point of this brief section is to emphasize the need for *continuous* Effective Communication by all levels of leadership. If all you do to communicate results is put out an Excel spreadsheet that shows the numbers, you fall short of what's necessary to lead and motivate. While an internal website for people to access is good and necessary, it's also not the complete answer. The problem is that it requires people to be proactive and search out information. In an environment where everyone's too busy to do their job, not enough people will take the time. Worthwhile information almost needs to be force fed to everyone in order for them to get on board and stay on board with the program. Regular reports and meetings help them understand what the organization has Prioritized as truly important and what to pay attention to.

The caution about force-feeding is that people will grow bored with the same approach week after week and begin to ignore the message. Get creative. Group meetings, posters, voice mails, emails, lunch talks, newsletters, video meetings, breakfast meetings, individual meetings, chain emails, pre-recorded announcements, flyers, gorilla-grams, monitors placed around the office with scrolling messages, and many more techniques can be used to spread the news in engaging and informative ways. If you present the information in a variety of ways, it also hits all the different learning styles, which makes it more effective.

Communication of results is also about management engagement and follow up. When you set out a goal that you expect people to reach, they'll be naturally curious as to whether the goal's on track to be reached or has been reached. Your job as a manager is to keep that curiosity alive. If you don't provide regular feedback, people will forget the goal even exists and gradually won't put forth the necessary effort to make it happen. You've got to stay engaged in any efforts that you started in the first place. That means Truly Prioritizing goal feedback so it becomes incorporated into your daily work life.

~~~~~~

Step 8 (Adjust as necessary. Maintain constant, unrelenting pressure . . .)

So now you've got all of the previous seven steps in place and they work like a well-oiled machine. You and your team have established key Principles, including Effective Communication, and you've Prioritized the right items for good, sound, rational reasons associated with customer satisfaction. Whether the goals are met or not, now isn't the time for the faint of heart. At all costs, keep the organization focused on what needs to be accomplished. See Step 7 for different ways to approach that.

If your goals become simply the flavor of the day, the management team will lose credibility with the employees and goals will become even harder to achieve. Don't fall into "The Customer Is King" trap in which the customer is king for a day and then the next day "Cash Flow is King" and then the next day "Safety is King." Think through your Priorities thoroughly before they're set and then stick to them, unless some big, dramatic event at odds with your Priorities imposes its will. For example, a core constant of customer satisfaction (essentially, the culture of the organization) is sustainable for many years and allows everyone to measure success against this core.

Let's talk again about how you also can't be blindly locked into your goals, except this time in a different context. I know it would be a remote possibility, so far from reality as to be virtually inconceivable, but maybe, just maybe, you set the goal incorrectly. Take that objective, third party, out-of-body consultant look at the situation and if the impossible proves to be possible, then step up, admit it, and change the goal. Are you in the middle of the year? It's okay. A mistake is a mistake and there's no point in compounding the issue by doggedly hanging onto an untenable position, especially when probably everyone in the company already has concluded management made a mistake. Credibility is critical for leadership.

Example: In an environment of rapidly changing technology in the telecommunications world, the ability to provide your customers state of the art data transmission speeds is critical to your long-term success. For discussion purposes, every time a customer requires more speed, a new, physical technological box is also needed at the customer's premises. In order to install these new boxes, upgraded test equipment is needed by the installer to ensure the customer's service works as promised.

After the annual budget had been developed at the XYZ Company, it became clear that not enough capital had been allocated for new test equipment. XYZ found that the demand for new services outstripped its supply of upgraded test equipment. The reaction by management? "Our hands are tied. The budget for this year has already been set and can't be changed." Consequently, they didn't purchase additional upgraded test equipment and the new high tech services were installed with less than optimal testing.

XYZ looked only at the financial factors and ignored the customer satisfaction factors. They could have reprioritized and simply moved capital from some other capital projects of less Priority, but they'd already put their stake in the ground and, by God, they weren't about to change, customer satisfaction be damned. Okay, maybe a bit dramatic, but hopefully you see my point. Flexibility's an attribute of excellent management.

Happily, however, you having to admit a mistake is likely the last option. We've spent a few chapters together; I know you pretty well by now, and, really, how often are you wrong? At the first sign of goal under achievement, you don't simply change the goal. Since you set the goal with a thorough vetting process that involved your leadership team, it's more likely that the procedures used to achieve the goal are at fault. Look for the root causes and continue to ask "Why?" as you investigate the causes of the lack of success. Keep the organization engaged to find the problems and, together, you will. Then, adjust the appropriate procedures to accomplish what you want.

~~~~~~

CURP

The other part of Step 8 is to maintain Constant, Unrelenting, Ruthless Pressure (or CURP) on the organization to keep everyone focused on the strategies, Principles, and goals. Language is a tricky thing, so a little explanation's in order about the true meaning of CURP. It's not ruthless as in cutthroat, it's ruthless in a good way such that all else falls by the wayside in your pursuit of your goal. It's a single-minded, determined focus with perseverance (Constant and Unrelenting). Think of the classic movie *Butch Cassidy and the Sundance Kid*. As a posse relentlessly pursued Butch and Sundance, Butch (Paul Newman) kept asking, "Who are those guys?" The posse followed doggedly on their heels over all kinds of terrain over many days, never giving up.

You need to be the posse. You Prioritized this goal (whatever it is or they are); you need to treat it as a True Priority and use whatever means possible to keep everyone engaged and on task.

The concept of CURP is useful at the basic task level as well as at the strategic level. At its core, it's really about holding people accountable. CURP isn't about getting in someone's face and screaming at them or standing on a desk and yelling at the top of your lungs. It's more about emulating a glacier. It's low key, but it's forceful. A glacier may move slowly, quietly, and calmly forward (at least in the days before global warming), but it's always moving forward, exerting tremendous pressure on whatever it encounters. It applies Constant, Unrelenting, Ruthless Pressure against any obstacle in its way and eventually overcomes the obstacle.

Let's say you have a project you need completed and you've agreed with Victor that he'll have it for you in two weeks. There are two ways to approach the two-week period. One, you can wait the two weeks for Victor to give you the results without any communication with Victor in that time. After all, Victor's a professional; he'll get it done. Plus he made a commitment to get it done in two weeks. Sure, you need the results before you can move on to the next step of your project, but it's not your job to babysit him. What you forget is that Victor's too busy to do his job. Unless Victor has an unblemished record of completing projects when he says he will, your project's already in jeopardy from the time you made the agreement with him.

Or, two, you can use CURP—a low key approach that actually helps Victor keep on track and increases the odds that you'll get what you need on time. **If an issue is important enough for you to raise, then what if it became important enough for you to follow up to see how it's progressing?**

CURP

*I*f the issue is important enough for you to raise, then it should be important enough for you to follow up to see if it's progressing.

Some might call this babysitting. Some are wrong. That would be the opposite attitude from what I advocate in this book. If you don't check in, that just means that you set Victor up to fail and, if he fails, then you can point the blame finger at Victor. "Hey, not my fault. But that Victor . . ." If you think follow-through is babysitting, then you've lost focus on the business issue, which is to ensure the project gets done on time. When you're off of business issues and on to personality or blame issues, you contribute to the company's inefficiency and to your own problem of being too busy to do your job.

If the issue is important enough to talk about and important enough to assign a due date, then you owe the issue the respect to do everything you can to ensure its completion. That's part of CURP. Don't blindly assume the other person will do their job. While some could view this as the opposite of trust (which is probably somewhat of a valid point), if you don't check in and the person needs help but doesn't ask for it, the result is a missed deadline. If CURP is viewed as teamwork in the spirit of help, all should be good.

Instead of "You screwed up" after the fact, make it "What can I do to help you not screw up?" before the fact. For example, you could send Joe an email that says "Joe, please call the customer. Thanks." On the other hand, you could send him this email: "Joe, please call the customer. Also, would you confirm that you're able to make the call or if I should make other arrangements? Thanks." In the former email, you've essentially set up Joe to fail if he didn't get the email, didn't read it, or couldn't call the customer. (But that's okay, says the wisdom at the XYZ Company. You can always point the finger at Joe and you'll be okay.) In the latter email, you've asked for confirmation, so when you don't hear back from Joe in a reasonable time, you can contact Joe again or do it yourself. The goal is to serve the customer and meet the deadline (the business issues), not point the finger at Joe. Why not help Joe and ultimately help yourself?

This is about teamwork and helping your fellow teammates be successful. No one goes through life alone. We all need a helping hand or reminder now and then. If your project's so important to you, then what if you did everything in your control to make it successful, including helping those on whom you rely? You can't necessarily control Joe, but you *can* control *your* actions.

Let's get back to the example with Victor and his two-week commitment to you. For this example, you can use your two-week period wisely to offer help or at least check in instead of sitting passively in a duck blind waiting for Victor to fly by so you can take a shot at him. After a week, contact Victor (in person is best, but circumstances may dictate a phone call or an email) and ask these questions:

- "How's the project coming along? We agreed that you'd be done by next Friday. Any problems that you can see to meet that deadline?"
- "Is there anything I can do to help you meet the deadline?"

Don't just routinely ask the questions without any real engagement. This is not a check-the-box process. You genuinely need to be ready to help if Victor says there are problems and he needs help. You also need to be ready to renegotiate a different due date if he says there's no way he can meet the deadline. But at least at this point, you'll have a week to rearrange things, which is more efficient than a scramble to recover *on* the due date.

With two days to go, check in with Victor again and ask this:

- "Hi, Victor. Our due date's close for that project and I just wanted to make sure things are still on track. As you know, there are a few departments downstream from you that are involved, so we've got several people who've scheduled work based on an on-time completion."

Note that these questions are gentle nudges, not an in-your-face inquisition. You don't bug him every hour of every day, but you *do* glacially remind him of his commitment. If you approach it with good intent and non-confrontational phrasing, defensiveness on Victor's part may not surface (subject to his individual personality). If you've established the culture of true teamwork with a focus on business issues versus personalities and blame and Victor has bought in to that culture, Victor won't even bat an eye. His capabilities aren't the issue, but the business issues of commitment and timeliness are.

~~~~~~~

As a leader in the company, at whatever level of management you are, follow up means that it's your job to keep the employees focused on the strategies, Principles, and goals. The company leaders own the strategies. The company leaders have accountability to see that the strategies are implemented. That responsibility can't be ducked. There can be no fingers pointed, no blame, no delegation.

A strategy by definition is long-range and broad in scope. That's the domain of company leadership. You, a leader, have responsibility to keep the employee body engaged in the strategies. This is your mission. You may delegate the tactics involved to implement the strategies, but you need to be sure the tactics are directly tied to the strategies.

That's what CURP is for. Don't shirk your responsibility to keep people informed and in alignment with the plan you've set out.

~~~~~~

Eight easy steps to operational brilliance, right? Wrong. Each step takes time and energy. Results won't come with the snap of a finger or an imperial decree. What'll get you there is to know what's really required for each step and to keep your eye on the ball with a little CURP thrown in.

Congratulations! At this point in the book, you've really got enough information to make your company (or department) almost all that it can be. But there's more meat that can be added to the bones to make all of what's come prior to this easier to implement. Read on, as we dig a little deeper. No one said it would be easy.

CHAPTER 10—CUSTOMERS
How to Satisfy Customers versus Service Them

While it's true that Profit feeds Management, Management feeds Employees, Employees feed Customers, and Customers feed Profit, every activity in virtually any company needs to have a direct link with Customer Satisfaction. As we learned in Chapter 9, Six Sigma management defines waste as any activity that doesn't contribute to value, "value" defined as what a customer buys. Customer Satisfaction is defined by how much value the customer thinks they get with your product. While it's a good thing for management to provide employees the tools they need to succeed, the somewhat cynical way to look at it (although no less true) is management doesn't really do that to make happy employees. They're motivated to make satisfied customers who will produce profits so that management's fed. Customer Satisfaction's the driver for both management and employees.

Most people talk about Customer Service, but there's actually a difference between service and satisfaction. Customer Service is more of an *internal* measure of what the company does to make the customer happy. It really doesn't even consider the customer, only the internal results of company actions. For example, if you answer calls in your call center within twenty seconds 80% of the time and you've set the goal for 80%, then you can fairly say that your Customer Service is what you want it to be. However, it's inwardly focused. It says nothing about how the customers view that level of service. It's as if you fear feedback from customers because they aren't really part of the company. It's almost xenophobic—that unreasonable fear of things foreign or strange to you (i.e., external to you).

Customer Satisfaction, however, is an *external* measure of how well the Customer Service works and how customers respond. It measures the only thing that counts—how happy the customer is.

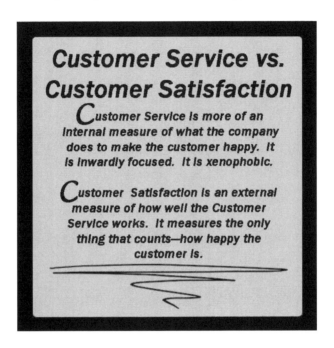

Satisfied Customers . . .

- ➢ buy more
- ➢ recommend you to other potential customers
- ➢ are retained longer (less churn)
- ➢ increase operational efficiency (cost reductions)
  - o fewer complaints to handle
  - o fewer repairs to make
  - o less time responding to needs
  - o fewer questions
- ➢ make for more effective or reduced marketing

Satisfied Customers keep your company in business and provide you personally with gainful employment. Everyone wins.

So why is it that so many vision and mission statements or

even main Principles don't incorporate Customer Satisfaction? At a minimum, you'd think that customers would respond favorably to companies that have that as an objective. How could you as a customer resist this? "Yes, excuse me, sir. Would you mind if I served your every desire?" Okay, maybe that's a little too much flair for the dramatic, but really, would you rather buy your car from a company whose vision is World Class Customer Satisfaction or one whose vision is to make the best cars? If you make a great car, but you treat your customers like dirt, you won't sell many cars over the long haul. However, if you provide World Class Customer Satisfaction, inherently incorporated in that concept is a quality car, otherwise customers wouldn't be satisfied.

Many people make the assumption that World Class Customer Satisfaction means perfection. That's far from the case. Everything's relative to your competition and perfection isn't required to make the vast majority of customers happy.

Take this example.

> Joe and Jim are on a hike in the woods. They carry fifty-pound backpacks and wear clunky hiking boots. They notice a bear some distance away, when suddenly the bear charges them. Both men start to run away from the bear, but Joe quickly stops, sheds his backpack, and takes off his hiking boots. Then he rummages through his backpack, pulls out a pair of running shoes, and hastily laces them on. Jim yells back to his friend, "Joe, what are you doing? The bear's getting closer. It's coming fast! You're losing time. The bear's gonna catch you and eat you even if you do have running shoes!" Standing, Joe takes off in a flash, passing Jim with the comment, "Jim, I don't have to be faster than the bear. I just have to be faster than you."

While this story's a good example of Prioritization (Joe knew the True Priorities, while Jim hadn't quite figured them out yet), it's really meant to point out the meaning of "World Class." You just have to be better than your competition. You may have all sorts of processes that need to be improved, but as long as your processes are better relative to all of your competitors, or at least equal to the best of your competitors, *as experienced by customers*, you're World Class. Since no one's better than you, you're by definition World Class, even if your processes have room for lots of improvement.

Garfield By Jim Davis

In a competitive world, there's no time to pat yourself on the back about the World Class nature of your business. Don't be complacent and satisfied with the status quo in an environment where, objectively, your processes really aren't that good. If customers only buy your product because there's not really a better alternative, then some competitor somewhere will eventually improve their processes and take your customers. The concept of continuous improvement needs to be a part of your organization as much as breathing's a part of living, regardless of how good you are relative to your competitors.

CHAPTER 11—TEAMWORK

How to Achieve True Teamwork

TEAMWORK

Ineffective communication often manifests itself as poor teamwork. It should be no surprise that teamwork has Effective Communication at its foundation. We've talked a lot about the hows and whys of Effective Communication, but in this chapter we'll talk more specifically around teamwork itself—what it means and what it takes to be successful as a team. Teamwork needs at least two entities, but those entities can vary in number and composition.

A COLLECTION OF INDIVIDUALS

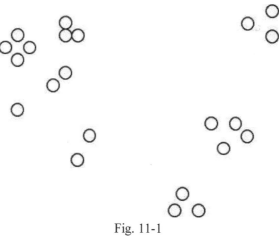

Fig. 11-1

In the above figure, all you have is a bunch of individuals

who occupy the same square footage of real estate. There's little or no communication among the individuals. Everyone has their own agenda. There's nothing to tie them together in a common cause. There may be cliques (the clustered circles in Figure 11-1), but there are no teams. From a success standpoint, if you look at the collection of individuals as a whole, the best they can be is equal to the performance of the best performing individual.

A COLLECTION OF DEPARTMENTS

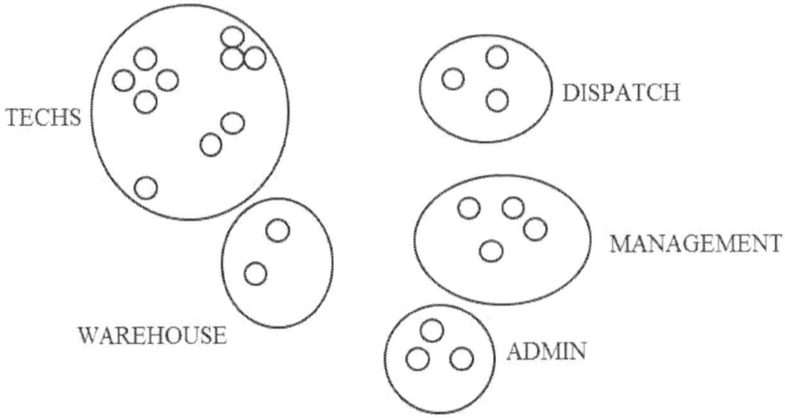

Fig. 11-2

In Figure 11-2, now we've organized the individuals into defined groups or teams. The techs now have something in common with each other and may now begin to act as a team in the best interests of the techs. The other departments can now operate similarly. The problem with this scenario is that each department acts in its own selfish interests to maximize its own individual performance. There's little or no communication among the various departments, although within a given department there may be plenty of communication. Each department's interaction and influence on other departments is restricted, as shown by the individual "bubbles" surrounding the team members. Again, with a look at the whole (i.e., the overall company), the best they can be is equal to the performance of the best performing department. Synergies may appear within a group, but not among groups.

AN EFFECTIVE ORGANIZATION

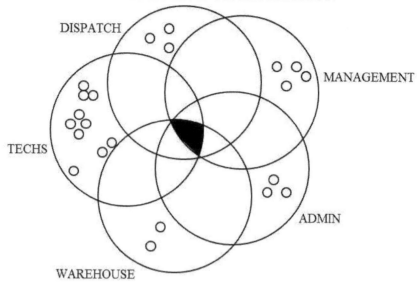

Fig. 11-3

In Figure 11-3, each department has made a conscious effort to expand its interaction and influence with other departments. While each department's still a department unto itself, they haven't isolated each other from each other. They work cooperatively with knowledge of what all other departments do and, perhaps most importantly, understand where overlaps occur. This company has become an effective organization.

The sweet spot of maximum teamwork is depicted by the black center of the diagram. Each department touches every other department so that no one works in isolation. Now the best the company can be is not limited by just the best one individual or department, but by the combined efforts of all. The whole is greater than the sum of the parts. That's synergy.

The above is a nice theoretical discussion, but the practical application to make it a reality is a different story. As a leader, you know that getting your direct report group to work together as a team is easier than trying to get different departmental groups to work together as a team. The reason's simple: you have more control over your own group than you do other groups. However, teams are ultimately a collection of individuals with individual personalities and motivations. Getting everyone in alignment with the common goals is the challenge of management. If everything worked correctly, there wouldn't be a need for management.

Let's get started: A good first step to get your group and other departments in alignment so that they truly become a team might be to present the big picture of what you want to accomplish with the use of the three diagrams above. The process here is no different from what we've already discussed about laying the big picture out first (vision, mission, Principles, values, and strategies) and then getting to the more tactical details of "how" in subsequent discussions.

The organization and structure of the initial meeting is important to get the players on the same page, so some thought should be given to it. When you pull together a team to work on a project, especially an interdepartmental team, the initial meeting needs to begin with some ground rules. Get everyone's buy-in now, in this first meeting. Here again, it starts with big picture and works down to the finer details. The big picture is the reason the team's put together. It's the mission or goal of the team, the problem you try to resolve. What if the purpose was simply stated and related back to either customer satisfaction or a critical business function?

Your meeting agenda might look like this. Let the team know the main purpose from the very beginning. Then go around the table and have people introduce themselves, along with why they think they've been invited to participate. Next, to help get buy-in to the process you want to establish, discuss the concept of teamwork and its role in solving the common problem. After that, you're ready to jump into the finer details of problem definition, who's involved in what aspects, questions that need answered, etc. The big point here is to get that foundation in place first before you jump into the details.

Teamwork has hundreds of definitions and descriptions. I think one of the most compelling is attributed to Andrew Carnegie:

"Teamwork is the ability to *work together* toward a *common vision*. Teamwork is the ability to direct *individual accomplishment* toward *organizational objectives*. Teamwork is the fuel that allows common people to *attain uncommon results*." [My emphasis.]

Let's break down these statements to point out some key phrases that can be used in that initial meeting when you discuss the importance of teamwork. Points to be made are:

- **Work together.** Here you can talk about the need for Effective Communication, not making assumptions or judgments, putting all issues on the table, accountability, doing what you say you'll do, stating your opinions, asking questions, etc.
- **Common vision.** The reason we ask people to introduce themselves and say why they think they've been invited to participate is to create an opening for discussion. You want to make sure that everyone knows their role and how they play a part in the problem to be solved. If someone doesn't know why they're there, they won't be an effective team member. You may find that some invitees really don't play a part and can be excused.
- **Individual accomplishment.** Here you can talk about personal responsibility and the need for full engagement by the individual members.
- **Organizational objectives.** Impress on everyone that the company has Prioritized this as something to be aggressively worked. Before the invitations went out to the participants, you should have met with their upper management and obtained their buy-in to the necessity of the project. You should have negotiated with them that they'll be okay with this project pushing some other items off the plates of the members and that sufficient time will be provided to make the project succeed. The department heads also need to

understand how you think their department can contribute to the resolution of the issue. Once the department heads know the issue, they should be able to recommend people who would be the best contributors.

- **Uncommon results.** Here again, you can trumpet that the problem impacts different departments and the company has Prioritized it for action. Frequently when a project team is formed, it addresses an issue that's been around for months or years. Be clear that this team's the one that'll solve the problem that no one else could. Create a sense of importance and *esprit de corps* for the team. If people take pride in their task, they're more likely to succeed.

For some motivational value, you could share some of the following thought-provoking quotes about teamwork. Know that in constructing this list, there were hundreds to choose from, which in itself lends credibility to the value of teamwork. Lots of people profess the importance of teamwork, so there must be something to it. I went through a Prioritization exercise to Simplify the list down to sixteen. I'm tellin' ya, the Big Four Principles have applications everywhere.

Teamwork Definitions and Observations

"In teamwork, silence isn't golden, it's deadly." [Purkey's note: in essence, Effective Communication is critical.]
—Mark Sanborn (motivational speaker)

"The way a team plays as a whole determines its success. You may have the greatest bunch of individual stars in the world, but if they don't play together, the club won't be worth a dime."
—Babe Ruth (professional baseball player)

"Gettin' good players is easy. Gettin' 'em to play together is the hard part."

—Casey Stengel (professional baseball manager)

"No matter what accomplishments you make, somebody helped you."

—Althea Gibson (professional tennis player)

"Light is the task where many share the toil."

—Homer (Greek poet, author of *Iliad, Odyssey*)

"There is no 'I' in 'TEAMWORK.'"

—Unknown [Purkey's note: . . . but there is an "I" in WIN.]

"One man can be a crucial ingredient on a team, but one man cannot make a team."

—Kareem Abdul-Jabbar (professional basketball player)

"Teamwork: the whole is greater than the sum of the parts."

—Unknown

"Teamwork divides the task and doubles the success."

—Unknown

"None of us is as smart as all of us."

—Ken Blanchard (management expert, author of *The One Minute Manager*)

"People who work together will win, whether it be against complex football defenses or the problems of modern society."

—Vince Lombardi (professional football coach)

"Coming together is a beginning.
Keeping together is progress.
Working together is success."
      —Henry Ford (founder of Ford Motor Company)

"We must all hang together or, assuredly, we shall all hang separately."
      —Benjamin Franklin (diplomat, inventor)

"Teams are successful when they are focused, have a short cycle time, and are ***supported by the executives***." [Purkey's note: my emphasis added]
      —Tom Bouchard (psychology professor)

"Effective teamwork will not take the place of knowing how to do the job or how to manage the work. Poor teamwork, however, can prevent effective final performance."
      —Robert F. Bales (social psychologist)

"I've got gaps, she's got gaps. Together we've got no gaps."
      —Rocky (Sylvester Stallone), from the movie *Rocky*

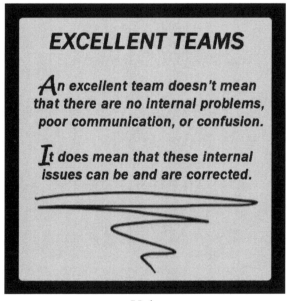

EXCELLENT TEAMS

An excellent team doesn't mean that there are no internal problems, poor communication, or confusion.

It does mean that these internal issues can be and are corrected.

—Unknown

If I Prioritized and Simplified even further to get down to just one quote, I'd keep the last one about Excellent Teams. It incorporates a lot of the concepts around Effective Communication that drive so many situations. It's a practical view of things, in that it recognizes that everything's not always perfect and that people are involved. The fact that "the internal issues can be and are corrected" encompasses continuous improvement, raising business issues, willingness to change, Effective Communication, and other concepts we've covered so far.

From Ronald R. Short in *Leading Groups: Models, Concepts, and Theory* (1988), an excellent team has these characteristics:

> ➢ Informed decisions are made.
> ➢ Individuals feel empowered.
> ➢ Communications are clear or can be cleared up.
> ➢ Expertise is shared.
> ➢ Members are committed to the task and the other members.
> ➢ Results are achieved; goals are met.

An important point not to be overlooked is that each point is related to Effective Communication, except perhaps the last, which is the culmination of the Effective Communication.

~~~~~~

The Foundations of Teamwork and Interdepartmental Interactions

Let's take a closer look at Kareem Abdul-Jabbar's comment that "One man can be a crucial ingredient on a team, but one man cannot make a team." Often overlooked in the hype about teamwork and its importance is that the team must have some level of excellent talent on it to succeed. Given equal individual talent on two teams, the one that better incorporates teamwork Principles will win. However, it's generally true that if the individual talent level on a team is sub-par, the team as a whole will be, too. Teamwork will allow that team to do better than the collection of separate individuals, but if the end product is sub-par, then what good was teamwork, really?

The construction of a team requires thought and an assessment of the talent level of the people chosen to be on the team. Abdul-Jabbar's "crucial ingredient" really means a talented individual, or, better, multiple talented individuals. As the manager who forms the team, you've got to ensure that appropriate people with the needed expertise are on the team and not just a collection of people who volunteered or you conscripted to take part for lack of volunteers. It's about engagement in the effort. If the team believes they'll succeed, they likely will. That belief's driven in large part by understanding that they have a collection of talented individuals to begin with.

So, choose your team members wisely. It's important to future success. But where do you start with that selection? In alignment with the Principle of finding root causes, start with yourself. Know yourself first. Know your group second. Know other departments third.

Objective self-assessment's a tough thing to do, but with some introspection and literally asking yourself what you're good at and what you're weak at, you'll find what the team needs. Of course, this is all relative to the vision or mission statement of what the team's supposed to do. As we've talked about, you need that North Star defined so that all actions can be put into alignment with that goal. Your self-assessment needs to be in terms of what you bring to the table relative to the goal/mission of the team.

Suppose you form a team to speed up assembly of a car. If you know you're great at organization, then perhaps you don't need other team members to have that strong characteristic, since you can provide organizational help as needed. If you know you're weak technically in your knowledge of how parts go together, then you'll want to select a person who's a mechanical or engineering wizard.

This all seems pretty obvious when written down, but I've seen plenty of ineffective teams thrown together in response to some boss's directive. Keep Purkey's Law of the Seven Ps in mind and approach the formation of the team deliberately. A commonly seen quote from an unknown source is "Planning's not about what we will do in the future, it's about what we will do *now* to make the future all we want it to be." For this step of team formation, the "now" is to assess yourself and your potential team members' skills properly relative to the goal you want to reach.

Like anything else, Simplification also plays a role to get a team together. You can spend so much time to try to get the exact, perfect players on the team and to understand everyone's strengths and weaknesses that the costs begin to outweigh the benefits. Don't get hung up in the briar patch of AT&Tization (see Chapter 9).

At the XYZ Company, annual evaluations had just been completed with one-on-one sessions between employees and their supervisors. Yes, it's a time-consuming process, but if built into the standard work schedule, it doesn't need to be disruptive to regular, daily work. That's a good practice in theory, but the XYZ Company does things a little differently. Just two months after the evaluations, Human Resources (HR) determined that it didn't have enough information on the necessary training needed in the company. If the evaluations were correctly structured and conducted, this information would have been captured, but HR found the information lacked specificity. They formed a team (composed of HR people only, which should have been a red flag) and determined that they wanted all technical employees to fill out a questionnaire in a one-to-one session with their supervisors. Each session would be scheduled to last up to two hours because, apparently, they needed excruciating detail. HR suggested it be comparable to an evaluation, even though they'd been done just two months ago. HR had just set up an interdepartmental conflict

HR lost their way in that they failed to look at the team goal in big picture terms. They failed to capture their real goal correctly at the start and consequently went down a rabbit hole of detail that was the opposite of administrative simplicity. Ultimately, XYZ had a big picture need—*macro* types of training needed and wanted by employees. However, HR attempted to use a *micro* methodology. Its proposal would have used up to forty tech-hours (a week of lost productivity) for some groups that had just gone through a very similar exercise with the annual evaluations. The proposal defined redundant and unnecessary.

Operations stated their concern about the additional tech-hours it would take to meet HR's interview requirements, particularly since customer installations and repairs would be impacted. Operations stayed focused on the customer.

Although both Operations and HR shared the common goal to assess training needs, they had conflicting opinions on how to get there. Operations suggested completing the questionnaire in a group environment and finishing the task in two-plus hours versus forty. This approach would still get feedback directly from the frontline, but it would take much less organizational time with less customer impact.

HR (out of alignment with the customer focus Principle) objected that the self-assessment of training needs represented a personal, individual task and should be done in private sessions so as not to embarrass any given tech. If a tech had a question as to his degree of competency on a given question, the tech might be reluctant to express that in a public environment, according to the HR theory.

HR hadn't accounted for the fact that management posted all technical metrics in the tech room, so everyone already knew each other's rankings and effectiveness. There were no secrets in this island of an open, communicating environment at the XYZ Company. (Even a company like XYZ has its shining moments.)

What if everyone knew how everyone else was measured so that they could all assist each other to meet their goals? This creates an interdependency and forces people to look outside of their own little personal world. It gets them to see the big picture and gets them to understand the strategies, as well as help them see exactly where their contributions rank with their peers. In a teaching, teamwork environment, peers can help each other with their weak spots, further reducing your workload as the manager.

HR's method assumed secrecy, the unwritten cultural standard at XYZ. Operations' method relied on open communication, combined with a need for operational efficiency (two-plus hours versus forty) to get the same result. Both departments ultimately agreed on Operations' method, but, this being the XYZ Company, the effort produced no new training programs due to it never being Truly Prioritized by either department.

Interdepartmental interactions are often tricky because each department may be invested in its own individual success without consideration of the grander team/company needs. This narrow, siloed view of the world isn't conducive to efficiency or effectiveness. The problem is that when a team is formed to accomplish a theoretically mutual goal, departments come to the table as peers. No one department has control over another department. Kind of like the United Nations. Once again, the value of strong and clear Principles comes into play. Alignment with Principles is what makes for successful teams with the use of:

- The ability to refer back to Principles that have already been agreed on;
- The ability to openly discuss how any given action or proposal by a department is or isn't in alignment with that already agreed to Principle;
- The willingness to change a proposal or re-prioritize it.

~~~~~~

An Example of Conflicting Departments

A quick caveat before you read this section. There are a number of different lessons incorporated in this one story. It shows how a single issue that starts with a surface symptom can mushroom into a tangled web of several causes. While the story is therefore necessarily a bit long, think of it as a mini-summary of how to apply various techniques you've learned so far.

The XYZ Company formed an interdepartmental team to make the process to dispatch technicians more efficient and to make the installers' daily routes more efficient so they wouldn't spend so much drive time between appointments. Organizationally, Dispatch and Installation constituted separate departments—peer departments with different individual agendas, but unrecognized common larger priorities. The managers of each department viewed themselves as separate but equal, versus players on a common team with common goals. On an org chart, the two functions didn't come together at a common leader until three layers up the management chain. Consequently, issues dragged on as disputes took longer to find a judge who could rule more impartially.

Dispatch developed the daily schedules for the techs and acted as an overall air traffic control to know the location of each tech at any given moment, ostensibly to help the installers. However, when changes to the schedule needed to occur, conflict erupted with the techs. Management had not clearly defined the roles of each group. In an environment where no one wanted to step on the toes of another department's perceived responsibilities or have their own toes stepped on, they couldn't act as an effective team.

Over the course of time, somehow the techs had usurped the authority to change the schedule on the fly and frequently just said "no" when asked to rearrange their route. Techs resented always being told to change the schedule and came to believe that the schedule at the start of the day held little relevance to their actual day. Techs look for some stability in their days instead of being yanked willy-nilly from place to place like marionettes. In the absence of clear direction from management, techs filled the vacuum with their own procedures that worked best for them, regardless of overall company (or customer) impact.

As this culture developed, Dispatch came to believe it didn't have the authority to order a tech to take another job outside of the initial schedule. They didn't want to plead and hassle with techs who said "no," so Dispatch simply turned the problem over to the Installation managers for resolution. Eventually the Installation managers became frustrated that Dispatch abdicated its "air traffic control" function, while Dispatch became frustrated that techs wouldn't take new work.

But more than frustration played a role here. Installation managers were too busy to do their jobs. They didn't realize that the additional time invested to supplement Dispatch's job contributed to that. As departmental conflicts became more frequent, the total amount of time lost from involving techs, dispatchers, Installation management, and Dispatch management greatly exceeded the time it took for Dispatch to just work it out with the techs—the original problem.

Finally, frustrations on everyone's part got to the point that Installation and Dispatch management sat down to correct the situation. Effective Communication ensued and management overtly agreed on a common Principle (Dispatch = air traffic control) that had been in place before, but which hadn't had the continuous engagement by management in order to see that it was worked in practice. Generally, if Dispatch said jump, the techs needed to ask how high.

Thankfully, managers went further and looked for not so obvious root causes. Both dispatchers and techs agreed that too many schedule changes occurred, so managers redirected the project team to reduce changes. Managers brought both dispatchers and techs into the same room at the same time and provided clear direction that techs could question changes, but dispatchers had the ultimate authority. Techs couldn't simply say "no" anymore. However, dispatchers also had the obligation to explain why they made the change and what alternatives they'd explored. Managers asked them to adjust their attitude towards schedule changes. Techs agreed to incorporate that as part of the job they were hired to do instead of thinking of it as something "extra" to do, with the *quid pro quo* that efforts would be made to reduce the number of changes.

Effective Communication, Alignment with Principles, clear direction, addressing both sides' concerns to find a middle ground, and a willingness to change all came together to smooth the troubled waters of Dispatch and Installation interaction. The sooner managers employ these basic Principles, the sooner interdepartmental wars are resolved. Had this work been done earlier, the interdepartmental war never would have occurred in the first place.

Working with customers is really no different from working interdepartmentally or even just working with others on your direct team. In order to get customers to buy your product or service, you need to persuade them that there's value for them to make a purchasing decision and then provide that value.

In order to get other departments to cooperate with you, you need to understand the motivations of that department. What are their goals? What are their Priorities? When you construct your team for any given project, you need to persuade the other department that what you're after is what they're after—that there's an alignment of common causes. If you can't do that by incorporating one of their stated departmental goals, then you have to go back to the larger Principles and goals set for the company and demonstrate how their assistance will further those Principles and goals.

As a side note to the above example, the project team decided to implement a more automated system for Dispatch to reduce the number of changes that needed to be made. However, lack of engagement by Dispatch management led to further complications. Remember, as a manager, if it's important enough for you to take your time to come up with a plan, it should be important enough to you to see that it's properly executed. See Chapter 2. Dispatch management forgot this basic premise. It was the XYZ Company, after all.

They had one person trained as part of a beta test on the new automated system for Dispatch. The test went very well, as the beta dispatcher outperformed (per measurable metrics) other dispatchers in his ability to route more jobs in less time and provide better route efficiency that required fewer changes.

However, other dispatchers had a reluctance to use the automated system. "I've always done it the way I do it." "The automated system isn't always reliable." "The automated system's too complicated." Dispatch management chalked it up to fear of change and tried to ease the new system into practice. They basically hoped that the beta dispatcher would spread the good word and others would jump on board when they saw the advantages. Dispatch management used this extreme laissez-faire approach because they were too busy to support the change. They hadn't really, Truly Prioritized effective implementation of the automated system, despite their advocacy for it in the project team meetings. Dispatch management clearly lacked integrity and accountability.

The lack of follow through meant that the other dispatchers didn't get the proper training on the system. The person trained wasn't comfortable training others, although Dispatch management *assumed* this would be the way forward. Dispatch management had let the vendor-provided automated system trainer leave, *assuming* since they'd trained one person, they'd trained everyone. Eventually the automated system got implemented fully, but the disengaged management team made it a bit more painful and slow than it needed to be. Be engaged.

CHAPTER 12—MEASURING
How to Use Goals, Deadlines, and Evaluations

We discussed the Eight Steps to Operational Brilliance in Chapter 9. Step 5 is to establish measurable goals and deadlines for the tactics at both group and individual levels. In this chapter, we'll expand on that topic a bit with a few more perspectives.

Let's start with deadlines. The XYZ Company had some problems with the timely delivery of the annual bonuses and employees became disgruntled. The owner correctly assessed the mood of his employees and met with Finance to determine a reasonable timeframe for them to produce checks. At the first of the month, the owner made the declaration that bonuses would be in people's hands no later than the 20th of the month, come hell or high water. While somewhat skeptical based on past performance, everyone accepted the 20th as a reasonable time, given the owner's passionate, public declaration. He had the ball clearly in his court and put the credibility and integrity of executive leadership on the line.

Doing what you say you'll do, when you say you'll do it is the essence of integrity. The owner wanted to make sure the deadline wouldn't be missed. Now, think of the credibility that would have been demonstrated by actually handing out the bonus checks on the 20th. Expectations had been set, everyone agreed to them, and if delivery occurred exactly on the 20th, he would have had hero status.

But his approach to that goal blended "more is always better" with Pendulum Management in his drive to be a hero. His thinking?

If a 20th delivery would make him a hero, a delivery even earlier, say on the 10th, would make him a god.

So, back to Finance he went and demanded that they produce the bonus checks by the 10th. Now, every department in any company has its own rhythms, its own business-as-usual processes. (Okay, granted that those rhythms often are chaotic, but they're rhythms nonetheless.) Disruptions to those rhythms cause frustrations and inefficiencies. I call them reactionary inefficiencies, because whenever you have to react to something (a problem, a new process, a new employee, etc.), by definition you don't do things in the fashion you'd planned. Additional effort's required to move off plan and re-orient to the new situation. That's inefficient. The owner didn't realize that he introduced inefficiencies into his business; he just thought he was doing a good thing and wanted the bonuses by the 10th. Finance had to figure out how to do that.

Needless to say, Finance moved into a full-on panic mode. The owner's arbitrary escalation had put them on an unnecessarily tighter schedule than what they'd already assessed they could comfortably do and agreed to. The owner might have wanted to gain credibility with the employee body at large, but he certainly ruined it with Finance.

Extra, unplanned work was introduced in order to speed up the process to deliver early. People had to be pulled from other projects in order to accommodate this new deadline. Accounts payable was delayed, which created late payments to vendors and affected company credibility. Accounts receivable delayed sending out bills, which decreased cash flow.

Finance was beset by unnecessarily created stress, chaos, and resentment as an unexpected, arbitrary deadline loomed, in an imprudent attempt to jam in something that really didn't need to be jammed.

If you have more control of your schedule, you'll be a more effective manager. You'll have time to do your job. With the "drop everything" approach, events take control of you (OBE—Overcome By Events). You don't plan, you don't think, you just do. Effective managers need time to plan and think. If you're efficient, you'll have that time, which will make you more efficient, which will give you more time.

As an effective manager, you need to assess whether the crisis of the moment is really a crisis that needs attention right now. Err on the side that it doesn't, since many crises are simply manufactured by the people who bring them to you. You need to keep your cool while others about you panic. Be the eye of the hurricane where winds are calm. It's your duty as a leader to model the 7 Ps. Use deadlines, but use them judiciously and with meaning. Commit to true engagement to help meet them.

~~~~~~

Scamming the Metrics: Example

Lean management has metrics at its core. Because Lean started in the manufacturing arena where tolerances of part sizes and assembly times are critical, numbers naturally lent themselves to find out if a process worked correctly. Humans, statisticians, and mathematicians being what they are and with the predilection for Pendulum Management always in play, Lean can get into grueling detail. It can almost become a statistics class. A non-statistician could wonder if an analysis is done for the sake of demonstrating mathematical prowess rather than to get some actual, useful, practical information with which to make management decisions.

Now don't get me wrong. I've already come down strongly on the side of metrics. See Chapter 7, among other references. Without them, your business simply can't improve. But they need to be the right metrics—ones with practical value. Remember the four Principles of a proper metric seen in Chapter 7:

1. Directly applicable to the behavior desired and used to coach that behavior—a behavioral metric
2. Largely in control of the person measured
3. Administratively simple
4. Used to uncover and correct process or efficiency issues

With any metrics, and in alignment with a skeptical manager

who questions, you need to ask yourself whether the metrics tell you what really happens or what you want to hear. Do they truly measure the behavior you seek to implement or improve?

The XYZ Company knew that being on time for installation appointments drove customer satisfaction. XYZ attempted to evaluate this notion by measuring the time it took to complete jobs compared to the standard, "by-the-book" time. They theorized that the faster a job was completed, the more satisfied a customer would be. Now why they chose to measure that instead of directly recording the time that the tech knocked on the door versus the time promised to the customer, I can't tell you. It violated the first Principle of a proper metric. But, for that particular metric they chose to measure, many techs had uncannily good results. In fact, some had a 100% on time completion record over lengthy periods, yet others couldn't seem to finish on time more that 75% of the time.

Management, working with Principle 4 of a proper metric, decided to dig in and find the root causes for the differential. They discovered that the techs had a little secret—the techs could manually input their time of completion and override the automated system. The 100% techs used the manual method to put in whatever time they wanted and the 75% techs had the integrity to let the automated system record the actual situation. The 100% techs weren't actually 100%, they just had gamed the system to make their numbers look good on their scorecards.

The XYZ Company hadn't yet established the culture in which employees raised their hands without fear of retribution when they saw business issues. While the lower percentage techs resented the 100% techs (which created its own set of personnel problems), they were afraid to spill the beans to management. So the problem continued.

Once the business issue found the light of day, management discussed integrity with the techs, gained agreement of all to use the automated system, and then addressed how to improve the completion times. While completion times improved as a result of using metrics to uncover problems—a good thing—the process did nothing to determine how to really improve customer satisfaction.

Use metrics to uncover problems, but also use the right metrics that tie employee behavior to customer satisfaction.

~~~~~~

Scorecards

Scorecards are simply a set of metrics that are tracked on either an individual basis or a departmental basis (regardless of the size of the department). Constructed properly, scorecards really are job descriptions put into numerical form. They Prioritize how people should spend their time and set more clear expectations that everyone understands.

Scorecards might be the ultimate application for metrics, with the caution that scorecards must be properly implemented. Primarily by that, I mean Simplified. Once you discover the power of metrics to induce the behavior you look for from your team (behavioral metrics), the tendency is to over use them. The thought often goes that if three metrics are good, then six must be better. And, well, if six are better, then ten must be simply "mahvelous" (with a nod to Billy Crystal). While we've talked about this tendency before, it bears repeating to not fall into that common trap.

Individual metrics must be linked to the departmental metrics and, in fact, they're often the same. If you want to measure *a person* on the accuracy of her order inputs, then it'll also be important to understand where your *department* is on order accuracy. All the metrics drive customer satisfaction or efficient critical internal processes.

Ideally, scorecards should be limited to five or so significant, measurable, accountable goals per person or department. Get many more than that and people won't be able to keep them all in mind, with the result of a lack of results. Focus on a few. Get good at those, make sure they're stable over time, and then maybe you can substitute (not add) a new metric into the mix.

Your job as a manager is to keep your team focused on those

scorecard metrics. Create communication around them. Publish results regularly. Reward top performers. Keep them alive and fresh to maintain people's engagement and perform to their best capability.

In addition to driving desired behavior, the other main benefit of scorecards is for annual (or more frequent, if your company's more enlightened) evaluation purposes. When people's raises and bonuses are inextricably tied to performance as defined by scorecards, those scorecards take on a level of significance that demands employee attention. They help keep people on the rails.

The main objection to scorecards in an XYZ Company environment is "You just want something to beat me up with come evaluation time." The level of paranoia that exists in business about the true motivations of management is surprising to me. Management's generally not trusted, often with good reason, so maybe the paranoia is justified. Just because you're paranoid doesn't mean they're not out to get you.

Your job is to buck that perception and show people that you have not only the company's best interests at heart, but theirs, too. While my cynical response to the "beat me up" objection is to say, "Well . . . yes," it's important to overcome that little devil who sits on your shoulder and keep that response to yourself, regardless of how amusing or true it may be. The real purpose of scorecards is to look for ways to improve (in a culture of continuous improvement) and to reward those who do what's expected of them. They're not a vendetta to punish people; they're there to help.

Another objection to scorecards is "I do a lot more than what those numbers say. It's not fair to evaluate me just with a scorecard." Those are true statements and must be honored. Pendulum Management often rears its ugly head here, too. Some companies attempt to make scorecards 100% of the evaluation. While that adheres to the Simplification Principle, this cut-and-dried approach isn't in the spirit of what an overall evaluation should be. For example, how do you quantify attitude or interaction with teammates or so many other subjective qualities that comprise the ideal employee? A person's contribution to the company simply can't be fully stated by metrics. Accordingly, as with most Pendulum Management situations, we've got to reject the extreme idea of evaluations based on 100% scorecards. Similarly, we've got to reject those evaluations that are 100% based on subjective opinions.

≈≈≈≈≈

A Word about Evaluations

What if evaluations were mostly objective in order to avoid favoritism or even perceived favoritism? While evaluations are theoretically supposed to be private, the practical reality is that people talk. When word starts to circulate that you've given someone a high rating only because you liked the person, your credibility as a manager drops dramatically. Cynicism starts to grow in the group. You'll find yourself confronted by a whole different set of problems that'll suck your time to deal with the perceived (true or not) group dynamics. The ability to back your ratings with observable, quantifiable metrics makes for a healthier team. The team members will know that it's their performance that determines their raise, bonus, and promotion opportunities, not whom the manager likes.

In a metrics-driven culture, I've found that a 70% metrics, 30% subjective mix to determine an evaluation rating satisfies both employees and managers. That subjective 30% is your responsibility as a manager to do with as you please (though most likely within some broad HR guidelines). Just remember that absolute power corrupts absolutely.

Managers aren't hired to be automatons that simply plug numbers into spreadsheets. They're hired to coach, guide, encourage, discipline, drive, and judge their teams. In theory, a manager has a bigger picture in mind and more overall business experience than a frontline employee. You get paid to put your expertise to use and that needs to count in that 30% subjective portion of an evaluation.

Somewhat ironically, this 70/30 mix is mostly a process to plug numbers into a spreadsheet and have a rating pop out—a decidedly objective, numbers-based process without any subjectivity.

Each metric needs to be weighted based on how you (and/or the company) perceive its importance to produce customer satisfaction or support critical internal business processes. Human Resources certainly needs to be involved to determine the weightings, mostly to ensure that peer groups are evaluated in the same way, regardless of manager.

This is pretty basic to most companies so I won't spend much time on it, but generally, a 1 to 5 rating scheme for each metric makes the most sense and is easiest to administer, with a 5 the best and a 1 the worst. HR will always assist to attach definitions to each rating. Just make sure they're clear.

For example, a 1 usually gets something like "needs immediate improvement" attached to it, while a 5 usually gets "outstanding" or "excellent" attached to it. A 3 rating should define the expected performance. In the interest of Effective Communication, it's helpful to elaborate about what observable behaviors constitute the ratings. For metrics ratings, it's really a matter of defining up front what the score means based on the performance relative to the goal. Note that, since nobody's perfect, perfection shouldn't be expected. Accordingly, with rare exceptions, goals shouldn't have an expected target of 100%.

The Appendix contains a detailed example of how this simple system would be implemented to produce an overall rating for Tom.

When you've completed this process for all of your team, you'll now have an accurate and convenient way to stack rank your employees so you can easily see who your best performers are and who will need more coaching. In the event of company personnel cutbacks, knowing who to keep and who to let go is critical. That decision can now be made based on measured performance instead of who's the boss's buddy.

This system can produce some surprising results when newly introduced into a company that uses predominately subjective appraisals. For example, as a new manager, in order to get the lay of the land, I asked each of my direct report managers to stack rank their employees from top to bottom and also asked them to explain their rationale. A few months later we introduced the 70/30 system and the order in the stack ranks shifted substantially from the favoritism-based subjective stack ranks originally submitted. It opened some eyes. Because we now had a predominantly objective-based evaluation system, we had much more confidence in who represented our best people and could focus our efforts on those who needed more help.

Something that also seems pretty basic but isn't seen in many companies is that goals should be in terms of percentages rather than absolute numbers (sales being an obvious exception). Absolute numbers generally drive the wrong behavior. For example, if you measure someone on the number of loan applications processed per day, you incent the person to push through as many as possible regardless of quality. Customers don't care how many applications a processor completes, they only care about the quality and timeliness of their particular application. A better measurement might be the percentage of applications without any errors. Carried to an extreme, a focus on absolute numbers can negatively affect the business, as banks found out with their "robo-signature" process during the real estate crisis in the 2000s, to the tune of millions of dollars in fines.

~~~~~

Excellent Companies

Ever notice the tendency of groups to proclaim their superiority over other groups, even without any objective criteria to back up the claim? "We're an excellent company!" is the refrain, but let's look at what that really means from a more logical, objective perspective.

At the XYZ Company (an "excellent company" per their marketing department), management believed that when it came to bonuses, high performers should get more than lower performers. That makes sense and is in alignment with the Principle of fairness. However, Finance, HR, and upper management wanted to limit the number of evaluations that could be rated a 5 (best). They demanded that, when they viewed all evaluations in totality, there had to be a bell-shaped curve distribution of ratings from 1 to 5, with the 3 rating (average) at the peak of the bell. Given that a bell-shaped curve describes the average situation by definition, XYZ had defined itself as average. If most of your employees are average, again by definition, you can't have an excellent company, you can only have an average company.

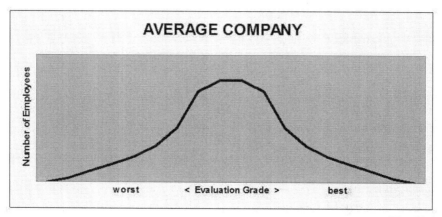

Fig. 12-1

Imagine the demotivating conversation with an otherwise excellent rated employee. "Gee, I'm sorry, Bob. I really wanted to rate you as a 5, but as you know, I've only been allotted one space for a 5 on my team. Unfortunately, I chose someone else, so I'll rate you a 4 this year. However, I really like the work you do, so please keep it up."

Consider what really makes an excellent company and you'll have to conclude that it's excellent employees. Therefore, a truly excellent company can't have the bulk of their employees be average; they must be better than that. Evaluations should reflect the nature of that situation. A distribution of all evaluation ratings in an excellent company should look like this:

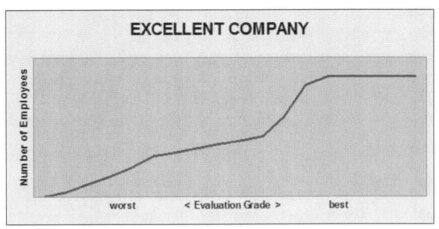

Fig. 12-2

The driver at the XYZ Company was the dollars budgeted for bonuses—including $10,000 for a 5 rating. The constraint of the bell-shaped curve was of their own design, a box they'd put themselves in but which they couldn't see. In their zeal to reward "the best" with a fantastic bonus—an amount they thought would make everyone strive to be a 5 in order to incent everyone to work harder—they'd set an arbitrary amount of bonus for each of the rating categories (more for 5s and less for others), developed a budgetary dollar total for each category, and capped the number of people who could be in any given category.

They'd essentially rated all of the employees before the actual evaluations took place.

The ABC Company, an actual excellent company, also had a budget for bonuses. However, they simply let the math determine how much of a bonus the employees received. Instead of a predetermined bonus dollar amount for any given rating level, they predetermined that a 5 should get twice the bonus of a 4 and a 4 should get twice the bonus of a 3, and a 2 should get half the bonus of a 3. Managers could rate anyone any rating level without constraint, based on the 70/30 Principle. They expected that the bulk of the employees would be rated 4s or 5s because ABC personified an excellent company, producing best in class financial returns and customer satisfaction.

See the Appendix for how the math works out for the various amounts of bonus for a given bonus money pool at each of the companies. If you're not mathematically inclined, I don't want to bore you here with that analysis. I'll bore you in the Appendix.

The major difference is that at XYZ, the top bonus was substantially bigger, but the number of people who could achieve it was substantially smaller. The top bonus at XYZ was akin to winning the lottery. ABC employees had a much greater motivation to achieve that 5 level, since it was realistically achievable with the right performance. That continuous improvement attitude is what allowed ABC to succeed where XYZ failed. Why?

- The top bonus at XYZ presented a nice shiny opportunity, but few could get it. With the arbitrary number of 5s pre-determined, management couldn't guarantee that if a 4 performed better next year that they would get the higher rating. Similarly, the 1s, 2s, and 3s had virtually no hope to reach a 5 rating because of the artificial cap on the numbers in each category. XYZ's management theory to motivate everyone to do better dissolved in the face of the employees' knowledge that even if they did do better, they'd never see the ten grand.
- Employees at XYZ viewed the process as inherently unfair, since their true performance often didn't get captured by the rating.
- ABC, through their metrics-dominated evaluations (70/30) actually identified the poor performers. At XYZ, many poor performers got lumped into the 3 category, but because they were "average" as defined by the 3 rating, no one paid attention to coaching them. ABC management could target the true poor performers and coach them up or, if necessary, coach them out.

ABC's method inherently focused on the bottom 10% of performers for improvement or dismissal. That meant the overall company performance could improve more than XYZ's method to try to motivate the top 10%. It's common knowledge in most management circles that you get more bang for the buck for overall company improvement by coaching up your bottom 10%. While you don't want to ignore the top 10%, the theory is they're already motivated, talented people, so they shouldn't need as much of your limited time. They can operate without much management interference.

The bottom 10%, however, can drag your company down into the muck. It's really an illustration of the old 80/20 rule that 80% of your problems are caused by 20% of your people. If you understand from a customer perspective that you can eliminate the vast majority of your problems by improving a minimum number of employees, you can take advantage of that leverage.

See the Appendix for the math that proves the truth of the theory. The bottom line is that if you want to move the needle the most on your company's overall performance, focus your energies on the bottom 10% of your employees.

With this focus on the bottom 10%, you'll quickly uncover the problem children and the incorrigible. Make no mistake that the best approach to the long-term health of the company and your limited time is first to coach these folks up to the standards you have.

But don't fool yourself that you can save everyone. You can put lipstick on a pig, but it's still a pig. Some people want to create chaos in their lives and others' lives. Some people thrive on the misery of others. Some people think if they take advantage of others ("There's a sucker born every minute" mentality), that bolsters their own place in society. Some people are lazy. Some people are incorrigible. After a legitimate effort (however undefined), if you can't teach them how a business succeeds from a focus on Effective Communication, people, and processes, then make a change. Lead, follow, or get out of the way. These types need to be moved out of the way.

~~~~~~

Certifications

Job title certifications are beneficial to create a sense of pride in the workforce. They fit hand-in-glove with excellent companies that use evaluations and metrics. Normally when a new person's hired into a position, they receive some limited formal training, then some on the job training, and then they're thrown to the wolves. It's *assumed* that they should know their job, but seldom are they tested for it. While evaluations should reveal weaknesses to be strengthened over time, who determines that the person is even qualified to do what they were hired to do? Certifications provide the answer to that.

Certifications are designed to say that a given person is skilled in the minimum requirements needed for their job title. Auto repair shops are generally great at getting their repair techs various defined certifications. National certification standards organizations exist to provide definition to the minimum requirements of competency, such as the National Institute for Automotive Service Excellence (ASE). However, most job titles don't have national certification standards. There simply aren't national standards for call center reps or administrative assistants or clerks or thousands of other job titles.

If you don't have certifications, create them. Take a hard look at what the minimum behaviors are for a given job (Prioritization), metricize them, document them, and put them into a certification program. Those criteria are really the first evaluation template for a new person in that job title. Once certified, then regular evaluations kick in to assess the degree of expertise beyond the minimum.

At the XYZ Company, Central Office Technicians (COT) had three different levels of supposed competency. A tech started as a COT I and, after some undefined period for undefined reasons (mostly because the boss liked him), eventually got promoted to a COT II. After some additional undefined period for still undefined reasons (mostly because the boss liked him), he eventually got promoted to a COT III. Each promotion came with an associated pay bump, but no one really knew why the promotions occurred other than political lobbying by the boss.

The ABC Company also had COT I, II, and III positions, but they also had a certification program with the minimum skills required for each level clearly outlined. Demonstrate through actions that you met the competency requirements for a COT III and you immediately got the promotion. No badgering the boss for a raise, no political wrangling by the boss on your behalf with HR, just prove your worth against a defined set of standards and you win.

As opposed to XYZ where you dead-ended at a COT III level, ABC created advanced certifications that tied to additional expertise and further tied to additional pay increases. ABC created lifelong techs who relished their work, could advance up the ladder, and were paid accordingly. How much time do you think the manager of a multiple certified COT III spent with that person? You want more time to do your job? Create a path of success for your people with defined certifications. The automotive industry has already laid out the plan for the rest of us. We just need to apply it to your company.

CHAPTER 13—MUSINGS

How to Round Out Your Management Expertise

~~~~~~

This chapter's really a potpourri of ideas to help you manage better. These miscellaneous musings deserve a spotlight of their own so that you can more clearly understand and incorporate them into your daily routines. Each one will help you find the time to do your job.

~~~~~~

Be Specific

Be specific and demand specificity from others. Don't settle for generalities. Generalities usually contain assumptions and we know where that leads. Generalities are used by those who want to spin the truth to make you believe what they want you to believe without actually doing what needs done. Generalities are used by those who don't necessarily have a good handle on whatever task they're supposed to manage. Generalities will require either additional follow up or clean up on your part as deadlines and tasks get missed. Generalities contribute to you not having enough time. Did I use the word "generalities" enough in this paragraph to make the point that you shouldn't settle for generalities?

"Soon" is the classic example of a generality. "Oh, yes, I'll have that done soon." "Soon" is not a number. "Soon" is not a deadline. Who defines what "soon" means in terms that are mutually understandable? Whenever you hear the word "soon," red flags should pop into your mind immediately. Stop the conversation then and there and get specifics as to what "soon" means in terms of hours, days, weeks, or months. Your job as a manager is to hold people (at all levels) accountable. That can only be done with stated specifics understood by all parties.

You: "What are you doing to train the techs?"

Them: "Oh, we work with the techs one-on-one" or "Oh, we're out in the field all the time."

You: "What do you do when you work one-on-one? What are your Priorities for topics to address? How often are you in the field? Who've you worked with in the last week and what did you work on?"

Now this may sound like the Spanish Inquisition to those on the receiving end, but remember that generalities mean that something's being hidden from you. In a culture with respect as a value and Effective Communication as a Priority, generalities show a lack of respect toward the person asking the questions. Whoever uses them needs to be brought back to the company's values and shown that they're out of alignment with those values.

Pronouns are another form of generalities. Don't get caught up in the pronoun game. Pronouns (e.g., they, someone, he, she, etc.) deflect accountability from the true source. Similarly, the department game (e.g., Finance made that decision, Operations did it, etc.) hides people from accountability. If you want to change a financial policy, you'll only do that with a discussion. That discussion can only take place with people, not some amorphous, ethereal entity. Get names, talk directly, be specific, and go from there.

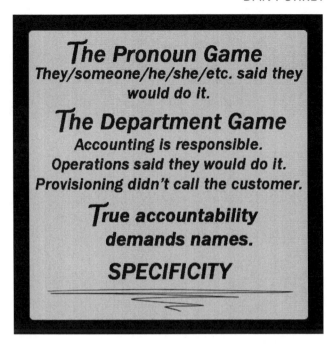

The Pronoun Game
They/someone/he/she/etc. said they would do it.

The Department Game
Accounting is responsible.
Operations said they would do it.
Provisioning didn't call the customer.

True accountability demands names.
SPECIFICITY

~~~~~~

Demand Accurate Communication

You: "Are you done yet?"

Them: "Oh, yeah. We've got it all done. All we've got left to do is . . ."

You: "Then you're not done yet, right? When will you be done?"

This one's a hair-puller for me. Maybe it's a reason why I'm follicly challenged. Drives me crazy. It's akin to a generality. The person really wants you to think they're done and they lead with that. Often it works. You only hear the first part and ignore the "All we've got left to do is . . ." part. You can't let this type of response slide. Require the person to say what they mean. It may be okay that they're not done yet if the deadline hasn't passed, but don't let them try to spin their lack of accountability or integrity.

~~~~~~

Be Consistent

Consistently send the message and keep your actions consistent with the message. This really is a form of CURP (Chapter 9, Step 8). As we've learned, if you've Prioritized your message, then it's not just your responsibility to follow up, but to follow up consistently. Otherwise, the message will get lost in the tyranny of the supposedly urgent versus what's really important.

For example, if one of your guiding Principles is to create a learning, improving environment, then you, as the leader, have to consistently

- Provide guidance
- Provide specific help
- Provide coaching
- Require *specific actions* to make things better
- Model the behavior you want

I once had a boss who talked the good talk about coaching improvement, but couldn't quite walk it. One day on the golf course, we paired up in a team best-ball competition. Now I rarely golf, but I've got some natural athletic talent. I'm used to being coached from playing team sports most of my life. So before we teed off, I made it a point to let my boss know that I was open to and actually expected coaching about what I could do with my swing to get better. I wanted to take advantage of the knowledge of someone better than me at golf. Disappointingly, his only advice through 18 holes was "Hit it in the short grass." While that might have been good strategic advice, it fell a little short of actually how to improve my game. As a leader, you consistently have to model what you expect from your people, including coaching.

~~~~~~

The Open Door Policy

The stereotypical open door policy's much like a Dilbert comic strip. An employee walks into their manager's office, offers a suggestion, turns to leave, and gets a knife thrown in their back for daring to bring up a problem (figuratively, of course, but I can see the comic strip now—GAAAH!). The term "open door policy" has gotten a bad rap over the years because many managers don't really mean what they say. Integrity, once again, or lack thereof. Employees spend too much time trying to interpret or look for hidden agendas when talking to their managers.

Despite that, you need an open door policy—a *true* open door policy—regardless of your management level. What if employees felt comfortable enough and empowered enough to poke their head into your office and say, "Got a minute?" If you want to model Effective Communication, an open door is critical. I'm not talking about anyone being able to interrupt you at any moment—that's an extremist, Pendulum Management view. There must be boundaries even with an open door, like when you're in a meeting, on the phone, or your door is, ironically, closed. There's the value of respect that comes into play. Most people will honor those common sense boundaries, but for those that don't, have them schedule a time when they can come back. Set the expectation up front about your boundaries, but also set the expectation that when people do talk to you, you'll listen and not shoot the messenger.

~~~~~~

Raise Your Hand When You See a Business Issue

Associated with the open door policy is the concept to create a culture in which no one's afraid to raise their hand when a business issue impacts their ability to do their job most efficiently and effectively. When you introduce a true open door policy for the first time, people are likely to be skeptical until you prove to them that you do what you say you'll do and that you won't shoot the messenger. Hear them out and take appropriate action (or not, so long as you're clear about your intentions).

Do you bury the messenger who might otherwise expose a problem that could help the company? I can see a comic strip now where a messenger-killer boss responds to a comment made by an employee who had raised his hand with an issue. "Yes, yes, Mr. Einstein, I heard you. 'e = mc squared.' Please don't waste my time. Do you understand the concept of an honest day's pay for an honest day's work? Now go back to work."

You've got to foster the culture where people will eagerly raise their hands when they see a problem or have a solution. You need contributions from the entire team and they need to know you expect that. Otherwise, you'll simply encourage brownnosers and suppress innovation.

The other side of the coin is that when people's hands are raised, management needs to listen. Don't confuse that with simply doing anything that anyone says. But ideas at least need to get a fair examination from open minds.

Dilbert By Scott Adams

~~~~~~

Speak Plainly

Obfuscation: meaning to make so confused as to be difficult to perceive or understand. The word itself is confusing, since it's one of those fifty cent words some haven't even heard before. What a great, ironic word. A one word oxymoron, since its use should be to clarify, but it often confuses. How much more effective would it be to a general population to say, "The politician hid the true situation" versus "The politician obfuscated the true situation?"

Remember that the goal every time you open your mouth or write words is to Effectively Communicate—to achieve a mutual understanding of the topic. The more gobbledygook you spout, the more credibility you lose with your audience. The more credibility you lose, the less likely people will be to follow you. The less likely people are to follow you means the more difficult task you'll have to achieve your goals. As I said in Chapter 4, bring the food down to where the dogs can eat it.

Another version of this, famous in marketing and political circles, is called spin. If a situation is something you don't like, the theory is to dress it up in an avalanche of flowery words and people will be diverted from the true state of affairs. Hopefully, most people see through these transparent attempts to disguise the truth. Yet, spin must work well enough to the satisfaction of the spinners because people continue to attempt it. Maybe those spinners are just self-delusional.

Spin creates assumptions, by design. You may have heard that assumptions are the silent assassins of Effective Communication. The spinners bet that the assumptions made are in their favor. The problems surface when the favorable assumptions are proven false. If employees generally are skeptical of management to begin with, spin that's exposed for what it is only serves to increase that skepticism and reduce management's credibility even further.

Spin tactics are used by people who believe in image over substance. It's where the phrase "empty suit" came from. Or "all hat and no cattle." There are a hundred sayings like those, all of which have their origins in derisive thoughts and comments about spinners.

The problem is that the more spin you produce, the less likely people will be to pay attention to you when you actually do say something important. A classic case of the boy who cried wolf. To be an effective leader, don't sink into the spin cycle. Plain speaking will best serve you to get the engagement and loyalty of your employees.

Political correctness is in the same category as spin, but a lesser evil. Here again, people don't say what they really mean, which can only lead to misinterpretations. Diplomatic speech is an even lesser evil than political correctness, but also suffers from the same problem. In an effort not to hurt someone's feelings, often the real message of what's intended is lost. An Effective Communicator will work to ensure mutual understanding. To be most effective, what if you could be straightforward without rudeness? Of course, rudeness is in the eye of the beholder, so there's another consideration to factor in. No one said Effective Communication was easy.

I once read an article that listed about a hundred "power" words that should be contained in correspondence. Supposedly, their use made you appear important and authoritative—the verbal equivalent of the power suit or power tie. As a joke, I decided to cobble together as many of them as I could and put them into a power memo—the ultimate of all memos by definition, since it contained such a huge amount of power words. Here's The Power Memo, for your amusement:

MEMORANDUM

To: Employees

From: Dan Purkey

RE: Integrated Operational Factors

Given our imminent embarkation into more fully enriched processes, I thought it important to analyze some of the integrated operational factors involved in our jobs on a going-forward basis. Reviewing the compatible organizational outputs of management has allowed me to see the reciprocal, albeit parallel, transitional guidelines in their full light.

Flexibility exhibited in a totally systematized, yet responsive, environment remains a key to the mobility concepts expressed in this logistical phase of the overall strategic endeavor. Functional contingency factors developed by management will enable creative capabilities to be synchronized with the modular components of the plan. Designed monitoring of the possible perturbations will allow us to implement this process with the maximum degree of freedom.

However, one must not oversimplify the issues. One school of thought holds that organizational transition is bilateral at best. The organizers' outputs and the operational inputs are rarely parallel, much less reciprocal. We must assure ourselves that the fallacies of managing diversity are not retroactive. In doing so, we must remain malleable and ensure that the dysfunctions of the corporate society do not create degenerative diseases of the working body.

Clearly, the headset of the team-unit on a forward-going basis must be to provide a synergistic environment for dialoging.

Please call me to discuss these thoughts in more detail.

I've shared this memo, presented as a real memo without any explanation, in a variety of venues with a variety of reactions. The sad fact is that, while most saw it as the farce that it is, many people took it seriously. It shows how ingrained spin is in business culture and how accustomed to it people are. I had a boss who didn't respond to it in any fashion for several days. Finally I asked him for his reaction. He confessed that he'd spent a lot of time with a dictionary and still struggled with what I meant to say, so he couldn't respond.

Now, in its own warped sort of way, The Power Memo actually does make sense and does have a message. Read it carefully, if the spirit moves you, and you'll understand. For example, "ensure that the dysfunctions of the corporate society do not create degenerative diseases of the working body" really means that a bad culture should be contained so that it doesn't impact daily work conditions. But what I use it for, besides amusement, is to help gauge how open people are in their communication, how eager they are to raise their hand when they see an issue, how much of an open door culture exists. If I get a bunch of comments from people, I know we've got some good attitudes to work on business issues. If few people comment, I know there'll be a lot of uphill work to do to implement change.

~~~~~~

The Tyranny of Perfection

We know people, as a general rule, resist change. One of the common ways they use to avoid change is to set the bar at "If it doesn't fix everything, then what's the point of doing it at all?" With this all-or-nothing mentality, they'll go to great pains to find the exception and then spin the exception into the general rule.

For example, take a good idea that'll work 60% of the time. In group discussions, someone will inevitably bring up that the solution won't fix an issue that occurs 1% of the time. However, they won't openly say it only applies to 1%. Instead, they'll spin it and present the issue just like any other, without quantifying it. Unless someone overtly says it's only a 1% issue, the group will collectively assume that the objection raised has as much validity as any other and torpedo the whole solution. This tactic's often used unintentionally, with the originator not even considering the magnitude of impact. This occurs in cultures that don't live by Names, Numbers, Dates, and Deadlines. Therefore, otherwise good ideas often go to an early grave. Be aware of this tendency and fight it. Ask pertinent questions and verify assertions.

As a manager, you can't expect perfection, despite Vince Lombardi's famous quote that "You don't do things right once in a while. You do things right all the time." His sentiment's correct—we should always strive for perfection—but we shouldn't expect it. Don't let a failure to be perfect prevent you from implementing solutions that can have a big impact on many situations and drive incremental improvement.

~~~~~

Coaching Thoughts

Give people respect, give them responsibility, give them help to carry out those responsibilities, and they'll respond. When an employee asks for help, give it to the fullest extent possible (versus "hit it in the short grass"). For some, it takes a lot of courage to approach their manager for help for fear of showing weakness, a weakness that might be punished in the performance evaluation. A better way is to reward the employee for raising his/her hand. The goal is to make things better, not repress ideas or the ability to question authority.

I know someone whose coaching advice to an employee who asked for help was, "You're a well-compensated manager and I pay you to figure that out." This person cried out for help and the manager basically turned his back on them. A strong, engaged manager would say, "How can I help?"

Yes, there's value in giving people the freedom and empowerment to let them try and fail in order to learn, but don't be the Pendulum Manager who lets people flounder in all circumstances. You don't have to do it for them, but guiding, coaching, and encouraging are skills respected by employees and necessary for a good manager.

Even worse is the manager who doesn't like to be questioned. Their typical response is "Just do your job! Don't ask me questions. Just do your job!" Ironically, as I laid out in Chapter 1, it's usually management that's set up the situation that the employee questions. The employee likely needs clarification from the source as to what exactly constitutes her job. Be that manager that takes the time to understand what the root cause of the problem/question is before you send an employee away without direction.

~~~~~

Group Coaching

A common adage in management is praise in public, coach in

private. Sound advice, as a general proposition. However, there can and should be group coaching. A key with that is to set expectations for the group up front. Before you begin a specific issue discussion, the group needs to understand that the coaching may be a refresher for some, but is directly applicable to at least a significant portion of the group. The message needs to be that the group coaching session's to get everyone on the same page and work together as a team.

Bring in the concept of *team* success. That'll help bring everyone into the conversation. Otherwise, there'll be those who think that they already do whatever the topic is and they'll mentally check out. You can engage these people by asking them to share how and why they work the process correctly and what benefits they see from it.

~~~~~~

Recognition and Rewards

We hit on this topic earlier, but here are some more thoughts on the subject.

Most people are satisfied with the public recognition of a well-done job. Rewards don't necessarily need to be elaborate and expensive. They just need to be symbolic of achieved success and really can be as minimal as trash and trinkets or even just a certificate of recognition of some sort. It's the thought that counts. At a minimum, recognition and rewards should be given in some form on a monthly basis with some degree of ceremony. Make them very public.

What you want to avoid is that the recognition degenerates into meaningless awards like participation trophies given out in tee-ball to six-year olds. If you want to recognize everyone, then come up with unique, but valid, reasons to provide individual awards for everyone.

At the XYZ Company, the sales department had a Breadwinner of the Month Award, presented to the person with the highest sales for the previous month. Seems reasonable, but when one person dominated month after month, the "losers" complained that they weren't recognized for their efforts. The manager then changed the Breadwinner Award to incorporate "contributions" to the sales group. That quickly devolved into the award being given on a rotating basis among the sales people. "I had it last month, so I know I won't get it this month." The manager manufactured reasons to justify the award, even to the unworthy, in order to make everyone at some point feel good for at least a month. It became a running joke among the salespeople and lost all motivational value.

Recognition shouldn't be rote or routine or equally allocated. If Jane hasn't been recognized for the past three months, then you should privately coach Jane for improvement, not give her a trophy.

~~~~~~

Cynics

Robb Graham, noted philosopher, says that cynicism breeds true enlightenment. Cynicism's the equivalent of telling the emperor he's wearing no clothes. It brings to light things that are otherwise hidden. In my terms, it's like raising your hand when you see a business issue that needs to be addressed, except presented less professionally with a bit of a raw edge to it. It's honesty with a sneer. Cynics question authority, a healthy attribute in any culture when used in moderation. Cynics can be amusing and I'm proud to count myself among them in certain circumstances, but they can be the source of ultimate dissention and a cause for loss of respect for management if carried to an extreme.

As a manager, if you think ahead and particularly try to think like a cynic, you can forestall those types of comments by overtly addressing them up front. Call out the potential comments first and you take the wind out of the cynics' sails.

Unlike Phil Connors' (played by Bill Murray) proclamation in the movie *Groundhog Day* that "Anything different is good," almost any change will likely engender cynical comments. The more change, the more cynicism. Therefore, limit change. Prioritize the really important changes you want to make and let others temporarily fall off the plate. Constant change starts to be viewed as a rearrangement of the deck chairs on the Titanic.

≈≈≈≈≈

Conflict Resolution

There are many methods to use for conflict resolution. Whole books have been written on the subject and I'm not about to recreate them here. What's important to understand is that when conflicts occur among your team (and they will), you'll likely get dragged into the situation and that eats up your valuable, limited time.

The best form of conflict resolution is to put the conflicting parties in the same room and tell them to hash it out civilly among themselves. Most people aren't trained in conflict resolution techniques, but the process to simply sit down and talk face-to-face doesn't take much training. It's a simple, effective method that can usually fix the problem if you have willing participants. It has the advantage that it won't take your limited time. You can have them just report their resolution to you.

If that doesn't work, here's a common conflict resolution tool that's been both effective (good results) and efficient (takes less time) for me and that puts some definition and structure around the resolution process. Emotions often run high when people disagree and, you, in the role of moderator/coach, need to establish a framework and boundaries to bring rational thought to the discussion. The tool to use to provide that framework is called VOMP.

It's composed of four defined sections, each with its own purpose. When taken together, the session usually ends with smiles and handshakes, with people confident in their ability to work peacefully together. VOMP's an acronym for Vent, Own, Moccasins, and Plan.

Let's use the simplest example of just two people (let's call them Becky and Pat) with a problem and you as the moderator. The first thing to do when you bring the parties together is to explain the following rules of engagement. You've got to maintain tight control as moderator to make sure each party stays within and follows the rules of engagement.

V = Vent. This is step one. Each party gets the same set amount of time (usually 3-5 minutes) to express their frustrations about the situation from their viewpoint. Because it's from *their* viewpoint, "I" statements need to be used by the speaker instead of accusatory "you" statements. Descriptions of the observable behaviors can be combined with "I" statements to provide more context. For example, "You're an idiot" is a "you" statement, doesn't describe an observable action, and so is out of bounds. As mediator, you'll need to have good awareness of this rule and keep tight control. Comments need to be phrased in such a way as to describe how the speaker feels when an action occurs. For example, "I feel really disrespected when you redo the work that I just did."

Usually the aggrieved party (let's say Becky) goes first, since sometimes the second party (let's say Pat), if venting first, will say, "I'm not sure why I'm here." Becky speaks without interruption to vent her feelings with appropriate language. Pat's required to take notes of Becky's venting. Once time's up, reverse the roles. It's the Venting section that can get out of control, so be sure to exert your authority as mediator to keep people on task.

O = Own. This is step two. Each party again gets their own dedicated time (3-5 minutes) to paraphrase what the other person said in the Venting section, using the notes they took. If the paraphrase isn't what the other person said/meant, then the other person can jump in with a clarification until the second person has more accurately paraphrased the issue. Part of the paraphrasing is to Own the paraphraser's contributions to the conflict. For instance, "I heard you say that I sometimes redo your work. I agree." It takes two to tango, after all. This is the mutual understanding phase, so it's important that both parties agree that their positions have been correctly characterized. Then the parties reverse roles.

Because interruptions are permitted, the mediator again plays a strong roll in reining in the paraphrasing and ensuing discussion or disagreement. The goal of this phase is to acknowledge areas of personal responsibility.

M = Moccasins. As in, can you walk a mile in the other person's moccasins? Again each party gets the same amount of dedicated time. The goal here is to take paraphrasing to the next level to describe not just their understanding of the other person's statements, but to turn it around into the form of "If I were you and someone redid my work, I'd be frustrated, too." This section's designed to bring empathy into the equation. Then the parties reverse roles.

P = Plan. Through the first three sections, the parties have expressed the issue from their perspective, acknowledged each other's perspective, and put themselves in the other person's place. Now they should be in a position to fix the problem. This is a more free form section, where the parties jointly plan on how to avoid the conflict in the future through an actual conversation. The discussion here should reference what they put on the table in the first three sections. It's helpful here to use the "what if" technique instead of the "you should" approach. See Tip #2 in Chapter 5. In the service of mutual understanding and Effective Communication, both parties should restate/paraphrase whatever agreement they reach at the end.

~~~~~~

Rewire Your Hot Buttons

Hot buttons are those things that happen to you that inevitably cause you to get angry, upset, irritated, or otherwise disturbed. For example, my wife gets irritated when people throw in the word "like" every fifth word in conversations. Like, overuse of the word "like" gets her, like, irritated. Remember that experience isn't what happens to you, it's how you interpret what happens to you. Your brain wires itself with your reactions to events, remembers them, and builds on them. Well, if your brain can wire itself, then it can also rewire itself. It's a matter of how you reacted and how you could have reacted. You control the horizontal, you control the vertical.

Most importantly, you also need to pay attention to yourself when in a more heated conversation. Does the volume of your voice rise? That's probably an indication that someone has just pushed one of your hot buttons. Do you feel irritated? Your hot button was pushed. Face feel flushed? Hot button. If your hot button's pushed and it negatively impacts your ability to Effectively Communicate, then what if you did something different than your usual response?

Recognize the personal signs that let you know your hot button has been pushed, acknowledge and understand the situation, then make the incredibly hard conscious decision to react differently. Perhaps "act differently" is a better description, since "react" implies a lack of control.

I know a manager whose head and neck literally turned red and his eyes bulged (not comically, but definitely bigger) when he got perturbed (i.e., someone pushed one of his hot buttons). In addition, his tone of voice and speech became much more clipped and measured. Since he's bald (which magnified his redness) and big, his physical changes intimidated others and tended to hinder further discussion. Everyone around him could see the obvious signs of his hot button reaction, but he didn't notice anything himself. Further, no one actually talked to him about the reactions when they occurred. However, after we talked about it (Effective Communication), he was able to tune in to himself and notice the physical and audible changes. He improved his ability to recognize his physical feelings associated with his hot button state. When his head turned red (others' observation), he felt warmer (his observation), which makes sense if you have a lot of blood rush to a spot. He clued in that his warm head meant he should dial down his emotions.

As another example, suppose you're driving and someone cuts you off. If that pushes your hot button, you may want to flip off the other driver. That could end up in a road rage conflict. Instead, if you know you're currently wired to flip off the other driver, rewire yourself to simply move farther away from that car for safety reasons.

REWIRE YOUR HOT BUTTONS

Fig. 13-1

This is much easier to say than do. It's the reason psychiatrists make lots of money, because rewiring can involve deep, deep psychological situations that you may not consciously understand. A deep look into your psyche can be scary for some, but when you understand the reasons for your actions, you'll be better able to choose how you want to react/act instead of allowing the situation to control you.

~~~~~~

Ready, Fire, Aim

Many people pride themselves on their ability to make decisions quickly. They don't spend days and weeks of study and analysis paralysis. Get some input, make a decision, and move on. It's a great attribute in a leader, except when it isn't.

The problem surfaces when the leader has so much hubris that they believe they don't need much input before they make a decision on anything. One school of thought is the leader's too busy to do her job, so she's Simplifying her life, in alignment with one of the Big Four Principles. Yeah, sure. Maybe that's a bit too much benefit of the doubt. Given that we know that communication is frequently ineffective, it would seem more prudent to want more, not less, information before you make a decision, if for nothing else than to verify the accuracy of your judgment.

"Ready, aim, fire" or "ready, fire, aim?" Quick decision making's often imperative to succeed, but it can't be used in every circumstance. It may be fast, but it might not be good. Good counts more than fast. Undue speed in all circumstances will eventually turn the culture to chaos and you won't have time to do your job. Just because you choose "ready, aim, fire" doesn't necessarily mean that decision-making will be slow. It's possible—easily possible—to do "ready, aim, fire" and do it quickly. Just ask Wild Bill Hickok.

The XYZ Company searched for marketing ideas to improve sales, so leadership decided to have a "green light" or brainstorming session. The boss unexpectedly brought several department heads from various disciplines together for an emergency meeting that needed to be held that very afternoon. They had no idea beforehand about the meeting, but when they gathered, the boss explained that sales had tanked and they needed to come up with some creative ways to increase sales and get them implemented immediately.

They formed three teams. The process development consisted of each team being locked (almost literally) in separate rooms for thirty minutes and, by God, they weren't leaving that room until they had some ideas to implement. Certainly a challenge for their creativity. Everyone nodded at the boss and proceeded to create.

In almost any group setting, the attitude of the room is to reach agreement, especially if the boss is there. There's an inherent, unstated social pressure to come out of meetings with results of some sort. In addition, in most businesses, there's a lack of true open and honest communication. People get defensive when their ideas are questioned. No one wants to offend, so everyone's agreeable. So when the boss says, as she did, "That's a great idea. Who disagrees?" who will actually disagree? If a person has been shot down before by the boss for disagreeing and the group has witnessed it—frequently the case at XYZ Company—who reasonably would have the courage to speak up in opposition? During a forced thirty minute session, people will commit to anything just to get out of the meeting unscathed and not appear uncooperative.

So they did their duty. Each team came up with ideas and initial processes and left the meeting promptly at the thirty minute mark. Keeping the meeting to the stated time at least showed good leadership. However, no real buy-in existed within the group. People said stuff they didn't really mean and had no real intention of doing. Therefore, follow up and follow through simply didn't happen. Other than the command to start implementation, the boss didn't really follow through either to see how the teams progressed in the execution phase and the whole effort came to naught. Thirty minutes of their lives they'll never get back.

The boss almost appeared to be more interested in the exercise for the exercise's sake than to get results. Brainstorming is a valuable tool, but to grab hold of the ideas generated in the space of thirty minutes and move directly to implementation is ludicrous. Now, maybe you can get lucky—after all, even a blind squirrel finds an acorn every once in a while. Apparently, though, the idea appeared not so ludicrous as to prevent some real world bosses from making an attempt.

The whole fiasco was akin to locking a group of people in a room, giving them the task of solving world peace in thirty minutes, and yelling "Go!" Now maybe some great ideas would be generated, but more than likely none would be practical for instant implementation.

CHAPTER 14—SUMMARY
Everything You Need to Know in Bullet Points

Well, you made it to the last chapter. Congratulations! While there's a certain amount of tongue-in-cheek involved in that congratulations (I mean, really, you only read about 300 pages. You learned to read in grade school. Don't get too enamored of your participation trophy.), the rest of it is heart-felt. You picked up this book when you didn't even have time to do your job. You made a conscious choice to do something different and make an effort to improve things for yourself and your business in spite of the heavy burdens placed on you by both life and work. That took commitment. That's what the congratulations are really for. It also demonstrated that when you put your mind to it, you can take action. Because after having read all of the words here, actually taking action instead of just talking about it is the best piece of advice you can get out of this book. All of the advice in the world won't help you unless you put it to use.

I don't know what you learned from our conversation, since this really was only a one-way monologue and I can't get feedback from you, at least at this point. (Feel free to provide any feedback via www.TheOpenDoorGroup.com.) However, I'm hopeful you learned the following things. Note that I've put these in Priority order according to my view of the world, going through the Bubble Sort process seen in Chapter 2. After all, I'm not only president of the Priority Club, I'm a member. I also numbered them for easier reference.

≈≈≈≈≈

Bullet Point Lessons

1. Actually take action instead of talking about taking action.
2. Effective Communication is the foundation for success in business and life.
3. Communicate openly and honestly, without spin.
4. Actively seek to ensure a mutual understanding of issues among all parties.
5. Actively seek to uncover assumptions and verify them. Assumptions are the silent assassins of Effective Communication.
6. Effective Communication is 50% sender and 50% receiver.
7. Personal change precedes organizational change. Expect both to take a while.
8. You must have a simple set of personal and professional Principles that provide overall guidance.
9. The Big Four Principles are Effective Communication, True Prioritization, Simplification, and Alignment with Principles. If these are your only guiding factors and you live by them, you'll go far.
10. Principles (including values, mission statements, and vision statements) provide the point of authority against which all actions can be evaluated as either in alignment or out of alignment. To correct an action out of alignment with Principles, begin by overtly questioning how the action forwards the cause of the Principle.
11. Priorities without follow up and follow through are useless. If an issue's important enough for you to raise, then it should be important enough for you to follow up on to see if it's progressing. CURP—Constant, Unrelenting, Ruthless Pressure.

≈≈≈≈≈

Let's take a break. You've already read about a page of bullet points and there's more to come. You've (hopefully) learned a lot from this book or at least reinforced practices you know that work. So reflect on the bullet points you just read. What can you do to put them into action? As part of your break, here's a little diversion: A horse walks into a bar. The bartender says, "Hey, buddy, why the long face?" (That one's for you, Jay Buhner.) Okay, back to more bullet points of things you've learned.

≈≈≈≈≈≈

12. True Priorities are those few items that you've identified and actively work on. Forget everything else and focus on your True Priorities if you really want to accomplish something.

13. It's okay for things to fall off your plate, so long as you and your boss know what they are and agree on them.

14. Regardless of how busy you might be, there are ways to find time in order to find even more time.

15. Have an unrelenting focus on Customer Satisfaction.

16. The five steps needed to achieve goals are:
    1. Prioritization
    2. Simplification
    3. Standardization
    4. Execution
    5. Verification

17. Change your and your team's language by talking in terms of Names, Numbers, Dates, and Deadlines.

18. Never leave a meeting, whether formal or informal, without knowing WHO will do WHAT by WHEN.

19. Goals need deadlines.

20. Good Behavioral Metrics have these characteristics:
    1. Directly applicable to the behavior desired and used to coach that behavior—a behavioral metric
    2. Largely in control of the person measured
    3. Administratively simple
    4. Used to uncover and correct process or efficiency issues

21. The Eight Steps to Operational Brilliance are:
    1. Establish a Principle of clear, continuous, open, and honest communication with and among all levels of employees.

2. Establish a business culture of unrelenting customer satisfaction with key Principles to follow.
3. Initiate departmental performance assessments—what works and what doesn't.
4. Prioritize issues that most significantly affect customer satisfaction. Assign accountable leads to resolve a limited number of the top Priorities.
5. Establish measurable goals and deadlines for the tactics at both group and individual levels.
6. Execute and track progress towards goals and deadlines.
7. Continually communicate clear expectations and results in various forms to all levels.
8. Adjust as necessary. Maintain constant, unrelenting, ruthless pressure to achieve strategic and tactical goals.

~~~~~~

Time for another break. If you try to assimilate a long list all at once, your eyes will glaze over and you won't actually internalize anything. So—a nun, a duck, a rabbi, and a lawyer walk into a bar. The bartender says, "Hey, what is this, some kind of joke?" Break's over.

~~~~~~

22. Raise your hand when you see a business issue and expect it to get a fair examination.
23. Encourage everyone to raise business issues without concern for reprisals.
24. Paraphrasing is one of the most powerful tools that facilitates Effective Communication.
25. Experience is *how you interpret* what happens to you.
26. Accept the reality that you may be wrong.
27. Leadership is creating the page and then making sure that everyone is on that page.
28. Be aware of the dangerous effects of Pendulum Management and find the middle ground instead.
29. What gets measured gets improved. Behavioral metrics are a key to success.

30. Excellent companies have more employees evaluated at an excellent level than average companies, assuming evaluations are based on metrics.
31. Coach 'em up first. If there's no improvement, coach 'em out.
32. Profit feeds Management; Management feeds Employees; Employees feed Customers; Customers feed Profit.
33. "Ready, aim, fire quickly" is better than "ready, fire, aim."
34. Management is the root cause of you and your fellow employees not having enough time. Fix management and you fix everything. [Note: Maybe this should have been first.]

~~~~~~

Summary of Practical Action Suggestions

Although I labeled some practical actions specifically as that, you've by now discovered that there are many other practical actions scattered throughout the book. What follows are just the ones that I numbered.

PRACTICAL ACTION #1: Resolve to turn words into actions.

PRACTICAL ACTION #2: Resolve to Prioritize your work and then act in accordance with your stated Priorities.

PRACTICAL ACTION #3: List your potential Priorities.

PRACTICAL ACTION #4: Prioritize your potential Priorities.

PRACTICAL ACTION #5: Resolve to be okay with things falling off your plate.

PRACTICAL ACTION #6: Communicate early with the people to whom you committed a result if the Priorities change and you can't meet the commitment.

PRACTICAL ACTION #7: Don't disengage from a conversation if you're unclear or sense the other person is.

PRACTICAL ACTION #8: Prioritize paraphrasing.

PRACTICAL ACTION #9: Stop the argument and find the assumption.

PRACTICAL ACTION #10: Involve both management and front-line personnel in the development of processes to make them more useful and successful.

PRACTICAL ACTION #11: Allocate your corporate energy in direct proportion to the Priority level of the component.

PRACTICAL ACTION #12: When dealing with problems, talk in terms of business issues, not personalities.

PRACTICAL ACTION #13: Never leave a meeting/conversation about someone doing something without exact clarity about

> ➢ Who will do
> ➢ What
> ➢ and When

≈≈≈≈≈≈

Significant Sentences

For this section, I pulled out some sentences from the previous chapters that carried some import that you might have overlooked, since they were generally just part of a paragraph without any particular emphasis. If you're one of those people who highlight sentences or paragraphs in a book, these are sentences you probably already highlighted. This section is for those who don't use a highlighter or maybe missed some important concepts. These are organized by the order in which they appear in the book for easier reference. I recommend you do your own Bubble Sort to determine their level of Priority for you.

1. Ineffective communication takes many, many different forms that can appear to the untrained eye as something other than a communication issue. The key to success is to have the realization that if you can't associate the root cause of a given problem with some type of communication, then you haven't dug deep enough. (Introduction)

2. A business leader must incorporate the human, emotional factors into whatever direction the leader leads. (Chapter 1)

3. Limit how often the term "Priority" is used. Reserve it for things that fall into the category of single-minded focus until completion. (Chapter 2)
4. Priorities without corresponding action are simply ineffectual words. (Chapter 2)
5. A True Priority is whatever you're doing at this exact moment. (Chapter 2)
6. True Priorities are defined by actions, not words. (Chapter 2)
7. It's the order and dependencies of your Priorities that are the important things. (Chapter 2)
8. Priorities are nothing without follow up and follow through. (Chapter 2)
9. If you say you'll Prioritize something, have the perseverance to follow it through to completion. (Chapter 2)
10. You can't do it all, so don't. Be ready to say "No." (Chapter 2)
11. If you say it, then do it. (Chapter 2)
12. It's important to Prioritize communication with your co-workers as one of those strategic Priorities. (Chapter 2)
13. Issues seldom have just a single cause that can be easily identified and attacked. (Chapter 2)
14. A problem transferred is a problem solved. (Chapter 2) [Note: Okay, that's a bit cynical, but an amusing phrase that I use frequently when commenting on an unresolved problem. I'm not recommending the phrase as a course of action.]
15. If you start at the real beginning and follow an order through in detail to the end (however you define an "order" for your business), you'll gain a better awareness of your business and what to Prioritize. (Chapter 2)
16. Decisions based solely on a short term, immediate financial impact are simply misguided. (Chapter 2)
17. Stuff falling off your plate's okay, as long as the stuff is non-prioritized items and your plate's otherwise full with True Priorities. (Chapter 3)
18. If everything is a priority, then nothing is a priority. (Chapter 3)

~~~~~~

Time for a break. You'll find this section's a few pages in length. A truism for speeches is to organize them such that, first, you tell them (the audience) what you're going to tell them, then you tell them, then you tell them what you told them. Chapter 14 is about telling you what I told you. Think of it as kind of a CliffsNotes version of the whole book.

Here's a classic joke for this break from Henny Youngman ("King of the One Liners"): "Take my wife . . . please." Now, back to it.

≈≈≈≈≈

19. Principles, Simplified in quantity by using Prioritization, provide that solid framework from which everything else flows. (Chapter 4)
20. Every individual action/task is taken because it will directly impact the strategic or tactical objectives. (Chapter 4)
21. Management is continuous coaching, or at least good management is. (Chapter 4)
22. Principles and Values allow management to coach desired behavior more effectively. (Chapter 4)
23. Effective Communication is the foundation for every function associated with business or even life as a whole. (Chapter 5)
24. The real world definition of Effective Communication is the achievement of mutual understanding among participants. (Chapter 5)
25. Most people assume that what they say is what's understood. That's far from the case. (Chapter 5)
26. Paraphrasing may be the most powerful tool to use to help ensure mutual understanding. (Chapter 5)
27. The brain does two things with memories: it alters them, and it believes it hasn't. (Chapter 5)
28. Accept the reality that you might be wrong and your filters might have deceived you. (Chapter 5)
29. Assumptions are the silent assassins of Effective Communication. (Chapter 5)

30. Make sure you really, truly understand the impact of assumptions to produce Effective Communication and actively work to find those assumptions. (Chapter 5)

31. Identify assumptions, let them see the light of day, and you'll give yourself a better opportunity to be understood for what you mean to be understood for. (Chapter 5)

32. If you can *describe the behavior*, rather than place a judgment, you'll have made great strides in interpersonal communication. (Chapter 5)

33. Don't accuse; do describe. Don't judge without examining why you've judged as you have. (Chapter 5)

34. Don't be a boss that asks a question whose answer you don't want to hear. If you ask it, be ready to assimilate an answer that's the opposite of what you expect. (Chapter 5)

35. Lead by example. Consciously model the culture you want to build. (Chapter 5)

36. Management is the most important component of business success. (Chapter 6)

37. Learn to breathe the processes. (Chapter 7)

38. In the absence of direction to the contrary, people will formulate their own ways to do things that are most comfortable for them. (Chapter 7)

39. The involvement (i.e., buy-in) of the people who will be measured by the metric is an important concept in the development of metrics. (Chapter 7)

~~~~~~

One more break, one more joke. A hamburger and a french fry walk into a bar. The bartender says, "I'm sorry we don't serve food here."

Oh, what the heck. It's your last break. One more joke for all you Latin majors. Who says that degree is useless? Julius Caesar walks into a bar. "I'll have a martinus," he says. The bartender gives him a puzzled look and asks, "Don't you mean a 'martini'?" "Look," Caesar retorts, "If I wanted a double, I'd have asked for it!"

~~~~~~

40. True accountability, in which names of responsible people are named (whether for good or bad actions), is a part of any well-managed business. Identification of a root cause is not finger-pointing; it's integral to fixing a business issue. (Chapter 7)

41. Everything rests on management. (Chapter 8)

42. An effective leader will continually communicate with a variety of methods, with all departments and employees about where things work well, where they don't, and what the benefits are to customers from an efficiently operating organization. (Chapter 8)

43. The issue's not whether communication takes place, but whether that communication takes place in such a fashion that both (or all) parties have the same internal understanding of what's said. (Chapter 8)

44. It's always better to take a current employee and coach them up versus throw out the baby with the bathwater, hire new, and start over. But it's also important to recognize when coaching has no effect and selectively cut the dead wood. (Chapter 9)

45. Self-assessment is a key to improvement. (Chapter 9)

46. If an issue is important enough for you to raise, then what if it became important enough for you to follow up to see how it's progressing? (Chapter 9)

47. The underlying premise of metrics is that if you measure something *and you Prioritize it,* you'll improve. (Chapter 12)

48. As an effective manager, you need to assess whether the crisis of the moment is really a crisis that needs attention right now. Err on the side that it doesn't, since many crises are simply manufactured by the people who bring them to you. (Chapter 12)

49. Since nobody's perfect, perfection shouldn't be expected. Accordingly, with rare exceptions, goals shouldn't have an expected target of 100%. (Chapter 12)

50. Be specific and demand specificity from others. Don't settle for generalities. (Chapter 13)

51. Remember that generalities mean that something's being hidden from you. (Chapter 13)

52. Your job as a manager is to hold people (at all levels) accountable. (Chapter 13)
53. Ask pertinent questions and verify assertions. (Chapter 13)
54. You don't have to do it for them, but guiding, coaching, and encouraging are skills respected by employees and necessary for a good manager. (Chapter 13)
55. Your brain wires itself with your reactions to events, remembers them, and builds on them. Well, if your brain can wire itself, then it can also rewire itself. (Chapter 13)
56. Good counts more than fast. (Chapter 13)

~~~~~~

Read It Again

We've talked about how education and true learning involve repetition and practice. My goal with this book is to have you take the practical techniques presented and turn them into actions. The better you understand the techniques, the easier it'll be for you to do that. Therefore, I encourage you to go back and read the entire book again immediately after you finish this round. Multiple times would be even better.

The basic reason for this is to overcome those filters that reside in your brain. With multiple readings, you'll find concepts that were fuzzy before or that didn't make any impression at all will now become clear. Ideas that initially were clear will become more set in your mind. Write notes in the margins, dog-ear important pages, use a highlighter on passages that resonate with you. Make it a true reference book. Beat it up. Use it. You can always buy another clean copy if you need one.

~~~~~~

Call to Action

Let's be honest. If you're the only one that implements this philosophy and practical actions in a sea of the uninitiated, your life will still improve, but real, solid, tangible gains for the company will be minimal (perhaps unless you're the CEO). It'll still feel like you're swimming upstream, as you look around at the insanity that seems to self-perpetuate and realize what could be. The more people there are that use these techniques, the easier everyone's lives will be.

So, here's the plan. First, identify a peer in another department that you work with frequently. Buy them a copy of this book, follow through, and actually give it to them. Make a pact between the two of you that you'll both do your level best to walk the talk of this book, particularly with your departments and one another, but also in general with anyone in the company. When they finish the book, have them enlist someone else. Meanwhile, you find another peer and repeat the same process.

Then engage your team. Give them (or have them buy) a copy of the book. Let them know that this is what you're trying to be as a manager and how you want to manage. Create the expectation that you're counting on them to keep you in alignment with the Principles of the book and that you also expect them to operate in this fashion.

Then give a copy to your boss (the Board of Directors, if you're the CEO) and say, "Boss, this is how I'll manage from now on. I'd like your support to keep me in alignment with the management Principles of this book." Once your boss is on board in a support role, now she'll almost have to incorporate the ideas in her own work life in order to help you keep on track with what you're doing. Then the boss will become a believer. Then she can enlist a peer.

Pretty soon you'll reach a critical mass and you'll have something. Ideally, by the time you get done, everyone in the company will have a copy of this book and you'll all be on the same page(s). Imagine what your company would look like then.

Final Thoughts

You learned earlier that personal change precedes organizational change. You're the one in ultimate control. It starts with you. Then persuade others to join you to effectively communicate, align with principles, truly prioritize, and simplify. Then you'll find you've got time to do your job really well.

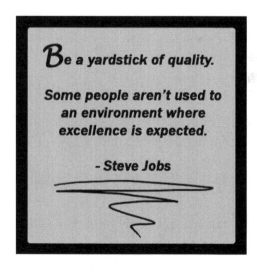

APPENDIX

In Chapter 12, we talked about evaluations and having them structured such that the overall evaluation score is 70% objective based on metrics and 30% subjective based on the manager's general assessment. What follows is an example of how the math works to produce an overall evaluation score. For this example, we'll use five objective metrics to comprise the 70% portion.

PERFORMANCE EVALUATION FOR TOM

OBJECTIVE METRICS – 70% OF OVERALL TOTAL
[NOTE: The weighting of each metric must total 100% within this Objective Metrics section.]
Metric A: Percentage on time to jobs.
Weight of Metric A: 35%
Goal for Metric A: 95%
Rating Definition: <85% = 1; 85% - 93% = 2; >93% - 96% = 3; >96% - 98% = 4; >98% = 5
[NOTE: Avoid overlapping range limits. For example, having a 93% result at both the upper end of one rating and the lower end of the next higher rating. Surprisingly, this mathematical illogic is still present in many evaluation systems, so is worth a mention. It's ineffective communication.]
Tom's Actual Performance: 95.6% = Rating 3

Metric B: Quality Control inspection pass rate.
Weight B: 25%

Goal B: 95%
Rating Definition: <85% = 1; 85% - 93% = 2; >93% - 96% = 3; >96% - 98% = 4; >98% = 5
Tom's Actual Performance: 98.9% = Rating 5

Metric C: Percentage of jobs without accidents.
Weight C: 20%
Goal C: 99%
Rating Definition: <97% = 1; 97% - 98.5% = 2; >98.5% - 99.5% = 3; >99.5% - 99.8% = 4; >99.8% = 5
Tom's Actual Performance: 100% = Rating 5

Metric D: Percentage jobs completed within time limit.
Weight D: 10%
Goal D: 95%
Rating Definition: <85% = 1; 85% - 93% = 2; >93% - 96% = 3; >96% - 98% = 4; >98% = 5
Tom's Actual Performance: 92% = Rating 2

Metric E: Percentage installs without a repair call within 7 days.
Weight E: 10%
Goal E: 95%
Rating Definition: <85% = 1; 85% - 93% = 2; >93% - 96% = 3; >96% - 98% = 4; >98% = 5
Tom's Actual Performance: 98.9% = Rating 5

Tom's Weighted Objective Metrics Rating =
(Weighted Metric A Rating + . . . + Weighted Metric E Rating) =
3*35% + 5*25% + 5*20% + 2*10% + 5*10% = 4.00

MANAGER'S SUBJECTIVE EVALUATION – 30% OF OVERALL TOTAL

[NOTE: While this section's more free form, there can still be categories to review, such as attitude, plays well with others, technical expertise, extra effort, etc. Similar to the metrics, each of the more subjective categories can have a weight associated with it. For example, if the manager believes attitude's more important than technical expertise, then attitude would be given a higher weight. Each of the categories in this section would also be weighted such that their total is 100%.]

Tom's Actual Subjective Rating: 5

Tom's Weighted Overall Evaluation Rating =
Weighted Objective Rating + Weighted Subjective Rating =
$4.00*70\% + 5.00*30\% = 4.3$

≈≈≈≈≈≈

In Chapter 13, I made some assertions in the Excellent Companies section around how to provide bonuses that motivate a larger percentage of the employee body. I also asserted that to create an excellent company, it's better to focus on and improve the performance of the bottom 10% of your employees than the top 10%.

This Appendix is devoted to the math and proof behind those assertions. It seemed a bit detailed to be included in the main part of the book, but at the same time, I believe that assertions need to be backed by facts or at least logical arguments. You should know that about me by now.

Refer back to Chapter 13 in the Excellent Companies section if that will help you make the connection with what follows.

≈≈≈≈≈≈

Bonuses and Evaluation Ratings

To orient you with Chapter 13, remember that the driver at the XYZ Company was the dollars budgeted for bonuses. The constraint of the bell-shaped curve was of their own design, a box they'd put themselves in and which they couldn't see.

Of the total bonus budget of ten million dollars, XYZ allocated two million for employees rated a 5. In order to achieve their pre-determined bonus of $10,000 for each 5, there could only be 200 employees (or 2% of the total employees) rated a 5.

Working the bell-shaped curve backwards, that meant that 200 employees would be rated a 1, 1s being the mirror image of the 5s. That left 9600 people to be rated 2, 3, or 4. Since the number of 2s and 4s had to be equal and the number of 3s had to be the biggest group, they decided that 2400 would be 2s, 2400 would be 4s, and 4800 would be 3s. They'd essentially rated all of the employees before the actual evaluations took place.

In this system, 5s got $10,000, 4s got $2100, 3s got $500, and 2s got $250. 1s got nothing.

At the ABC Company, an actual excellent company, they, too, had a budget for bonuses. However, they simply let the math determine how much of a bonus the employees rated a 5 received. Instead of a pre-determined bonus dollar amount for any given rating level, they pre-determined that a 5 should get twice the bonus of a 4 and a 4 should get twice the bonus of a 3, and a 2 should get half the bonus of a 3. Managers could rate anyone any rating level without constraint, based on the 70/30 Principle. They expected that the bulk of the employees would be rated 4s or 5s because ABC personified an excellent company, producing best in class financial returns and customer satisfaction.

So, of 10,000 total employees, 5,000 rated a 5, 2,000 rated a 4, 1,500 rated a 3, 1,000 rated a 2, and 500 rated a 1. They pre-determined a budgeted bonus of $10 million. The math works like this. If X is the base bonus amount, then a 3 gets the base amount, a 4 gets 2X, a 5 gets 4X, a 2 gets 0.5X, and a 1 gets zero (You want a bonus? Then you need to contribute at a level that doesn't need immediate improvement.). The equation's easy:

(# of 5s)*4*X + (# of 4s)*2*X + (# of 3s)*X + (# of 2s)*.5*X = $10 million.

Solving for X, we get $384.62 as the bonus if you're a 3 rating. A 4 gets $769.24, a 5 gets $1538.48, and a 2 gets $192.31.

You'll quickly notice that all of the bonuses at XYZ were

greater than at ABC. You'll also notice that only 2600 people at XYZ got more than $500, but ABC had 7000 such people. ABC had a much greater overall employee motivation to improve, to achieve that 5 level. That continuous improvement attitude is what allowed ABC to succeed where XYZ failed. Why? See Chapter 13.

≈≈≈≈≈

Focus on the Bottom 10%

Let's see how math proves the truth of the theory that you should focus your management energy on the bottom 10% performers. Okay, maybe the following is a little over the top and too detailed, but I put it together and, by golly, I'm gonna use it, even if it's relegated to the Appendix. For those whose eyes glaze over at the mere mention of math, just remember this bottom line conclusion: spend your time to coach up your worst performers instead of your best ones and, if coaching up proves impossible, then find replacements. For those looking for some math fun (such as it is), proceed.

In Figure Apx-1 below, we look at what happens to the overall evaluation rating for the company if you coach up the top 10% of your employees. For this example, you really can't coach up those who are rated a 5, since there's no 6 rating. Therefore, you need to look at the top 10% starting with the 4s. They have the opportunity to move to a 5 with some coaching.

See the shaded cells in Figure Apx-1 for the Rating of 4. To begin with, we have 20 employees rated a 4. The Total Points is just the Rating times the Number of Employees, or 4 times 20 = 80. Assume in Year 1 that you can coach up 10 (the top 10% of 100 total employees) of the 20 employees rated a 4 to be 5s. At the end of Year 1, you'll have 10 less employees rated 4 and 10 more employees rated 5. In Year 2, you coach up the remaining 10 people rated 4 to be 5s. At the end of Year 2, now you have no one rated 4, but you have 30 people rated 5, versus the 10 rated 5 you started with. Looking at the Average Rating row, you can see that you started with an average company rating of 3.00, but by the end of Year 2, you've moved that to a 3.20. Congratulations! You've improved the company by 0.20 rating points.

Mathematical effect of coaching up Upper 10%						
RATING	# EMPL.	TOTAL POINTS	YEAR 1 # EMPL.	TOTAL POINTS 1	YEAR 2 # EMPL.	TOTAL POINTS 2
1	10	10	10	10	10	10
2	20	40	20	40	20	40
3	40	120	40	120	40	120
4	20	80	10	40	0	0
5	10	50	20	100	30	150
	100	300	100	310	100	320
AVG. RATING		3.00		3.10		3.20

Fig. Apx-1

Now let's look at what happens when you focus on the bottom 10% in Figure Apx-2 below. You have ten people rated 1. Let's fire them. You've coached them enough and they'll just never get it. We'll hire new people, but let's assume that they pan out to be rated on the same a normal distribution as the company as a whole. That means of the ten new people you hired, at the end of Year 1, you'll have one of the ten rated as a 1, two rated a 2, four rated a 3, two rated a 4, and one rated a 5. In Year 2, you work with the new bottom 10%. Of those ten people, one of them is rated a 1 and the other nine are rated 2. By the end of Year 2, you've coached them up to the next rating level.

Now look at the overall company Average Rating at the end of Year 2. You've increased it to 3.36 from a starting point of 3.00, an increase of 0.36 rating points. 0.36 is more than the 0.20 increase from working on the top 10%, so, *ipso facto*, you've improved the company more overall with a focus to improve the bottom 10%.

| | | | YEAR | TOTAL | YEAR | TOTAL |
| | # | TOTAL | 1 # | POINTS | 2 # | POINTS |
RATING	EMPL.	POINTS	EMPL.	1	EMPL.	2
Mathematical effect of coaching up or replacing Bottom 10%						
1	10	10	1	10	0	0
2	20	40	22	44	13	26
3	40	120	44	132	50	150
4	20	80	22	88	25	100
5	10	50	11	55	12	60
	100	300	100	320	100	336
AVG. RATING		3.00		3.20		3.36
Note: Assumes new hires distributed same as original population.						

Fig. Apx-2

ACKNOWLEDGEMENTS

Roger Taylor, thank you. I had many instructors during my MBA education, but he was by far the most influential. He pushed me to places I'd never explored before. Roger opened my eyes to the power of Effective Communication and how to make it happen. Without that foundation, this book wouldn't have been possible. Of course, Roger was part of the faculty at City University of Seattle, so credit also goes to the university for the vision to have Managerial and Organizational Leadership as part of their MBA curriculum.

I know a lot of smart, talented people. Some of them helped edit this book to make it more understandable. They gave me clarity about what needed to be changed and why. Before them, I had a lump of clay; after them, I had a book. Those primary contributors are Terrie Purkey (Editor-in-Chief, who, over many hours of work that she Prioritized over other activities, meticulously scoured the drafts for lack of clarity, inconsistencies, and grammar. Her best editorial comment to make me rethink phrasing was a succinct "Huh?") and Robb Graham, who challenged me with open and honest communication on many points in the course of many discussions to help make things more clear.

Bob Pentico provided some pithy quotes that helped make the points in an entertaining fashion. He takes to the management philosophies in this book like a duck takes to water. It's nice to have a kindred spirit.

Mark Reynolds helped me bring the food down to where the dogs can eat it. That phrase formed the basis for Simplification. Mark also deserves thanks for seeing my potential early in my career and providing a helping hand to make use of it.

Dave Abbott helped me realize that clearly the headset of the team-unit on a forward-going basis must be to provide a synergistic environment for dialoging. That phrase, cynically coined after a training session we were in together, formed the basis for the opposite of Simplification and inspired The Power Memo.

Thanks, again, Kim Standerfer, for taking the risk and being the great sport you were in the "argument" role play. Talk about being out of your comfort zone!

Mark Charles provides a different view on life. He succinctly summarized the process to achieve the goal of improved operational efficiency with the labels of starting in survivor mode, then moving to productivity, then to efficiency, and finally to proficiency (seen in Chapter 1). Where's your business on that continuum?

Carolyn Tschida taught me the concept of "What if . . . ?" instead of "should." I still don't use that tool as much as I should. What if I used it more?

Special thanks to Mark Kettering, Robb Graham, Rick Hess, Bob Pentico, Doug McElroy, and Kevin Person for reviewing the book and providing testimonials about how this book fits with your proven expertise in making your own business operations successful.

I've got a few quotes in here where the origin was unknown to me. My apologies to those originators for my inability to get the research done down to the root cause. If anyone knows, please contact me via TheOpenDoorGroup.com website. I can make the changes in future editions.

While the dedication at the beginning of the book might seem generic to some, my intent is truly heartfelt. Any person is the sum of those they interact with and learn from over the years, whether consciously or unconsciously. It's not practical to list everyone who's influenced my life and in what manner, but I recognize I wouldn't be the person I am today without those influences, even if I've taken what you sent and received it differently. Really, I thank you all with whom I've crossed paths on life's journey.

"No matter what accomplishments you make, somebody helped you."
—Althea Gibson (professional tennis player)

≈≈≈≈≈

If you'd like help to implement the concepts of this book in your business, please contact me through TheOpenDoorGroup.com website.

ABOUT THE AUTHOR

Usually this section is written in the third-person, as if we have to pretend the author didn't actually write it himself, but some other unknown entity did. Pretending is not open and honest communication. I think this third-person scenario exists because, culturally, it could appear egocentric to use the word "I" so much in describing yourself. However, it's really only the English language that creates that construct. I don't intend to appear egocentric, but there aren't many options other than "I" when I'm writing about me. This book has the premise of a casual coaching conversation, as if I was talking to you, the reader. Being in alignment with that premise, let me tell you about me.

At my core, I'm a teacher. While I might not have known it at the time, I can go all the way back to elementary school to find the beginnings of that. I've always enjoyed passing on my knowledge to others and seeing them grow from it. I've also always enjoyed having knowledge shared with me and growing from it. This book is the culmination of that experience.

Over the years, I actually got my teaching degree and taught high school math. I taught a business the most efficient way of doing an oil change in ten minutes, once I learned from them how to do an oil change in the first place. I taught customers about finding the best benefits and solutions to meet their telecommunications needs. I taught utilities commissioners, attorneys, and Fortune 100 companies the fairest way to implement processes that had never existed before. I was enlightened to the foundational power of Effective Communication in my MBA education and how to theoretically move organizations to achieve goals. That then turned into practical reality as a VP of Operations, consultant, and business owner to help companies reach goals not thought possible before. I authored a novel (*Trackers*), a short story (*The Legend of the Groundhog Day Hearing*), and many editorials, speeches, and testimony in various venues. Now, as a teacher and author of *Uncommon Sense Management*, I'm hopefully teaching you how to get control of your work life and create a better reality for everyone. The potential for real, sustainable change is exciting for me and I hope it is for you, too.

Terrie, my wife of thirty-plus years, is a talented interior designer. She dabbles as a pretty good artist on the side. Those right brain activities are balanced by an exceptional left brain organizational capability, making her an extraordinary editor. We have two sons, Adam and Eric, who reside in Seattle, and of whom we're very proud. For recreation, I ride a bicycle, brew beer, and play Disc (please don't call it Frisbee) Golf, basketball, and chess—all with varying degrees of success.